The New Liberalism
Reconciling Liberty and Community

CW00968021

The "new liberalism" of the late nin[
an unjustifiably neglected strand of
sizing community as well as rights and liberty, thinkers sucn as 1. 11.
Green, J. A. Hobson, and L. T. Hobhouse support – but in distinctive
ways – recent challenges to the established dichotomy between
communitarianism and liberalism. These essays examine new liberal
thinking and conclude that liberal and communitarian concerns are
compatible, even mutually reinforcing. The "common good," the
empowerment of individuals to exercise their freedom and a regulated
free market are among the new liberal "basket of ideas" which, these
essays argue, can revitalize the liberal tradition. This collection of
essays by leading scholars provides exciting new insights into current
debates within the liberal tradition, and will be of great interest to
scholars of political theory and the history of political thought.

AVITAL SIMHONY is Associate Professor in the Department of Political
Science, Arizona State University. She has published in the field of
political theory, with articles in journals such as *History of Political
Thought*, *Political Theory*, *Political Studies*, and *Utilitas*.

D. WEINSTEIN is Associate Professor in the Department of Political
Science at Wake Forest University. His recent publications include
Equal Freedom and Utility (1998) as well as articles in journals such as
Journal of the History of Ideas, *Political Studies*, *Utilitas*, and *History of
Political Thought*.

The New Liberalism

Reconciling Liberty and Community

edited by

Avital Simhony

and

D. Weinstein

PUBLISHED BY THE PRESS SYNDICATE OF THE UNIVERSITY OF CAMBRIDGE
The Pitt Building, Trumpington Street, Cambridge, United Kingdom

CAMBRIDGE UNIVERSITY PRESS
The Edinburgh Building, Cambridge CB2 2RU, UK
40 West 20th Street, New York, NY 10011–4211, USA
10 Stamford Road, Oakleigh, VIC 3166, Australia
Ruiz de Alarcón 13, 28014 Madrid, Spain
Dock House, The Waterfront, Cape Town 8001, South Africa

http://www.cambridge.org

First published 2001

Printed in the United Kingdom at the University Press, Cambridge

Typeface Plantin 10/12pt   *System* 3b2   [CE]

A catalogue record for this book is available from the British Library

Library of Congress cataloguing in publication data

The new liberalism: reconciling liberty and community / edited by Avital Simhony
and D. Weinstein
    p.   cm.
Includes bibliographical reference and index.
ISBN 0 521 79083 2 – ISBN 0 521 79404 8 (pb)
1. Liberalism. 2. Communitarianism.
I. Simhony, Avital. II. Weinstein, D. (David), 1949–

JC574.N4895   2001
320.51 – dc 21   00-065157

ISBN 0 521 79083 2 hardback
ISBN 0 521 79404 8 paperback

For Abisi and Gale

Contents

Contributors

MICHAEL FREEDEN, Mansfield College, University of Oxford

GERALD GAUS, Department of Philosophy and Murphy Institute of Political Economy, Tulane University

REX MARTIN, Department of Philosophy, University of Kansas

JAMES MEADOWCROFT, Department of Politics, University of Sheffield

JOHN MORROW, School of History, Philosophy and Politics, Victoria University of Wellington

ALAN RYAN, New College, University of Oxford

AVITAL SIMHONY, Department of Political Science, Arizona State University

ANDREW VINCENT, Department of Politics, University of Sheffield

D. WEINSTEIN, Department of Political Science, Wake Forest University

Acknowledgments

This collection emerged from a panel on the new liberalism we organized for the 89th Annual Meeting of the American Political Science Association that met in Washington, D.C. in September 1993. Then, as now, we were keen to retrieve an unjustifiably neglected strand of liberal theorizing. To retrieve new liberal thinking is, we believe, to take seriously the fecundity of the liberal tradition, not least because new liberals have much to offer the current phase of the liberal–communitarian debate.

We would like to thank Michael Freeden for his steady support and the interest he has taken in our project from its inception. His important work on the new liberalism has been a constant source of inspiration to us. Our thanks also go to Peter Nicholson. Though he declined our repeated entreaties to contribute to this volume, his encouragement and valuable work on T. H. Green spurred our efforts. We owe a special debt to Abisi Sharakiya who urged us, during a genial summer evening's conversation in 1995, to put our thoughts about the importance of the new liberals onto paper by doing a collection, and who supported the project throughout. The constructive criticisms of two anonymous reviewers improved the text significantly and we are grateful accordingly.

Finally, we would like to express our deep gratitude to each of our contributors for their patience in staying with the collection to its completion.

A.S. and D.W.

Introduction: The new liberalism and the liberal–communitarian debate

Avital Simhony and D. Weinstein

Some contemporary liberals now acknowledge, partly in response to their communitarian critics, that they must "tap neglected characteristics of the liberal tradition" if they are to revitalize liberal political theory.[1] We seek to do just this by retrieving the new liberalism. We agree, in other words, with Stephen Macedo's claim that liberalism "contains the resources to mount a positive response to the communitarian critics."[2] The new liberalism, we hold, is just such a valuable resource. It transcends the discourse of dichotomies that dominated the early phase of the liberal–communitarian debate. It also has much to offer the current phase of the debate which is propelled by the widely accepted claim that, far from being opposed, communitarianism and liberalism are mutually supporting.

Retrieving the new liberalism as an unjustifiably neglected strand of liberalism serves, moreover, as a timely reminder that there never has been *a* liberalism but rather a family of liberalisms. Hence, not only should we hesitate to identify liberalism with the contemporary dominant strand of philosophical liberalism, but we should take more seriously the richness of the liberal tradition.

The first part of our Introduction suggests possible reasons why contemporary liberalism became vulnerable to the caricature that the first round of earlier communitarian criticism was prone to make of it. The second part contends that the debate between liberals and communitarians is misconceived in two fundamental ways regardless of which side deserves the greater blame. Part three explores how new liberals such as Green, Hobhouse, Hobson, and Ritchie accommodate liberal and communitarian concerns, thereby fortifying our contention that this debate has been misconceived from the start. In particular, part three claims that the new liberalism is distinctively non-individualist insofar as

---

[1] Alfonso J. Damico, "Introduction," in Alfonso J. Damico (ed.), *Liberals on Liberalism* (Totowa, NJ: Rowman and Littlefield, 1986), p. 1.
[2] Stephen Macedo, *Liberal Virtues: Citizenship, Virtues and Community in Liberal Constitutionalism* (Oxford: Clarendon Press, 1990), p. 284.

1

2   *Avital Simhony and D. Weinstein*

it takes community and common good seriously without abnegating liberalism's traditional devotion to the cultivation of individuality. In the fourth part, we introduce each of the contributions to this volume with the aim of weaving them together according to the foregoing themes.

The liberal tradition

The self-understanding of contemporary philosophical liberalism

"So why," asks David Miller, "did we start talking about a liberal–communitarian debate?"[3] Miller is surely correct in suggesting that much of the answer lies in the fact "that a certain widely held form of liberalism, which for the sake of convenience rather than historical accuracy I shall call standard or mainstream liberalism, does have a natural affinity with individualist anthropology." For Miller, "liberals of this sort characteristically defend their political positions by invoking an individualistic view of the self."[4] But liberalism's individualistic anthropology has not been the exclusive impetus for the communitarian reaction. Liberalism's historical forgetfulness has likewise, we suspect, probably encouraged this reaction.[5]

Much contemporary philosophical liberalism has been largely analytical. Contemporary liberals have consequently inherited the ambitions of analytical philosophy, namely conceptual precision in building and defending systemic political theories. They have too often abjured history and politics in the name of what Rawls has come to disparage as "metaphysical" once-and-for-all grand theoretical edifices.[6] Contemporary liberalism has, in short, been disposed to abstract severity and inflexibility.

The analytic nature of much contemporary liberalism, by featuring solitary abstract individuals who find fulfillment in separation from each other, has probably contributed to its individualistic anthropology. No

---

[3] David Miller, "Communitarianism: Left, Right and Centre," in Dan Avnon and Avner De-Shalit (eds.), *Liberalism and Its Practice* (London: Routledge, 1999), p. 173.
[4] Ibid.
[5] As a self-confessed left communitarian, Miller holds that the left communitarian "like the liberal communitarian and unlike the right communitarian, values personal autonomy, but whereas the liberal picture is of each individual choosing which way of life to adopt after encountering several possibilities, the left picture is of us choosing our way of life together, through critical reflection on the one we now have in common." (Ibid., p. 179.) Miller regards Kymlicka and Raz as representative liberal communitarians whereas he regards Walzer as a like-minded left communitarian. Typically, nonetheless, he completely overlooks new liberals who are as much liberal communitarians as they are left communitarians.
[6] John Rawls, "Justice as Fairness: Political not Metaphysical," *Philosophy and Public Affairs*, 14 (1985), 223–51.

wonder, then, that first-generation communitarians found contemporary liberalism such an inviting target for violating what Charles Taylor calls the "social thesis."

But just as significantly, contemporary liberalism's analytic nature has also encouraged its partisans to ignore important moments of their past, compressing the entire liberal tradition into an unbroken celebration of individualism. No wonder, too, that first-generation communitarians also found receptive ears for their overly simplified portrayal of the liberal canon.

But communitarianism, in turn, may be prone to the same aspirations plaguing contemporary liberalism, despite communitarianism's Hegelian roots and its purported greater deference to historical context and situatedness. Contemporary communitarianism and contemporary liberalism are arguably opposite sides of the same analytic coin. The partisans of both sides are members of what Kevin Mulligan calls the same "Anglo-Saxon club," causing the contest between them to risk becoming overly exclusionary and therefore excessively inbred.[7] Hence, we should be unsurprised by the unvarnished nature of the struggle, especially in its formative rounds, between liberals and their communitarian foes.

Moreover, too few contemporary liberals have taken seriously Terence Ball's contention that the meanings of concepts are unstable and that they have histories.[8] Thus, we should find it unremarkable that contemporary liberals have often abused their own tradition, forgetting that the terms of today's political philosophical discourse mean things to us that they didn't mean for our predecessors. And this is no less true for the term "liberalism" itself as for any other political philosophical term.

---

[7] Kevin Mulligan, "The Great Divide," *TLS* (June 26, 1998), 7. Mulligan's review of recent books on twentieth-century analytical and continental philosophy is a succinct depiction of the differences between these two traditions.

[8] According to Terence Ball, the "linguistic turn" in philosophy structured the character of Anglo-American political theory over the last half-century. During its first phase, linguistic political theory echoed the ambitions of logico-positivism in seeking to purge political discourse of its metaphysical and normative conceptual baggage. In its subsequent phase, in Ball's view, ordinary-language analysis beguiled political theorists as they tried clarifying what *we* mean when deploying concepts like justice, liberty, and power. In its next phase, Anglo-American political theorists sought inspiration in W. B. Gallie's view that certain types of concepts are "essentially contested," making hopes of discovering, once-and-for-all, what we mean by the cardinal terms making up our political philosophical discourse illusory. Finally, in its most recent phase, political theorists began embracing "critical conceptual history" as a modified version of essential contestability. Accordingly, political philosophy is thoroughly contextualized, both historically and culturally, making conceptual metamorphosis and ambiguity unavoidable. As Ball observes, "words do not have histories but concepts do." See Terence Ball, "Political Theory and Conceptual Change," in Andrew Vincent (ed.), *Political Theory* (Cambridge University Press, 1997), p. 41.

Contemporary liberalism too often seems impervious to the conceptual permutations that the term "liberalism" and its constituent concepts have enjoyed in the past. By becoming unwittingly mesmerized by the meanings of the basic terms of *our* political philosophical discourse, including especially the meaning of liberalism, contemporary liberals have become too parochial and therefore prone to an anachronistic understanding of their own tradition. Parochialism, whether of the ordinary-language variety or even of the more recent "political not metaphysical" variety, promotes anachronistic insensitivity to liberalism's variegated past, causing us to forget it.[9] To domesticate parochially is to take too much for granted and then to forget. And to forget who we have been is to risk wasting precious intellectual energy reinventing ourselves but again.

In sum, contemporary political philosophy, particularly its American variant, has been prone to debilitating anachronism because analytic political philosophy seems to encourage anachronism. Contemporary liberals seem disposed to view their own past through the prism of their infatuation with *something* they insist on calling "liberalism."[10] Consequently, contemporary liberalism domesticates its richly textured past in the image of its current, analytic self-understanding. Contemporary liberalism thus risks becoming reified, and the liberal tradition, an overly myopic, canonic narrative it keeps retelling itself. Liberals would do better to heed Conal Condren's admonition concerning the abuse and misuse of political philosophical traditions:

A tradition is itself a context for its putative members. It is correct to say that some sense of traditionality will provide illuminating, even necessary, contexts for given texts in political theory. Nevertheless, The Tradition – in which, for example, Machiavelli provided a context for Hobbes, Aquinas for Machiavelli, by virtue of being, for us, the previous thinkers of real note – has proved particularly vulnerable to accusations of anachronism. It has meant mislocating a late-nineteenth- and twentieth-century sense of intellectual tradition, the convenient construction maintained partly for educational purposes, and superimposing it upon the past-awareness of earlier times.[11]

---

[9] See, however, John Rawls, "Introduction," *Political Liberalism* (New York: Columbia University Press, 1993), pp. xxi–xxx where Rawls historically contextualizes the kind of liberalism he advocates.

[10] J. G. A. Pocock has criticized enthusiasts for Rawls for deploying the terms "liberal" and "liberalism" as if their meanings have always been unambiguous and consistent. For instance, at her talk entitled "Communitarian Critics of Liberalism," The Johns Hopkins University, March 1985, Pocock pressed Amy Gutmann emphatically: "What is this 'liberalism' *thing* which you keep referring to?"

[11] Conal Condren, "Political Theory and the Problem of Anachronism," in Vincent, *Political Theory*, p. 54. Of course, while insisting that the new liberalism has much to offer liberals laboring to respond to their communitarian critics, we must concede that the essays in our collection are invariably tainted by a measure of anachronism. Our

Retrieving the liberal tradition

We have been suggesting that the liberalism vs. communitarianism debate quickly flared into an overheated contest between two over-simplified conceptual dualisms. Earlier partisans on both sides neglected Alfonso Damico's warning that while "formal political discourse aims to produce a more careful and systematic inquiry," it too often "proceeds according to some elementary oppositions."[12] Early on, contemporary liberals also contributed more than enough to causing the rivalry between liberalism and communitarianism to evolve into a rivalry of philosophic stereotypes by domesticating historic liberalism and thus reifying it. Their historical myopia has only exacerbated dualistic theorizing. For instance, by forgetting our new liberal past, contemporary liberals are just now rediscovering that strong rights and devotion to the common good need not be ineluctably opposed values. New liberals embraced strong rights as enabling powers which guaranteed all citizens the opportunity to flourish and thereby contribute to the common good. Similarly, by forgetting our new liberal past, too many of us are just now reappreciating that liberalism and perfectionist politics are not mutually exclusive and may even be mutually required. New liberals never doubted the state's role as an active moral agent charged with indirectly making ethical personalities out of us all.[13]

Forgetting our new liberal past has, in addition, made communitarianism's initial response to contemporary liberalism seem both much more *original* and debilitating than is warranted. Its criticisms were less penetrating than appeared because the new liberalism had already reformed the liberal tradition internally by incorporating many of the concerns of present-day communitarians.[14] And precisely because the new liberalism had *already* absorbed so many of these concerns decades ago, communitarian objections, as well as recent liberal efforts to accommodate them, are considerably less imaginative than their respec-

---

contributors have done their best in exercising what Condren calls "historiographical damage control."

[12] Damico, "Introduction," p. 2. Damico continues: "such 'divisions' are seen as antonyms implying some necessary invidious contrast between the two sides of the division, giving pride of place to one or the other." (p. 3.) Moreover, he adds that insofar "as the quarrel between liberalism and its critics persists, it should now be seen for what it is: a judgment about how best to combine the practices and values signaled by various concepts and categories, not which set to choose." (p. 4.)

[13] See, in particular, James Meadowcroft's contribution to this volume.

[14] In highlighting the new liberalism's corrective role within the liberal tradition, we do not mean to exaggerate its coherence particularly with respect to the practical policies new liberals recommended. As Gerald Gaus' contribution to this volume, on Bosanquet, reveals, the kind of moral perfectionism endorsed by new liberals need not justify extensive welfarist public policies.

tive advocates assume. Perhaps the most that can be said, then, of the liberal vs. communitarian debate is that it constitutes the latest round in the "eternal recurrence" of rhythmic corrections of liberalism of which the new liberalism was an earlier, but now largely ignored, predecessor.[15]

Recently, contemporary liberals have begun appreciating how the contest between liberalism and communitarianism has produced an overly stylized and fantastic account of the liberal tradition that merely reinforces the cartoon earlier communitarians drew of the purported essence of contemporary philosophical liberalism. Indeed, partisans on both sides of the debate have grown fatigued by its predictable tedium and have begun seeking avenues of theoretical accommodation. For their part, contemporary liberals have begun reexcavating the liberal tradition in order to remind us that its variegated complexity has always incorporated conceptual features advanced by communitarians. For instance, Stephen Holmes has vigorously insisted that liberalism does not exemplify the caricature imputed to it by communitarians insofar as liberalism has always privileged communitarian concerns such as common good, community, and the social nature of humans. But Holmes restricts his reexamination of the liberal tradition to canonical figures like Locke, Kant, and J. S. Mill.[16] Likewise, Donald Moon has recently argued that liberalism has never championed many of the positions attributed to it by communitarians. In particular, according to Moon, liberalism has never valorized the ideal of radical, unencumbered self-determination. But, like Holmes, Moon appeals to the familiar liberal canon, invoking first Mill and then Rawls as if liberalism between Mill and Rawls was a philosophical dead space devoid of interest and originality.[17]

And, similarly, Thomas Spragens has recently argued that liberalism's communitarian values have "often been obscured or denied by careless readers who anachronistically read twentieth-century premises" or "ideological proclivities" into the classical liberal tradition.[18] Values like

---

[15] See Michael Walzer "The Communitarian Critique of Liberalism," in Amitai Etzioni (ed.), *New Communitarian Thinking* (Charlottesville: University of Virginia Press, 1995), p. 70. For Walzer, communitarianism is "doomed" to the not unworthy fate of repeatedly correcting and repairing the disassociative excesses that are forever threatening liberalism.

[16] See Stephen Holmes, "The Permanent Structure of Antiliberal Thought," in Nancy Rosenblum (ed.), *Liberalism and the Moral Life* (Cambridge, MA: Harvard University Press, 1989).

[17] J. Donald Moon, "Communitarianism," *Encyclopedia of Applied Ethics*, 4 vols. (San Diego: Academic Press, 1998), vol. I, pp. 553–4.

[18] Thomas A. Spragens, Jr., "Communitarian Liberalism," in Etzioni, *New Communitarian Thinking*, p. 40.

the cultivation of virtue, community, and civic solidarity featured prominently in the thinking of classical liberals like Locke, Condorcet, and J. S. Mill. Unfortunately, according to Spragens, liberalism began changing in the late nineteenth century, eventually splitting into today's libertarian and egalitarian camps that are both individualistic and rights-oriented. In short, liberalism became "divorced from its original moral culture" and consequently became the atomistic brute contemporary communitarians rose up to slay.[19]

To be sure, Spragens is correct in holding that the late nineteenth century marks the splitting of liberalism into libertarian and egalitarian camps, both of which have been overtly individualistic. But the late nineteenth century also marks the expansion of liberalism in the very communitarian direction which Spragens holds contemporary liberalism should continue taking.

So, like Holmes and Moon, Spragens looks back to liberalism's canon in order to prove that the liberal tradition is heterogeneous and is therefore incompatible with the simplistic picture that first-generation communitarians eagerly claimed for it. And, like Holmes and Moon, Spragens appeals to the liberal canon, squeezing out of it communitarian preoccupations while ignoring altogether the new liberalism as a much richer resource for the "communitarian liberalism" he seeks to defend.[20] Indeed, the new liberalism is arguably more than an under-valued resource for Spragens' reformed liberalism and is, instead, its prototype.[21]

[19] Ibid., p. 42. Moreover, according to Spragens, neither "libertarians nor the egalitarians, it might be noted, give much attention either to the problem of human virtue or to the goal of community." (p. 44.) Both "extract a single element of the good society from its context and offer it as the dominant if not exclusive goal of political organization and policy." (p. 45.)

[20] Spragens' insensitivity to the new liberalism as an anticipation of the kind of communitarian liberalism he advocates is reflected in his claim, already noted, that late nineteenth- and early twentieth-century liberalism split into two individualistic and rights-oriented camps, namely libertarianism and egalitarianism. But this assessment totally forgets the new liberalism's prominence as a dominating mode of political philosophical discourse roughly one hundred years ago especially in Britain.

[21] For example, see Spragens' contention that the communitarian liberalism he advocates takes both individuality and community seriously:

First, a reformed liberalism could recapture some of the normative complexity of earlier liberalism by insisting upon the importance of all of the three goals of its Enlightenment predecessors: liberty, equality and fraternity ... *Fraternity* in this context should be understood as standing for "civic friendship within a flourishing community." And against this backdrop, liberal individualism would be understood not as a kind of empirical or normative atomism but simply as an insistence upon the moral autonomy of each liberal citizen and upon the crucial value of personal development. (Ibid., p. 47.)

Spragens continues:

Fraternity in this expanded sense should in fact, I would argue, be construed as the capstone goal of a liberal society. For that reason, my preferred version of liberalism is quite properly characterizable

The new liberals transformed liberalism by ridding it of its self-centered, narrow individualism, though each did so from different resources. Whereas Green brought together Kant, Aristotle, and Hegel, Hobhouse relied on biology and sociology, while Ritchie sought to reconcile Darwin and Hegel. Both idealism and biology converged at the close of the nineteenth century, disconnecting liberalism from narrow individualism and instead connecting it with what we, including Spragens presumably, would now call communitarianism.

According to Spragens, "There never was *a* liberalism" but "only a family of liberalisms."[22] We agree and suggest that the liberalism of the new liberals is a great store within the "family of liberalisms" which contemporary liberals can draw from profitably. Its omission from contemporary liberal reassessment of the liberal tradition is, therefore, unfortunate.

We have been suggesting that the tendency among philosophic liberals to understand the liberal tradition anachronistically, ignoring liberals who do not fit within contemporary liberal self-image, is one source of this omission. And to the extent that T. H. Green is not ignored, we contend that his liberalism has been tainted by Isaiah Berlin's condemnation of positive freedom as illiberal as well as by Green's misunderstood claim that individuals have no rights against the state.

Our collection aims, in the first place then, to retrieve the new liberalism from the shadows of the liberal tradition where contemporary liberalism has discarded it. Hence, this volume is intended as a curative to the partial and debilitating amnesia afflicting contemporary philosophical liberalism's historical self-understanding. It aspires to help liberals remember all that liberalism has been so that they can avoid as much as possible reinventing themselves, in their bid to accommodate liberalism with communitarianism, as if such accommodation were a fresh discovery. Our collection, in short, is primarily retrospective, but not entirely.

Even though our collection by no means aspires to "solve" some if any of the problems identified by communitarians as plaguing contemporary liberalism, our collection is invariably prospective, at least implicitly. Though this volume aims to avoid committing, as best it can,

---

as communitarian. But what makes this normative theory genuinely liberal at the same time is the insistence that civic friendship cannot be attained without extensive equality and that communities cannot flourish without extensive liberties. This recognition distinguishes communitarian liberalism from both conservatism and socialism and their own distinctive modes of community. (p. 47.)

A better summary of the salient ambitions of the new liberalism could not be easily written.

22 Thomas A. Spragens, "Reconstructing Liberal Theory: Reason and Liberal Culture," in Damico, *Liberals on Liberalism*, p. 36.

the sins of anachronism, of domesticating the liberal tradition according to recent liberal preoccupations, it likewise seeks to avoid falling victim to the opposite exegetical sin of antiquarianism. We want, to borrow from Condren, to "enrich the theoretical world we now inhabit."[23] We want contemporary liberals and communitarians to cease ignoring the new liberalism, not just because they need to understand better their shared intellectual past for its own sake but because we also hope that the new liberalism will assist liberals in bridging their differences with communitarians. We believe the new liberalism is a neglected and uniquely rich reserve within the liberal tradition itself which contemporary philosophical liberals can exploit in their struggle to come to terms with communitarianism.[24]

Santayana once remarked that if we want to learn from a crowd of faces, then we ought to focus on the unfamiliar faces rather than on the familiar and comforting ones. Otherwise, we risk simply mirroring back to ourselves our own parochial and limited concerns. Similarly, if we, as liberals, want to learn from our liberal past, then we ought to concentrate our interpretative gaze on its less familiar phases such as the new liberalism.[25] But we must at least be aware that these less familiar phases once existed and flourished before we begin focusing on them for assistance. Unfortunately, contemporary liberals have largely forgotten their own new liberal past, so little wonder they should not bother to appeal to it for encouragement and inspiration.

A misconceived debate

We seek to retrieve the new liberalism in light of the current liberal–communitarian debate because we concur with Ryan who says in his

---

[23] Condren, "Political Theory and the Problem of Anachronism," p. 56.

[24] In this respect, our collection shares Damico's ambitions for his earlier collection of essays on the liberal tradition. However, Damico explicitly says that his collection is more prospective rather than retrospective, whereas our intentions are more the reverse. Ironically, Damico claims that the essays gathered in his collection "recover[ed]" what he labels "new liberal themes" though by "new liberal" he is not referring to the historical new liberalism. See Damico, "Introduction," pp. 1–2.

[25] For a similar claim, see Ball's defense of the benefits accruing to political theory from doing conceptual history:

As one among many approaches to the study of political theory, conceptual history serves to alert us to features of our world that familiarity has obscured. It supplies us with the distant mirror of past practices and beliefs that seem strange and alien to our modern (or perhaps post-modern) eyes. To encounter and attempt to understand these beliefs and practices in all their strangeness requires the stretching of our own concepts and categories. The conceptual historian aims to address this sense of strangeness, of difference; not to make it less strange or different, but to make it more comprehensible. The aim is to shed light on past practices and beliefs, and in so doing to stretch the linguistic limits of present-day political discourse. (Ball, "Political Theory and Conceptual Change," pp. 42–3.)

contribution that it "is by now not much disputed that the so-called 'liberal–communitarian debate' was nothing of the sort ..."[26] The debate is misconceived, first of all, because liberals have recently begun accepting crucial communitarian tenets, admitting that liberalism has always been capable of accommodating them though it has not always been *overtly* sensitive to them. Second, the debate is misconceived because both sides have too often argued at cross-purposes.

Communitarian liberalism

According to Simon Caney, modern liberals have "developed a liberalism" combining "the best in communitarianism with traditional liberal commitments."[27] Therefore, much of the debate has grown misplaced because both sides do not realize how much they have always shared. Then "Why," Caney wonders, "did communitarianism arise?" It arose, he insists, because "in many ways political thought in the 1970s seemed to be taking the same course as political thought had in the last two centuries."[28] That is, in the last two centuries, liberalism moved from utilitarianism to Kantianism to Hegelian communitarianism. Likewise, since the 1970s, liberalism has moved from utilitarianism to Rawlsian neo-Kantianism to Hegelian-inspired anti-Kantianism. But, in retracing this move a second time in the twentieth century, liberalism purportedly learned from its previous mistakes by more self-consciously and effectively integrating many essential communitarian concerns with traditional liberal commitments.

Stephen Mulhall and Adam Swift strongly disagree. They claim that it is Caney who misconceives the debate because he "tends to over-emphasize the unity of the liberal tradition and under-emphasize the degree to which liberalism's self-understanding has been importantly altered by its engagement with the communitarian critics."[29] Caney's characterization of the overall unity of the liberal tradition may indeed be overexaggerated as Mulhall and Swift suggest. They may be correct in contending that liberalism has recently and significantly changed,

---

[26] Alan Ryan, "Staunchly Modern, Non-Bourgeois Liberalism," in this volume, pp. 188–9. See also his "The Liberal Community," in John W. Chapman and Ian Shapiro (eds.), *Democratic Community, Nomos XXXV* (New York University Press, 1993), p. 91 where he argues that "the conflict between liberalism and communitarianism that the 'debate' supposes is a figment of the imagination."

[27] Simon Caney, "Liberalism and Communitarianism: A Misconceived Debate," *Political Studies*, 40 (1992), 289.

[28] Ibid.

[29] Stephen Mulhall and Adam Swift, "Liberalism and Communitarianism: Whose Misconception? A Reply to S. Caney, 'Liberalism and Communitarianism: A Misconceived Debate,'" *Political Studies*, 41 (1993), 654.

thereby displaying considerable discontinuity, thanks to its encounter with communitarianism. But Caney is not overexaggerating if we consider the new liberalism. In short, Mulhall and Swift's criticism loses much of its force with regard to new liberals. Their modified liberalism shows the extent to which liberalism had *already* succeeded in becoming sufficiently communitarian thus revealing the extent to which the current round of the debate is misconceived. For one thing, new liberals demonstrated that the relationship between liberalism and communitarianism need not be one of simple opposition. For another, their communitarian liberalism produced a change in liberalism's self-understanding though this self-understanding afterwards lost much of its force. Thus, our case for retrieving the new liberals seems very strong indeed.[30]

Our case goes something like this: whereas Rawls' earlier liberalism (the chief target of communitarian critics like Sandel) has a great deal of affinity with individualism, new liberals aimed at ridding liberalism of its self-centered individualism. That is, Rawls' earlier liberalism assigned priority to right over good, relied on individualist understanding of the self as an unsituated chooser, and defended contractarian justice and state neutrality. Early Rawlsian liberalism thus held community and the common good in suspicion. By contrast, the new liberals defended traditional liberal commitments, all-the-while taking community and common good seriously. They accorded individuals pride of place while simultaneously situating them socially. They conceived justice as constitutive of the kind of community where mutual commitments flourished without which individual freedom would never thrive in turn. New liberals also featured rights but recast them from a communitarian perspective. In sum, new liberals combined communitarian zeal for common good and community with traditional liberal concerns for basic rights, justice, and freedom. Hence, our strong case for retrieving new liberal thought gains special importance in light of the individualistic character of Rawlsian liberalism which the liberal vs. communitarian debate has plainly revealed.

Our strong case for retrieving the new liberalism is, however, not without limitations. Whereas Caney overexaggerates the unity of the liberal tradition, our position risks overexaggerating its discontinuity by making the relationship between new liberals and contemporary philosophical liberals too dichotomous. Our position, that is, risks assuming too sharp a contrast between the new liberalism, which is innocent of communitarian charges, and contemporary philosophical liberalism,

---

[30] However, inasmuch as our case for retrieval focuses on the new liberals, rather than liberalism as a whole, we also avoid artificially exaggerating the unity of the liberal tradition.

which is not. It risks substituting a false dualism between new liberalism and contemporary philosophical liberalism for the false dualism between new liberalism and contemporary communitarianism. The former dichotomy would be just as misleading as the latter.

Our strong case, in other words, risks overlooking the extent to which Rawls and other leading contemporary liberal theorists have been quite widely regarded as not subscribing, either explicitly or even implicitly, to a rigidly individualist, abstract, and ahistorical kind of liberalism. This view is well established in Mulhall and Swift's widely read guide to the liberal vs. communitarian debate, *Liberals and Communitarians* (2nd edn., 1996). They even show that, far from instrumentalizing politics, Rawls has always defended the intrinsic good of political community. Furthermore, according to them, Rawls never really held that it makes sense to view individuals as socially unsituated.

Consequently our case for retrieving the new liberalism may be somewhat weakened, but it is by no means demolished. Retrieval remains attractive, nonetheless, even if new liberals are not alone in avoiding the errors that communitarians attribute to liberalism. Contemporary liberals now struggle to avoid these errors too. Retrieval remains attractive insofar as new liberals constitute an unjustifiably marginalized tradition of liberal thinking that avoids communitarian charges but in interestingly and importantly different ways. In our view, no contemporary liberal thinker (with the possible exception of Raz) has reconstructed liberalism along communitarian lines so systematically as the new liberals did. At a minimum, therefore, the new liberals constitute an invaluable resource for contemporary liberals trying to show that liberal and communitarian approaches are compatible and mutually reinforcing. New liberal conceptions of community make this abundantly clear.

Contemporary liberals, like past liberals, worry about how thick kinds of community can threaten traditional liberal values such as individual choice, toleration, and pluralism.[31] Yet, as noted previously, even Rawls values community especially where it serves as "a fair scheme of mutual cooperation between free and equal citizens." Likewise, Raz and Kymlicka take community seriously.[32] But new liberals had already defended complex and subtle views of liberal community long before, partly because, no doubt, theory and political practice were so intimately connected for them whereas contemporary liberals tend to keep the nitty-gritty of politics at a distance. Freeden, for example, has discerned

[31] Stanley I. Benn, *A Theory of Freedom* (Cambridge University Press, 1988), pp. 213–35; Holmes, *The Anatomy of Antiliberalism* (Cambridge, MA: Harvard University Press, 1993), pp. 198–200.
[32] Miller, "Communitarianism: Left, Right and Centre," pp. 175–6.

four senses of new liberal community that are capable of serving as a promising resource for contemporary liberals as they endeavor to make their liberalism more community-friendly.[33]

Our case for retrieving new liberal thought is also propelled by the important division within contemporary liberalism between perfectionism and neutrality which Mulhall and Swift hold that Caney ignores in his insistence on liberal unity. The issue of neutrality, especially, is the focus of much communitarian criticism of Rawls. But unlike Rawls, new liberals are invulnerable to communitarian criticisms that liberal neutrality is inviable. Their perfectionist liberalism demonstrates the distinctive way in which they are not guilty of communitarian charges. Though new liberals differ from Rawlsian liberalism on this score, their perfectionism also anticipates Raz's perfectionist liberalism. By contrast, Mulhall and Swift connect the communitarian nature of Raz's liberalism with his perfectionism, maintaining that Raz is doing something new and interesting. But, we suggest, Raz's perfectionist liberalism is not so exceptional and, Rawls notwithstanding, neutrality is not an essential feature of liberalism.

The new liberals, then, anticipated recent liberal maneuvers aimed at accommodating the communitarian challenge. They did so systematically, incorporating subtle and complex notions of community with robust forms of perfectionism. On the other hand, their maneuvering was not a defensive, almost artificial reaction to some perceived external communitarian threat as is the case with contemporary philosophical liberals. Rather, they did this from *within* the liberal tradition itself thereby testifying to its remarkable, natural flexibility.

Thus, communitarian criticisms of liberalism are unwarranted and the most that we can say on behalf of communitarianism is what Ryan claims in suggesting that "the parodic picture of liberalism offered in Michael Sandel's *Liberalism and the Limits of Justice* served only one valuable purpose, that of forcing liberal political theorists to say more clearly than they had bothered to before just what the sociological and cultural assumptions of their theory were."[34] That a body of theory has not, until challenged, bothered to set out its sociological and cultural assumptions does not establish that it is totally unaware (or has not been or cannot become aware) of those assumptions.

---

[33] Michael Freeden, "Liberal Community: An Essay in Retrieval," in this volume.
[34] Ryan, "Staunchly Modern, Non-Bourgeois Liberalism," in this volume, p. 189 See also Stephen Mulhall and Adam Swift, "The Social Self in Political Theory: The Communitarian Critique of the Liberal Subject," in David Bakhurst and Christine Synowich (eds.), *The Social Self* (London: Sage Publications, 1995), pp. 103–22.

Arguing at cross-purposes

The liberal–communitarian debate is also misconceived because, as Taylor contends, the two sides argue at cross-purposes.[35] That is, both confuse ontology with normativity.

Every political theory must have two components: ontology and advocacy (philosophical anthropology and prescriptivity). Ontologically, atomism and holism are principal rivals. Regarding advocacy, individualism and collectivism oppose each other fundamentally. The essential issue concerns the relationship between ontology and advocacy which is typically viewed either as analytical or supportive, either as logical or as one of affinity. Analytic connection holds that prescriptive principles are somehow derived from, and justified by, social ontology. Relations of affinity hold that political advocacy is not conceptually derived from social ontology. Rather, such relations are much weaker, with ontology merely supporting, or setting the boundaries for, prescriptive principles.

The latter, weaker relationship informs the cross-purposes argument. According to the latter, communitarian criticisms of liberalism's individualistic nature, such as Sandel's, are essentially ontological. They are directed chiefly at liberalism's purported atomist, ontological foundations. Rejecting atomist ontology, however, does not necessarily entail rejecting individualist advocacy (liberalism as a substantive moral and political doctrine). Being committed to liberal values such as normative individualism does not entail being committed to atomism. Partisans on both sides of the liberal–communitarian debate are confused in thinking that ontological atomism and normative individualism are inherently linked. Thus, Taylor holds quite plausibly that liberal values may be best supported by a holist rather than an atomist social ontology, giving us holist individualism.[36] According to Taylor, communitarian criticisms are typically directed at liberalism's atomist ontological foundations. But normative liberalism does not presuppose such foundations. Indeed, liberal values flourish best on holist and communitarian ontological foundations.

New liberal thought, which rejects atomist social ontology while embracing liberal individuality, perfectly exemplifies Taylor's holist individualism. For new liberals, as with Taylor, the development of individuality depends on thick communal nurturing.

While the new liberalism exemplifies and anticipates Taylor's holist individualism, the new liberalism also reveals its limitations. Briefly,

---

[35] Charles Taylor, "Cross-Purposes: The Liberal Communitarian Debate," in Rosenblum, *Liberalism and the Moral Life.*
[36] Ibid., p. 163.

Taylor's holist individualism rests on the premise that any crossover position from ontology to advocacy is possible thus denying a strong linkage between ontology and advocacy. That is, holist individualism may commit the opposite error to that of the strong relationship it rejects. Strong linkage between ontology and advocacy entails either atomist individualism or holist collectivism as the only symmetrical and therefore tenable options. By rejecting strict linkage, Taylor effectively concedes that complete crossover positions, that is atomist collectivism and holist individualism, are equally viable possibilities. Asymmetry is just as plausible as symmetry. Because holism is the ontological opposite of atomism and individualism is the normative opposite of collectivism, either ontological position can support opposite advocacy positions.

To appreciate this difficulty more fully, we need to recognize another possible dimension of Taylor's argument that he does not. He focuses on communitarian ontological criticism of liberal atomist ontology. It is also possible, however, to look at communitarian normative criticism of liberal individualism. The core of that criticism is that liberal individualism (as a substantive moral and political doctrine) purportedly fails to recognize genuine shared goals or the common good but instead regards social life merely as a framework for competitive private interests. But as we have been suggesting, Rawls regards political community as intrinsically as well as instrumentally good. Normative communitarianism, for its part, is no less complex insofar as there is no single communitarian political doctrine. There is conservative (right) communitarianism, socialist (left) communitarianism as well as liberal communitarianism.[37]

Not only is there no single communitarian doctrine (normative communitarianism), there is also no single coherent ontological holism or communitarianism that supports liberal values as Taylor's holist individualism seems to suggest (unless, of course, we contrast holism with general or crude atomism). As Gaus shows in his chapter on Bosanquet, even economic individualism can be defended on organicist ontological foundations. His analysis suggests, furthermore, that the relationship between holist ontology and economic individualism need not be necessarily straightforward. Bosanquet does not simply invoke holism but rather a particular form of it which stresses not so much the whole but its articulation in unique individuals. This articulation, then, leads to economic individualism instead of socialism.

Freeden's chapter on community in new liberal thought likewise demonstrates that there is no single coherent communitarian holism. He shows that whereas Hobson's communal ontology supports the norma-

[37] Miller, "Communitarianism: Left, Right and Centre," pp. 174–8.

tive claim that society itself possesses rights, Green's communal ontology does not. Their normative positions differ depending on the
"thickness" of their holist ontology.

In sum, unpacked and unqualified, holist individualism holds that
holist/communitarian ontology best sustains normative individualism.
However, once holist/communitarian ontology is unpacked, it becomes
abundantly clear that there is no one coherent communitarian holist
ontology. As Miller says, "The relationship between the philosophical
anthropology and the prescriptive principles is one of support rather
than entailment ..."[38] Yet, as he also correctly allows, "what emerges
from my analysis is that the claims such as 'community is constitutive of
personal identity' which are loosely bandied about in discussions of
communitarianism actually need a good deal of unpacking before it is
clear what they mean ..."[39]

Taylor's holist individualism shows how the debate between liberals
and communitarians is misleading by being at cross-purposes. But holist
individualism is itself not unproblematic in suggesting that ontological
holism and normative individualism can be linked so facilely. Thus, at
the same time that holist individualism exposes the confusion of the
"debate," it must nevertheless be unpacked in turn. The new liberalism
reveals not only the force of holist individualism but also its limitations.

Reconciling individuality and sociability

Intellectual roots

We have been claiming that new liberals sought to disassociate liberalism
from self-interested competitive individualism insofar as they held that
individuality flourished best on a holist understanding of society committed to stimulating greater cooperative interaction. The new liberalism, in short, aimed at reconciling individuality and sociability.

Reconciling individuality and sociability rests on the distinction new
liberals drew between individualism and individuality. Individualism
conceives individuals as competitive, self-centered, and independent,
and social life simply as an arena for coordinating the competitive
pursuit of private interests. By contrast, new liberals espoused the
development of individuality which could flourish only where social life
was understood organically and cooperatively. Thus, the new liberalism
was not so much a form of normative individualism as a form of
individuality-cultivating sociability.

---

[38] Ibid., p. 172.   [39] Ibid., p. 180.

The new liberals, then, made a double move. First, they rejected the atomist picture of individuals which, second, entailed rejecting the view of social life as little more than an aggregative gathering of dueling self-interests. Instead, they reconceived individuals in developmental and relational terms stressing social life's sociability as key to sustaining new liberal individuality. Though repudiating competitive individualism, new liberals championed strong rights as internal to, and essential to, the realization of individuality. Individuality and rights were both integral to the new liberalism's new individualism.

The new liberalism's double rejection of narrow individualism was equally a double affirmation. Reconceptualizing individuals as mutually self-developing entails reconceptualizing social life as a cooperative and mutually enhancing venture rather than as a competitive one. The two moves are not only inseparable but also reciprocally reinforcing. The development of individuality requires a certain kind of cooperative sociability which requires, in turn, the flourishing of a certain kind of mutually enriching, other-directed individuality. Mill initiated the first conceptualizing move but he failed to embrace fully (or at least consistently) the second move connecting the development of individuality with promoting thick, cooperative sociability.[40] New liberals embraced both moves fully.

J. S. Mill and the importance of individuality

Mill reconstructed the liberal individual by locating individuality, rather than self-interest, at its conceptual center. This reconstruction stemmed from what he regarded as Bentham's and James Mill's overly-narrow and mechanical view of human nature.[41] According to Mill, Bentham held that humans were primarily interested in maximizing pleasure and minimizing pain. Mill claimed that Bentham regrettably omitted our interest in excellence of character and personal worth from his table of the springs of action. By contrast, Mill emphasized our inner life and our capacity for personal growth which, in turn, required recognizing that we were potentially self-transforming. The pursuit of individuality consisted, accordingly, in exercising and successfully developing our capacities. Mill, then, laid the foundations, which new liberals built upon, for reconceptualizing liberal individualism in terms of liberal

---

[40] Gerald F. Gaus, *The Modern Liberal Theory of Man* (London and Canberra: Croom Helm, 1983), p. 270.

[41] J. S. Mill, "Bentham" [1838], in John M. Robson *et al.* (eds.), *The Collected Works of John Stuart Mill*, 33 vols. (University of Toronto Press, 1963–), vol. X, pp. 75–115. See also Alan Ryan, *J. S. Mill* (London: Routledge & Kegan Paul, 1974), pp. 104–6, 131–3.

individuality. But he did not fully make the second complementary move of linking individuality with sociability.

Bosanquet explained Mill's failure to make this second move as stemming from his "internalist" understanding of individuality. For Mill, according to Bosanquet, individuality "is not nourished and evoked by the varied play of relations and obligations in society, but lies in a sort of inner self, to be cherished by enclosing it."[42] Though Bosanquet overexaggerates, he nevertheless has a point. He over-exaggerates inasmuch as Mill does recognize the importance of sociability.[43] In *Utilitarianism*, Mill insists that a major cause for individuals not enjoying meaningful lives is selfishness, in "caring for nobody, but themselves . . ."[44] Similarly, in *On Liberty*, Mill insists that his plea for individual liberty is not a defense of "selfish indifference," instead claiming that "there is need of great increase of disinterested exertion to promote the good of others."[45] Bosanquet, however, is correct insofar as Mill does not seem to locate social relations at the core of his conception of individuality, Hobhouse's assessment of Mill notwithstanding.[46]

According to Richard Norman, Mill's devaluing of social relations as constitutive of individuality accounts for his failure to integrate individual and general happiness convincingly. As Norman says, "The transition from individual happiness to the general happiness cannot be made, so long as we start from the idea of the isolated individual." We can successfully "bridge the moral gap between self and others only when we understand the self as a social self."[47] Such an under-

---

[42] Bernard Bosanquet, *The Philosophical Theory of the State*, 2nd edn. (London: Macmillan, 1910), p. 61.

[43] Gaus, *Modern Liberal Theory*, pp. 107–8; Michael Freeden, *Ideologies and Political Theory* (Oxford: Clarendon Press, 1996), pp. 149–51; Ryan, "The Liberal Community", pp. 93–4.

[44] J. S. Mill, *Utilitarianism* [1861], in Robson *et al.*, *Collected Works*, vol. X, p. 25.

[45] J. S. Mill, *On Liberty*, in John Gray (ed.), *On Liberty and Other Essays* (Oxford University Press, 1991), p. 84.

[46] L. T. Hobhouse, *Liberalism*, in James Meadowcroft (ed.), *Liberalism and Other Writings* (Cambridge University Press, 1994), p. 60. A further explanation, which cannot be pursued here, concerns Mill's "punctual self." Though Ryan holds that Mill's "punctual self" does not dictate his conception of moral agency and hence does not settle the question of how communitarian Mill was, Ryan himself concedes that "*Something* . . . carries from the metaphysical disagreement" between Mill and Green regarding the nature of the self. ("Liberal Community," p. 94.) That "something" might go some way to explaining why, though Mill recognized sociability, it is nevertheless not constitutive of his view of individuality. Or, as Hobhouse put it, at the heart of liberalism lies "the organic conception of the relation between the individual and society – a conception toward which Mill worked . . . and which forms the starting point of T. H. Green's philosophy . . ." See Hobhouse, *Liberalism*, p. 60.

[47] Richard Norman, *The Moral Philosophers: An Introduction to Ethics* (Oxford: Clarendon Press, 1983), p. 156.

standing, Norman adds, is defended by Bradley, for whom the self is not isolated but "is penetrated, infected, characterized by the existence of others, its content implies in every fibre relations of community."[48] Moreover, this social understanding of the self, which bridges the "moral gap between self and others" engendered by individualism, suggests a way out of the dualism of practical reasoning which troubled Sidgwick so greatly.

Organic sociability

Organicism is frequently viewed by liberals as incompatible with, and indeed hostile to, individuality, and therefore inconsistent with liberalism. It suggests a one-sided relationship between individuals and society, between parts and the whole. Social wholes are viewed as greater than the sum of their individual parts, and consequently are sometimes said to possess a collective consciousness of their own independent personality. The ontological and ethical status of individuals thus risks being subordinated to that of society. Indeed, the organic metaphor has often been wielded against the mechanistic metaphor which has been used to defend atomistic social structures privileging the primacy of the individual. Hence, it is, perhaps, regrettable and ironic that new liberals deployed the organic metaphor to promote what the metaphor is often said by liberals to devalue, namely liberal individuality.[49]

However, new liberals deployed the organic metaphor in rejecting atomism (individualist social structure) without embracing holism (supra-individual organicism). The later kind of holism is not the sole alternative to atomism. New liberals defended what may be described as "relational organicism" in contrast to both atomism and full-blown holism.[50] Relational organicism embraces the following: the interdependence of the self-development of individuals, the interdependence of individuals and society, and the mutual recognition of each as a personality.[51]

Relational organicism thus enabled new liberals to break with self-

[48] F. H. Bradley, *Ethical Studies*, 2nd edn. (London: Macmillan, 1927), p. 172.
[49] For a similar claim, cast in different terminology, see Philip Pettit, *The Common Mind: An Essay on Psychology, Society, and Politics* (Oxford University Press, 1993), pp. 172–5. Herbert Spencer, whose liberal credentials are unimpeachable, likewise deployed organicism to defend traditional liberal values. See especially Herbert Spencer's "The Social Organism," in Herbert Spencer, *Essays: Scientific, Political and Speculative* [1868–74], 3 vols. (London: Williams and Norgate, 1901), vol. I.
[50] See Avital Simhony, "Idealist Organicism: Beyond Holism and Individualism," *History of Political Thought*, 12 (1991), 515–35.
[51] See Gaus, *Modern Liberal Theory*, p. 72; Freeden, *Ideologies and Political Theory*, pp.

centered narrow individualism and to reconceptualize liberalism. First, relational organicism highlights how self-development is so thoroughly reciprocal. By rejecting the atomism of older liberalism, according to which individuals are supposedly full human beings outside of society, organicism insists that we see social relations as constitutive of each individual's identity and well-being. The organic metaphor reminds us that individuals depend on each other for the development of their capacities and that enjoyment of relations with others partially constitutes the realization of these capacities. Hence, new liberals emphasize mutual dependence over competitive independence and appreciation of common enjoyment over private enjoyment. Because we can enjoy self-development together, and because the participation of all in that enjoyment is partly constitutive of the enjoyment of each, self-development is worth pursuing as a common goal.

Second, relational organicism also helps us appreciate the importance of building the right kind of communal relations in order to accommodate concern for our own good with our obligations to others. Thus, membership in the kind of society that fosters self-development, especially moral self-development, is intrinsically valuable and a matter of common enterprise and is therefore also a reason for common action, which, in turn, justifies a positive conception of the state as an enabling agency. Third, for relational organicism, the good of self-development, though enjoyed by distinct individuals, is nevertheless a common good whose collective value is more than merely aggregative. And far from expressing the will of some pseudo social entity, our shared social interest is simply the mutual interests of freely cooperating individuals taking interest in each other's development. Relational organicism thus tempers our tendency to see interests as fundamentally competitive and conflictual.

The relational organicism of new liberals, like their emphasis on the cultivation of individuality, shows just how much new liberals recast liberalism from within the conceptual parameters of the liberal tradition itself. The new liberals learned to say on their own what contemporary liberals have had to be admonished into saying.

The essays

Michael Freeden's "Liberal Community: An Essay in Retrieval" introduces our collection. Setting the tone for the essays which follow his, Freeden urges us to question our provincial assumptions about the identity of liberalism given that the new liberalism was no less commu-

203–6; Simhony, "Idealist Organicism," 519–23. See also Hobhouse, *Liberalism*, pp. 60–3, 65.

nitarian than it was liberal. Focusing primarily on Hobhouse and, to a lesser extent, on Hobson, Freeden argues that the new liberals deployed sophisticated versions of community at the core of their thinking. For Hobhouse, according to Freeden, our need for community is a natural impulse whose significance, for most of human history, has been ill-appreciated. Eventually, this impulse evolved into a common sentiment and more recently into a rational aim grounded in our conscious recognition that the flourishing of each is dependent upon the flourishing of others. We now cultivate community deliberately as an arena of ethical partnership and mutual respect. Moreover, in Freeden's view, the new liberals also anticipated recent liberal theorizing, like Will Kymlicka's, in trying to balance the importance of smaller communities within larger communities as a source of individual fulfillment against the value of individual liberty.

Rex Martin's "T. H. Green on Individual Rights and the Common Good" is propelled by the claim that Green's theory of rights is worth exploring not only because it is one of the finest theories of rights developed to date, but also because of the way Green's idea of rights is conjoined with the idea of a common good. Communitarians tend to pit the idea of rights against a commitment to the common good. Martin's essay shows, however, that Green seeks to reconcile the two within a single liberal perspective. Martin also holds that since Green's account of rights includes the requirement of social recognition in addition to the idea of common good, a potential tension afflicts his overall theory inasmuch as either of these two components could plausibly exist in the absence of the other. Martin suggests that Green resolves this tension as well. For Green, while the idea of social recognition belongs to the concept of rights, the notion of the common good belongs to the dimension of justifying something as a right. According to Martin, Green's notion of an institutionally justified right of each and all provides the basis for his new liberal conception of individual rights that, far from being antithetical to, is compatible with the idea of the common good. Although he criticizes Green for failing to develop an adequate institutional framework necessary for his reconciliation rights and common good to work, Martin nevertheless believes that this deficiency can be repaired by developing a particular account of democracy which is fully compatible with Green's ideas.

Avital Simhony's "T. H. Green's Complex Common Good: Between Liberalism and Communitarianism" holds that Green's notion of common good is worth studying not only because it is the centerpiece of his liberalism but because he introduced this idea to modern liberal thinking. Simhony examines Green's idea of common good against recent liberal vs. communitarian theorizing that continues to pit, though less irreconcilably, the "politics of rights" against the "politics of the common good" made famous by Sandel. She argues that we ought to understand Green's common good as a complex idea. Its complexity is revealed in our inability to classify it as belonging neatly to either the liberal or communitarian points of view whose purported opposition it therefore defies and transcends. Simhony explores this complexity from three perspectives. Morally, Green's common good is an ethic of joint self-realization that is best understood as bridging the dualism of self-love and benevolence. Politically, Green institutionalizes this ethic in terms of justice and citizenship which form the basis of the good society and also constitute the common good. Finally, Green appeals to both liberal and communitarian resources (Kant as well as Aristotle and Hegel) in carrying out his common good project. A full appreciation of this project shows, first, that the relationship between liberalism and communitarianism (and republicanism for that matter) is not, and cannot be, one of simple opposition. Second, such an appreciation reveals that the liberal tradition can unproblematically and readily embrace Green's complex notion of common good. Green's complex common good, in other words, is not just immune to traditional liberal anxieties about common good but actually extends liberal sensibilities.

John Morrow's "Private Property, Liberal Subjects, and the State" offers a thorough and comprehensive analysis of how new liberal thinkers (Green, Bosanquet, Hobhouse, and Hobson) defend private property in some form as necessary to the development of liberal subjects. Central to Morrow's argument, however, is his claim that new liberals do not see property rights as purely private claims. In that sense, Morrow's examination of property rights buttresses and illustrates our fundamental argument, namely that new liberals take rights seriously though they reject the individualistic, private society account of social life. Indeed, as Morrow shows, new liberals held that we value rights because they promote a common, rather than a purely personal, conception of good. The right to private property exemplifies this basic understanding of rights. Morrow also contends that new liberals grounded property rights in the social embeddedness of individuals. They believed that private property was essential to self-development precisely because of our inherent sociability. Morrow additionally shows that, despite variations in their accounts of private property, all new liberals followed Green in arguing that property rights provided opportunities for individuals to pursue a common good which simultaneously constituted their personal good. Moreover, according to Morrow, their treatment of property, in contrast to the abstract cast of many approaches to property rights, focused on concrete issues of public contention and was meant to provide a basis for policy-making.

In "Neutrality, Perfectionism, and the New Liberal Conception of the State," James Meadowcroft contends that insofar as our identities are socially constituted, we ought to promote mutual interdependence by promoting common good, understood as the good of each and every individual. Promoting each individual's good means maximizing everyone's opportunities to prosper as self-realizing personalities. Maximizing these opportunities requires, in turn, empowering perfectionist government policies as well as politically active, engaged citizens. Hobhouse, in particular, defends the kind of perfectionist liberalism that Meadowcroft finds attractive. Moreover, for Meadowcroft, since Hobhouse is nevertheless a genuine liberal through and through, we ought to be wary of reducing liberalism to simplistic formulas that purportedly capture its essence while ignoring the conceptual complexity of some of its historical variations. Meadowcroft concludes that the liberal tradition's actual conceptual complexity suggests, furthermore, that it is as much constituted by its common reference to symbols, icons, causes, and authorities as it is by any substantive conceptual continuity.

Gerald Gaus' "Bosanquet's Communitarian Defense of Economic Individualism: A Lesson in the Complexities of Political Theory" challenges the new liberal claim that because our identities are communally constituted, we must commit ourselves to collective action. Bosanquet's challenge is intriguing since, like Hobhouse for instance, he rejects individualist accounts of society and likewise embraces an organic (communal) account of social life. However, Bosanquet vigorously criticizes the new liberal welfare state and defends economic liberalism. Gaus argues that Bosanquet's combination of a thoroughgoing, organic (communitarian) social metaphysics with a strong defense of economic individualism is not only coherent, but is also a more plausible communitarian political program than the semi-socialist program of the new liberals. Gaus' argument depends on a particular interpretation of Bosanquet's conception of the social organism. According to Gaus, Bosanquet conceived it as a complex whole that (in Hayekian fashion) no member can adequately grasp, though the life of each is informed by, and is reflective of, the social organism's social will. Gaus claims that two insights follow from this understanding of Bosanquet. First, notwithstanding communitarian criticisms of liberalism, it is far from clear that communitarians can dispense with liberalism's property-based market order. Second, new liberalism's sympathizers should reexamine their belief that communitarian liberalism is incompatible with economic individualism.

In "The New Liberalism and the Rejection of Utilitarianism," David Weinstein contends that the new liberalism is considerably more indebted to nineteenth-century utilitarianism than the received view has recognized. The new liberalism, both as moral and as political theory, is less a rejection of nineteenth-century utilitarianism and more a modification of it. Consequently, the new liberalism has much to offer not just liberals laboring to modify liberalism and defend it from the fusillades of their communitarian critics, but also modern utilitarians struggling to accommodate utilitarianism with liberalism.

Alan Ryan's "Staunchly Modern, Non-Bourgeois Liberalism" shows how new liberal theorizing characterized John Dewey's political thought, making Dewey a critical bridge linking English new liberalism with political philosophical currents in the United States during the first half of the twentieth-century. Despite contemporary American liberalism's insensitivity to its own historical tradition, the new liberalism once enjoyed an insistent voice in Dewey whom Ryan has elsewhere referred to as a "midwestern T. H. Green."[52] For Ryan, greater familiarity with Dewey should entail better appreciation of a way of liberal theorizing that has, regrettably, faded from our memory.

Andrew Vincent's "The New Liberalism and Citizenship" completes our collection by depicting how the new liberal "active" conception of citizenship, which dominated English political thought and policy prior to World War I, gave way to a "passive" notion of citizenship over two phases after the war. Whereas new liberals theorized citizenship in terms of civic duties as well as rights, later liberals impoverished liberal citizenship by devaluing strong civic duties as correlative of rights. As a consequence, citizenship became less of a self-realizing activity in the service of the community and more of a passive entitlement alienating citizens from their community. This impoverishing of citizenship began, nonetheless, with new liberals themselves, especially Green and Hobhouse, who deployed the rhetoric of rights in the formative phase of the new liberalism in order to accent its continuity with classical liberalism. Thus, even from its very inception, the new liberalism exhibited a complex tension between civil and civic citizenship; between market individualism and rights on the one hand and social solidarity and mutual duty on the other.

Conclusion

Regrettably, the new liberalism is too often treated by contemporary liberals, insofar as it is treated at all, as some kind of aberration, as an

---

[52] Alan Ryan, *John Dewey* (New York: W. W. Norton and Co., 1995), p. 12.

intellectual epiphenomenon barely worth acknowledging but never to be taken overly seriously.[53] Taking the new liberalism seriously, we believe, is a liberal task long overdue. To be sure, we do not believe that the non-individualist liberalism of the new liberals is the "true" or "authentic" liberalism; we do not claim that it is the "real" mainstream of the liberal tradition. Rewriting the history of the liberal tradition is not our goal. Recovering it is. Our goal, therefore, may be modest but we believe it is crucial. First, the new liberalism is an *essential* moment in the history and theory of liberalism and ought to be so recognized. Second, such recognition is not merely historically significant. It also carries a sharp normative edge insofar as it suggests ways in which contemporary liberal theorizing can enrich itself by tapping into its own fertile liberal resources.

The new liberalism is an undervalued episode in *our* liberal tradition. Liberalism has become unduly monochromatic as a consequence, making it unduly vulnerable to criticism. Communitarians in particular have exploited our historical myopia regarding the richness of liberalism's conceptual treasures in order to give liberalism a bad theoretical name which contemporary liberals have only recently begun trying to repair by rediscovering much of the theoretical ground already traversed by new liberals. Hence, much of liberalism's bad name rests on the bad name of a historical caricature. This volume aims to join the battle against this bad theoretical name by doing battle against this historical caricature. Our aims, then, are hardly modest after all.

[53] See, for instance, Anthony Arblaster, *The Rise and Decline of Western Liberalism* (Oxford: Basil Blackwell, 1984), pp. 6, 143, 335.

1   Liberal community: an essay in retrieval

Michael Freeden

The liberal–communitarian debate, that intellectual companion and topological *vade mecum* of Anglo-American political philosophers in the 1980s and early 1990s, has left a residue that is still difficult to expunge. At its worst, it has created a new generation of students unable to think about liberalism in terms other than the contrast in which the terms are presented, and a contingent of politicians who have eagerly assimilated communitarianism or anti-communitarianism to their short-list of sound bites. At best, it has encouraged professional philosophers to reengage with issues of social responsibility, respect for individuals, and the quasi-anthropology of human nature. But facile dichotomies, however attractive to the pedagogue and categorizer, are the bane of understanding social life in its complexities; monolithic interpretations assigned to political concepts obfuscate the varied indeterminacy of the meanings they contain; and abstractions from concrete human conduct are a hindrance to the moralist who is also a social reformer, as well as a hindrance to the political theorist who is also an analyst of the actual political thought of a society and its key thinkers.

The purpose of this chapter is hence manifold. It attempts to put recent philosophical discussion in a comparative historical perspective. It endeavors to suggest that other conversations about liberalism existed before the current, ahistorical and asocial, version and that to ignore those conversations is not only to turn a blind eye to a cumulative ideational discourse but to impoverish our comprehension of current issues. And it proposes that the concept of community – an intricate, term possessed of multiple and not necessarily compatible meanings – was, and perhaps still should be, central to the mature liberal traditions of the West, rather than external to them. This latter viewpoint is now more in evidence among political theorists who have entered the debate.[1] As yet, however, the discussants have not engaged in detailed

---

[1] For some instances, see C. Taylor, "Cross-Purposes: The Liberal–Communitarian Debate," in N. Rosenblum (ed.), *Liberalism and the Moral Life* (Cambridge, MA: Harvard University Press, 1989), pp. 159–82; A. Ryan, "The Liberal Community," in

textual examinations of the structures of arguments employed diachron-ically, in particular at the point when the relationship between liberalism and communitarianism became central to the liberal tradition. In what follows, that relationship is therefore not (re)invented but retrieved through an examination of some key British liberal theorists of the late nineteenth and early twentieth centuries. Nor is the intention to suggest that the moral theory behind contemporary philosophical liberalism is superior or inferior to the one underpinning British new liberal theory. Rather, it is claimed that the former is not wholly or even mainly representative of what earlier liberals included in their creed, of what they believed they were talking about, or of what they bequeathed to mainstream liberal thinking.

I have contended elsewhere that conceptions of sociability, some stronger, others weaker, are to be found in the writings of the main shapers of British liberalism, in the utterances of Locke, Mill, and T. H. Green; indeed, that a total absence of the concept of sociability must raise serious doubts as to whether the theory before us is liberal.[2] Here I shall examine in greater detail how, in the writings of key new liberals, sociability appears in the form of community. Community, however, did not embrace a single meaning for new liberals, and its diverse nuances were attached to other core liberal concepts in such a way as to produce variations within the new liberal family of political thinking. In order to understand these variations, we need to appreciate on which dimensions of meaning "community" underwent changes. And in order to under-stand why these dimensions played an important role, we need to recognize that the ontological assumptions and methodological con-cerns of the new liberals differed considerably from those adopted by contemporary East Coast philosophical liberals.

Hence a brief reference to current theories of community within the mainstream of those who have attempted to address the problems of contemporary philosophical liberalism is necessary. The most central feature of those theories is that community – if liberals can speak of it at all – is the consequence, not the cause, of social arrangements, that it is largely (and for some, entirely) the product of human volition, and that its role is to augment the autonomy of the individual, now understood as related to group culture. The heuristic intention of philosophical liberals has been to construct reasonable and persuasive arguments in favor of specific conceptions of justice and distribution, of autonomy and iden-

J. W. Chapman and I. Shapiro (eds.), *Democratic Community, Nomos XXXV* (New York University Press, 1993), pp. 91–114.
[2] M. Freeden, *Ideologies and Political Theory: A Conceptual Approach* (Oxford: Clarendon Press, 1996), chs. 4, 5.

tity, of self-expression and rights-protection, and of resolving potential conflict among groups, through the modeling of logical possibilities and their alternatives.[3] They have addressed these issues by establishing framework rules through which solutions incorporating principles of fairness and equality are mooted. The project of the new liberals, however, was importantly different, but these differences only become clearly focused if we are prepared to recognize that liberalism is not only a philosophical enterprise but an ideological one, that it not only equips us with reasonable or valuable ways of approaching complex social problems but contains conscious and unconscious cultural and ideational assumptions that respond to, and seek to shape, salient concerns of individuals and groups at particular times and in particular spaces. Needless to say, these ideologies help in understanding why some ethical solutions to the questions that have preoccupied both contemporary philosophical, and new, liberals are preferred to others, because they assist us in appreciating why specific questions were asked.

Many of the considerations new liberals brought to bear on their political theories were forged in an era which, while sharing some of the aims of current philosophical liberals, differed on many others. The new liberals came to political thinking equipped with a strong sense of beneficial historical change. They attached to rationality a confidence not only in its survival value but in its continuous enhancement. They believed in the power of politics to improve human lives. They claimed to discover that the social costs of human immiseration through subscribing to unfettered laws of supply, demand, and individual initiative were intolerable. And on that edifice they constructed their various views of community, because they believed that human beings prospered best when socially benign interaction was permitted full rein. But contemporary liberals live in a rather different world. They take as given that encouraging individual life-plans is the aim of a civilized society, and that people differ sufficiently in such plans, preferences, and capacities to install pluralism as a fact of social life, and a desirable one at that. They believe that choice-making is not merely an essential, but a dominant, feature of human nature, and that the multiplication of opportunities for choices in current societies carries with it enormous potential for human self-expression. Many of these liberals, through the power and mystique of the American constitution, believe that suprapolitical and largely supra-historical constructs are not only in evidence, but offer the best hope for reducing, if not overcoming, the discord present in pluralism. And even when such liberals are concerned with

---

[3] I exclude conservative theories of community such as A. MacIntyre's from the current discussion.

groups, at least with the cultural groups that have dominated the socio-political landscape of North America (because these groups are believed to be crucial carriers of pluralism), they are concerned because they question the monopoly of ethical legitimacy of the group on which many individuals still bestow emotional allegiance – the national community.

Community in current debate

The multi-layered concept of "community" may benefit from an analyt-ical perspective that addresses both its historical and structural dimen-sions. These have been notably absent, on the conscious, intentional level, in recent characterizations of community. Instead, conceptions of community have been constructed so as to exclude compatibilities with many of the *ethical* ends attributed to liberalism, but they also are selective about certain *ideological* assumptions. "Philosophical" commu-nitarianism is thus seen by its critics to blur the distinction between the political and the civil; it is seen to uphold an untenable majoritarianism against the justified claims of minorities; it is seen as a homogeneous and exclusivist structure through which a common good is sought and the basis of individual identity is furnished, often by recognizing the cohesive force of existing practices and traditions; and, of course, it is seen as introducing considerations irrelevant to liberal argument.[4] Again and again, we find a tendency to speak of "the communitarians" as one entity. Unsurprisingly, one theorist asserts: "Examining community from the perspective of American constitutional theory is highly instruc-tive … the longing for community is a chimera – romantic, naive, and, in the end, illiberal and dangerous."[5] Community is thus constructed out of what liberalism is not.

Many communitarians, on the other hand, proffer conceptualizations which establish the paucity of liberalism both as an ethical and a social theory, and they notably fashion communitarianism as a counter-project to liberalism. For Sandel, membership in a community is a constituent of individual identity, and it is an attachment which shapes at least in part the ends of the self, prior to the exercise of choice by that self. A "community must be constitutive of the shared self-understandings of the participants."[6] In his most recent book, Sandel reiterates the view that liberalism purports to be neutral towards particular visions of the

---

[4] For an example of the latter point, see A. Gutmann, "Communitarian Critics of Liberalism," *Philosophy and Public Affairs*, 14 (1985), 316.

[5] Compare H. N. Hirsch, "The Threnody of Liberalism: Constitutional Liberalism and the Renewal of Community," *Political Theory*, 14 (1986), 424.

[6] M. Sandel, *Liberalism and the Limits of Justice* (Cambridge University Press, 1982), pp. 149–50, 173.

good life, substituting fair procedures for specific ends. But he does invite the reader to distinguish between two meanings of liberalism. The first is liberalism in "common parlance" (what others might term liberal ideology): "the outlook of those who favour a more generous welfare state and a greater measure of social and economic equality." The second refers to the historical tradition of thought of liberalism which "runs from John Locke, Immanuel Kant, and John Stuart Mill to John Rawls."[7] Having thus made an important distinction, Sandel immediately renders it ineffectual. For "common parlance" liberalism is merely contemporary, its historical development having been overlooked, while the historical tradition Sandel traces is highly selective and, one might add, ahistorical. Any acquaintance with the new liberals demonstrates that "common parlance" had clear historical roots. On the other hand, the sequence from Locke to Kant to Mill to Rawls is a particular historical construction adapted to the United States, but while Locke and Mill are arguably major players in forming the basic ideology of contemporary American politics, both Kant and Rawls are relative newcomers, if not rank outsiders.[8] Moreover, when we look at alternative horizons of the European liberalism which inspired its American counterpart, chosen from multiple readings of liberalism's history, another sequence could equally, if not more, persuasively be traced from Locke to Bentham to Mill to Green to Hobhouse, and result in a very different interpretation of liberalism's features.

As a counter to a liberalism which is based on a largely negative conception of liberty, assuming the ultimate capacity of the individual as choice-maker, Sandel posits a republican communitarian theory which, he argues, has been replaced with liberalism. One can understand why, on Sandel's account, that dichotomization is a necessary outcome of his particular interpretation of historical traditions. For republican communitarianism is not only participatory but engages civic virtues: "a sense of belonging, a concern for the whole, a moral bond with the community." This version is to be distinguished from "the liberalism that conceives persons as free and independent selves," manifesting a voluntarism which casts them "as the authors of the only obligations that constrain."[9] Moreover, Sandel promotes the case for strong communal obligation and a conception of the common good which, in his view, is not part of the liberal case for the welfare state. That case, according to Sandel – drawing almost entirely on the writings of Rawls – depends "on

---

[7] M. Sandel, *Democracy's Discontent: America in Search of a Public Policy* (Cambridge, MA: Harvard University Press, 1996), p. 4.

[8] Compare Freeden, *Ideologies and Political Theory*, pp. 236–41.

[9] Sandel, *Democracy's Discontent*, pp. 5–6, 12.

the rights we would agree to respect if we could abstract from our interests and ends."[10]

Walzer's communitarianism is conspicuously different from Sandel's. Sandel employs community in order to reestablish the source of the ethical ends individuals invariably carry with them, and in focusing on that aspect of deontology he reintroduces the political into our understanding of individual identity, which a neutral liberalism ostensibly eliminated. Walzer's sympathetic approach to communitarianism is distinguished by its readiness to examine, and to dispute, not a disembedded liberal neutralism, but an older and more historically authenticated liberalism. He locates that liberalism on two dimensions: first, the model of fragmented free choice supposedly representing liberalism; second – and more significant – the actual social and political practices which liberalism purports to embody. Walzer's focus is thus not on community as the basis of individual identity but on communiti*es* as the expression of social networks. His communitarianism is not a challenge to liberalism's assumed estrangement from the political, but a challenge to the social unit of analysis employed by political theorists, an attempt to move away from the individual to "patterns of relationship, networks of power, and communities of meaning."[11] In recognizing the social power and political reality of the liberal fragmented model, Walzer shifts the debate on to the level of concrete ideological and sociological practices. And in so doing, unlike the more extreme anti-liberals, he acknowledges that much of the language of liberalism is "inescapable": rights, voluntarism, pluralism, toleration, privacy. His solution – a more realistic and historically more accurate one than Sandel's – is a liberal communitarianism. Walzer sums up his view in a plea: "It would be a good thing ... if we could teach those [liberal] selves to know themselves as social beings, the historical products of, and in part the embodiments of, liberal values."[12] That is precisely what the new liberals had already achieved in their own manner.

Really existing liberalisms: alternative communities and naturalist ontology

Many of the above communitarian or republican attributes are central features of British social liberalism (and of many of its continental counterparts). In claiming this it will of course be necessary to argue

[10] Ibid., p. 16.
[11] M. Walzer, "The Communitarian Critique of Liberalism," *Political Theory*, 18 (1990), 10.
[12] Ibid., 15.

that these European doctrines were still liberal on any reasonable understanding that does not narrowly equate liberalism with a spurious
atomistic model of human conduct that – as we know from historical
evidence – mainstream liberalism did not espouse,[13] nor with the opus
of Rawls and his intellectual circle.[14] Specifically, by insisting on
drawing a line between political and comprehensive liberalism, Rawls
removes any notion of community from ontological assumptions linked
to human nature, replacing them with a willed cooperation as an option
reflecting a rational but contrived overlapping consensus. Instead, community is relegated to a feature of a comprehensive doctrine, that is, to a
position of adjacency to the core features of political liberalism.[15] For
the new liberals, a notion of community was, to the contrary, one of the
fundamental constraints within which choice would be exercised. It is,
however, also the case that, within the new liberal family, frames of
reference which were partly different engendered disparate conceptualizations of a liberal communitarianism.

To maintain that the new liberalism was a communitarian body of
thought is not necessarily to adopt recent characterizations of community, let alone the role of "community" in promoting certain kinds of
political argument. To begin with, the new liberals' view of community
was constructed on the basis of historical and scientific theories about
the structure and growth of societies. At the historical level, they
subscribed to quasi-naturalistic accounts of social relations and social
development, which served as the cause of, and hence genetic explanation for, certain attributes of human conduct in society. At the structural
level, they subscribed to theories concerning the primacy and intensity
of social bonds which offered an interpretative framework for their
human and social values. Each particular theorist might have had a
somewhat different understanding of the components of these theories
but nevertheless operated within a recognizably shared discourse.
Beyond that, on a heuristic level, the new liberals assumed that a viable

[13] Thomas A. Spragens, Jr., while recognizing the importance of sympathy, benevolence,
mutual obligations, and social solidarity in developing a liberal sense of community in
the period stretching from Locke to J. S. Mill, unfortunately vitiates his argument by
remarking that the picture began to change in the late nineteenth century away from
community, totally ignoring the developments in liberal thought in that latter period
(T. A. Spragens, Jr., "Communitarian Liberalism," in A. Etzioni (ed.), *New Communitarian Thinking: Persons, Virtues, Institutions, and Communities* (Charlottesville:
University of Virginia Press, 1995), pp. 37–51).
[14] Another argument which cannot be ignored, but which is beyond the remit of this
chapter, is that the "procedural," neutralist liberalism which Sandel identifies as at the
heart of American public philosophy is an illusory stance based on myths and self-
deception as well as on a bracketing out of crucial aspects of the American liberal
tradition. See Freeden, *Ideologies and Political Theory*, ch. 6.
[15] J. Rawls, *Political Liberalism* (New York: Columbia University Press, 1993), pp. 40, 201.

political theory should achieve two aims. First, it should be grounded on empirical evidence. Second, it should foster and enhance the moral conduct that, in their view, could be deduced from an evolutionary and, occasionally, psychologically based explication of a well-functioning society. Human will was neither antagonistic to nature, nor was it to dominate nature.

Those aims of political theory were superimposed on – though the new liberals professed to derive them from – accounts of the empirically ascertainable structure of society and, in particular, the identification of the social unit as one of crucial and constitutive importance in fashioning human ends. But the new liberals, far from adhering to the homogeneous conception of community apparently detected by contemporary critics of communitarianism, subscribed to a broad range of communitarian positions and identified a variety of attributes of community, some mutually compatible, others not. Moreover, all of these were tenable within the family of late-modern British liberalisms.

One of the more sophisticated versions of community may be found in the mature thought of L. T. Hobhouse, particularly in his post-war trilogy.[16] Hobhouse approached human societies as predicated on psychological impulses which evolved into more complex expressions of feeling and eventually into a rational consciousness. Dismissing, as did his contemporary new liberals, any suggestion of a society-forming contract and hence of society as a voluntary association, he explained a community as an initially unconscious elaboration of sexual, parental, and sociable impulses. Human development was hence tantamount to the development of a nexus of social relations. This naturalistic explanation of the social impulse ("society grows out of human nature") took, however, an interesting turn. Although the community and its organizing rules grew unconsciously, the natural social development of human beings culminated in the emergence of a "common sentiment" and a "common interest," in which "the development that each man can achieve is conditioned in kind and degree by the development of others."[17] This was brought about by the appearance, at an advanced evolutionary stage, of rational consciousness, conscious effort, and, above all, deliberate purpose.

[16] L. T. Hobhouse, *The Rational Good* (London: Allen & Unwin, 1921); *The Elements of Social Justice* (London: Allen & Unwin, 1922); *Social Development: Its Nature and Conditions* (London: Allen & Unwin, 1924). Many of these themes are to be found in Hobhouse's pre-war writings as well, though they are more developed and more carefully argued in the later work.
[17] Hobhouse, *The Rational Good*, p. 90.

Community as interactive structure

At this point, the second feature of community entered the picture. The naturalness of sociability and of group membership was joined by the specific input of human rationality into social behavior. Human rationality was a thick rationality, closely associated with the adjacent concepts of harmony, commonality, and welfare. It would be far too simplistic to explain these links as a particular kind of biological, or psychological, or moral theory. The interconnections among these disciplinary perspectives were the defining feature of Hobhouse's new liberalism, and this epistemology itself separates it from current concerns. He viewed rationality as the property of exercising self-consistent judgments. Such judgments were based on subjective grounds and were tested against other subjective judgments in terms of their mutual consistency. That process accorded them objective rational status. The crux of this intersubjectivity was, in effect, a particular notion of consistency as harmony, namely, the mutual support of a system composed of component judgments. This complete system of interconnecting parts supplied the rational self-evidence of a system of complementary truths, which would otherwise be partial. Put differently, and crucially for Hobhouse's conception of community, reason was "an organic principle in thought," incomplete but progressive. The reality which this reason identified and reflected was likewise an organic whole. In sum, the ethical principle of the good involved a harmony between feeling and action, reflected both in the internal make-up of an individual and in social relationships. Rationality entailed the attainment of balance, which for Hobhouse meant both fundamental similarity and a single system of purposes, which held human diversity in check, thus minimizing conflict. Finally, this ethical principle of organic, interrelated complementarity was both embedded in experience and superimposed on it. It emanated from knowledge of the world, and directed it as well, for to say that something is good was both a judgment of value and an assertion of fact.[18] That, ultimately, was the optimistic lesson the new liberals drew from evolution. Community was a sociological reality in a strong sense completely absent from recent debate, but it was also an ethical partnership if accompanied by a rational respect for individuality and for cooperation.

Central to rationality were its social implications, "the conclusion that the belief that we owe allegiance to a wider life than our own is justified in reason." These implications had at an earlier evolutionary stage been present in the social instincts of mutual forbearance and mutual aid.

---

[18] Ibid., pp. 65–6.

Now, however, the rational good could be attached to sociability as a direct consequence of its interpretation as "one in which all persons share in proportion to the capacity of their social personality."[19] The result was a complex conception of community, explored by Hobhouse at the developmental stage of modern societies, and one which allowed for both individuation and integration, precisely the elements which late twentieth-century political philosophers have allocated either to liberalism or to communitarianism or, when combined, have held these up as a project political theory may take on board *in future*. A community informed by an organic harmony among its parts led inevitably to a carving out of that element of harmony as the common good. Specifically, the organic relation was one of mutual service, constituting a harmony in which each part assisted the fulfillment of the others. Hence a community was, in Durkheimian fashion, "a system of parts maintaining themselves by their interactions."[20]

Whether or not a community was merely the dynamic interaction of individuals in their social, structurally interdependent mode, or a distinct social entity, was a matter of some difference, even altercation, among new liberals. Hobhouse tended to subscribe to the former; Hobson, as we shall see, to the latter. But the implications of Hobhouse's preference of the attribute "organic" to the entity "organism" were nevertheless considerable. It supplied a sufficient basis to identify the community as a rights-bearer, and consequently required individual liberty to be limited by the rights of the community. The shared element of the common good took on an identity of its own, an identity absent in most late twentieth-century versions of communitarianism. But this constraining communitarianism was far from being repressive. Methodologically, its constraints need to be appreciated as a general recognition of the limits of permissible ranges of political values and the conduct that embodied them. An unlimited liberty had long been rejected by all except extreme individualist anarchists. What had changed, however, was the constraining object, and what demands probing is the extent to which liberalism could place its faith in the rational self-limitation of a community, having preached as a matter of course the rational self-limitation of the individual. Undoubtedly, individual constraint could more easily be secured through the power of a collective body, in particular the state. Could liberals rely on parallel and sufficient constraints on the community? Their response was a compound based on the ethics of commonalties, social self-interest, social utility, the demo-

[19] Hobhouse, *Elements of Social Justice*, p. 117.
[20] Hobhouse, *Social Development*, p. 70.

cratic alertness of the individual members of a society, and an appeal to the facts of social structure and evolution.

On the first criterion, referring to the nature of social ethics, Hobhouse was confidently optimistic:

> a rational ethics starting with the web of human impulses is forced to discard those which are blind or contradictory, and retain as reasonable those only which form a consistent whole ... It cannot confine the good to any section of humanity ... it sets the consistent body of human purposes before each individual as the good, which he as a rational being must recognise and support, and within which alone can his own good be reasonably sought. The good of all others enters into his own, and by the same logic his good enters into theirs. Thus the rational system in the end is one of mutual furtherance, or what we have called harmony ... social development and ethical development are at the end the same.

Crucially, this ethics did not ignore the centrifugal tendencies of individual existence. Hobhouse insisted that, though human beings were social animals, they do not "see social life steadily and see it whole." Human interests were "fragmentary and often inconsistent," and their harmonization could never be total. Yet Hobhouse vested so much value in the individual that, in a strong echo of hermeneuticist holism, he could claim that in "his social potentialities each constituent individual holds the germ of the whole social order."[21] Here individuality was endowed with the entire human potential, while concurrently human sociability was elevated to a supreme attribute. But to assert this was not to insist that the individual was complete in itself. Quite the contrary: because each individual member of a society was incomplete, yet also endowed with the capacity of self-direction, a state of organic interdependence was a conscious aspiration in an individual's quest for self-development *through* community. To consider people apart from the society which they formed was a false view of social development.

Similar arguments are of course integral to socialist ideologies, yet Hobhouse was no socialist. At most, he saw himself as a liberal who incorporated some socialist perspectives in articulating his beliefs.[22] Occasionally he even extended his purview. A rational social order had to assimilate three philosophical principles: philosophic conservatism required a communal system that could actually sustain itself and offer a semblance of continuity; philosophic liberalism required liberation of vital impulses so that personalities could grow; and philosophic socialism required the principle of similars because of the importance of sharing significant goods. Hence equal treatment of individuals and

---

[21] Ibid., pp. 63, 67, 88–9.
[22] L. T. Hobhouse, *Liberalism* (London: Williams & Norgate, 1911), p. 165.

groups applied, unless essential differences could be produced. This was a recognition both of human equality and, as a lesser constraint, of the diverse claims of groups.[23]

For Hobhouse a community was neither a single, nor a static, entity. Communities developed on four different levels: population size; the efficient coordination and discharge of their functions; freedom for thought, character, and initiative of their members; and participation in mutual services. These developments did not occur at the same pace, allowing for a range of configurations of the conceptions constituting community, only a few of which carried Hobhouse's seal of approval.[24] In his more pessimistic moments he was unable to ignore the divide between the ethical and the sociological. For although a notion of complete ethical development could be conceived as form rather than specific content – as the fulfillment of the mutually compatible aspects of personality – the historical process, according to Hobhouse, shuddered and stumbled. Hobhouse was after all no Hegelian, neither in his assessment of the political consequences of Idealist theory nor in his personal, war-induced, abhorrence of German philosophy. As he commented, "while social development in its completeness corresponds to the ideal of a rational ethics, partial development may diverge from it, and ... the historic course of change includes what from either point of view is mere arrest, retrogression or decay. Hence if progress means the gradual realisation of an ethical ideal no continuous progress is revealed by the course of history."[25] This was a far more subtle position than the crude perfectionism now often attributed to teleological political theories.

According to Kymlicka, reinforcing commonly held views of what constitutes liberalism, "there seems to be no room within the moral ontology of liberalism for the idea of collective rights ... Individual and collective rights cannot compete for the same moral space, in liberal theory, since the value of the collective derives from its contribution to the value of individual lives."[26] If that schematic and dichotomizing feature is intended to characterize actually existing liberalisms, it must be conclusively rejected, if only because self-described and other-recognized liberals such as Hobson and Hobhouse persuasively argued the contrary. They could do so because they identified both the individual and the group-cum-nation (and occasionally the nation as separate from the group) as coequal units, capable of harmonious coexistence and

[23] Hobhouse, *The Rational Good*, pp. 132–4.
[24] Hobhouse, *Social Development*, pp. 78–9.   [25] Ibid., p. 90.
[26] W. Kymlicka, *Liberalism, Community, and Culture* (Oxford: Clarendon Press, 1989), p. 140.

mutual sustenance. Hobson, in an early piece entitled "Rights of Property," argued concurrently for the requirement of individual property in order to underpin what was necessary to express the vitality and developmental nature of human beings, and for the requirement of social property in order to service the cooperative needs of a society. As both the individual and society had a share in the bestowal of value on individual productivity, they both had a claim on the product.[27] Hobhouse echoed this argument: "if private property is of value ... to the fulfilment of personality, common property is equally of value for the expression and development of social life."[28]

Hobson's conception of community differed from Hobhouse's, and it is arguably the case that on occasion Hobson transcended the boundaries of liberal debate in his firm adherence to the analogy between society and an organism.[29] Though he incorporated elements of Hobhouse's empiricist and developmental approach to social interdependence, Hobson focused on the existential structural features of human societies. Thus, an organic community was one in which the activity of each part had, in holistic fashion, an important bearing on society in its totality. However, Hobson assigned a separately discernible identity to society in a strong version of organicism that plainly exceeded Hobhouse's and was an attempt to harness scientific knowledge in a bid to redefine the boundaries of a viable social ethics:

this organic treatment of Society is ... still more essential, if we consider society not merely as a number of men and women with social instincts and social aspects of their individual lives, but as a group-life with a collective body, a collective consciousness and will, and capable of realising a collective vital end ... The study of the social value of individual men no more constitutes sociology than the study of cell life constitutes human physiology.[30]

Justice as a good

What then of justice, that mainstay of recent philosophical theories of liberalism? For Hobhouse, justice occupied a complex position adjacent to and derivative from the core concept of the common good, yet concurrently playing a part in constituting it. If it still is necessary to persuade contemporary political theorists that, historically, liberalism

---

[27] J. A. Hobson, "Rights of Property," *Free Review* (November 1893), 130–49.
[28] L. T. Hobhouse, "The Historical Evolution of Property, in Fact and in Idea," in C. Gore (ed.), *Property, its Duties and Rights* (London: Macmillan, 1913), pp. 30–1. See M. Freeden, *The New Liberalism* (Oxford: Clarendon Press, 1978), pp. 45–6.
[29] See especially J. A. Hobson, "The Re-Statement of Democracy," in J. A. Hobson, *The Crisis of Liberalism* (London: P. S. King & Son, 1909), pp. 71–87.
[30] J. A. Hobson, *Work and Wealth* (New York: Macmillan, 1914), p. 15.

has not been neutral among different conceptions of the good, Hobhouse provides one of many clinching examples. Demonstrating that there are useful distinctions between neutrality and impartiality, Hobhouse declared that "justice ... is the impartial application of a rule founded on the common good." Rather than holding to a Rawlsian assertion of just rules that precede the good, Hobhouse commented: "Now the rules (applied by a state) themselves may be wise or unwise, just or unjust. If they are such to serve the common good ... they are wise and good." The good preceded the right, but one aspect of the right helped in determining the good. That aspect was a conception of equality which may be described as impartiality in the application of rules. So the structure of the argument runs as follows. There is a complex conception of the common good – a harmonious, individual-developing sociability – and the system of justice in societies which abide by that common good requires impartial rules to apply that good. Impartiality is hence not neutrality, because the good itself cannot be neutral. Impartiality is a wise way of dispensing a (non-neutral) good. In addition, however, the good itself is partly constituted by the idea of impartiality. Were the good wholly constituted by impartiality, the argument would indeed begin to resemble Rawls' notion of fairness. But Hobhouse's impartiality emerges from a clear idea of ethical ends which are not contained in it, and its version of equality-cum-universality is a crucial *component* in the project of realizing the common good. That component is that "all members of the community ... simply as members have an equal claim upon the common good, while any difference in what is due to them or from them must itself be a difference required by the common good."[31]

Unlike Rawls' second, difference, principle, Hobhouse's notion of difference was based on a substantive test which rational actors who are *conscious and informed* members of a society could agree to, and it was further based on the ontological assumption, buttressed by sociological evidence, that communities exist and that they are manifestations of human rationality. We are not invited to engage in a thought-experiment to determine a morally compelling position but in a concrete extrapolation from already existing practices. We are not invited to conceive of a rational individual actor, for whom limited cooperation but not association or community is the sign of a just order,[32] but to conceive of an

---

[31] Hobhouse, *Elements of Social Justice*, pp. 105, 108.
[32] Rawls, *Political Liberalism*, pp. 40–3. Because Rawls conceives of community only as a political society that affirms the same comprehensive doctrine (p. 146), he cannot incorporate into his argument any nuances of social structure that obtain between such an extreme totalitarian option and the minimal cooperation he endorses.

evolutionarily given rationally cooperating society. We are not invited to
reduce the sphere of the political to that of respect for foundational
processes or constitutional arrangements, but to extend it to an increasingly deliberate pursuit of policies designed to augment well-being. As
the liberal Idealist philosopher D. G. Ritchie cogently put it, within the
context of discussing justice, "With regard to equality, as with regard to
freedom, people are very apt to fall a prey to abstraction, and in pursuit
of the form to neglect the reality, preferring shadow to substance."[33]
The new liberal substance was linked to concerted state action as well as
to individual involvement. For Ritchie, on the one hand, state interference had to be considered from the viewpoint of its probable effect on
the welfare of the community as a whole, for "[a]ll salutary State action
must be such as will give individuals so far as possible the opportunity of
realizing their physical, intellectual, and moral capacities." On the other
hand, the adage that man is a political animal meant that "if cut off from
the life of active citizenship in a constitutional state, human nature fails
to attain fully the best things of which it is capable."[34] Rawls' first
principle also failed the new liberal test of justice, because "if no man
may ever justly do what interferes with the equal liberty of any other
man, this seems to me to bring us to a deadlock ... This 'equal liberty,'
therefore, if in any subordinate sense it is recognized, is not an absolute
and primary, but a derivative principle, dependent on some idea of
common good or advantage."[35]

Constraints on community and the question of autonomy

We turn now to two kinds of questions: how did the new liberalism
address problems of the relation of society to individuals, and how did it
address problems of the relation of society to groups? The first issue was
addressed by Hobhouse by means of his emphasis on personal development. Such development was only to be sought through an individual's
rational choice, but rational choice also entailed contributing to the
common good. A dual role of the state required the protection of
personal rights as well as the attainment of common objects. Indeed, in
a rationally engaged society, the protection of individual rights was not
merely, as with many philosophical liberals, lexically prior to social
welfare but an element of social welfare.[36] As Hobhouse famously put it

---

[33] D. G. Ritchie, *Studies in Political and Social Ethics* (London: Swan Sonnenschein, 1902), pp. 36–7.
[34] Ritchie, *Studies*, pp. 57–8, 69.   [35] Ibid., pp. 58–60.
[36] Hobhouse, *Elements of Social Justice*, pp. 37, 82, 85.

in his classic *Liberalism*: "Mutual aid is no less important than mutual forbearance, the theory of collective action no less fundamental than the theory of personal freedom."[37] In employing these two mutually decontesting and interdependent terms, Hobhouse dissociated himself from a conception of autonomy as self-regarding action, a conception which slowly crept back in favor as the twentieth century drew to a close. Liberty meant inward growth and entailed external enabling conditions which, crucially, involved combined action: "every liberty rests on a corresponding act of control. The true opposition is that between the control that cramps the personal life and the spiritual order, and the control that is aimed at securing the external and material conditions of their free and unimpeded development."[38]

The second question is linked to the first, but it raises an issue of more specific concern to communitarian discourse, and it is through its exploration that another set of distinguishing features marking off current debate from the new liberal thinking becomes visible. In substance, it demonstrates that present concern with individual autonomy was at best a problematic issue for the communitarian liberals on which we are focusing, and at worst an obfuscating category which cannot be superimposed on their analyses. Mulhall and Swift have rightly suggested that there exist current brands of liberalism, among them that of Raz, that limit the supremacy of autonomy within a field of liberal values.[39] Indeed, Walzer is forced by the logic of his communitarian position to resort to an unsatisfactory term such as "relative autonomy" which, whether applied to distributive spheres or to individuals, illustrates the ill fit between the concept and its explanandum.[40] But these reservations were the meat of liberal debate for most of the twentieth century in Britain, France, Germany, and Italy.[41] Nor is the issue a matter of choice between autonomy and heteronomy, as the dichotomy posited by these terms is inadequate in capturing the structure of discourse – and hence the conceptual equipment – at the disposal of communitarian liberals. Rather two dimensions of problematics emerge: is autonomy the primary end of individuals, rather than development or welfare; and among pluralist communitarians, is autonomy a concept that can express the structural relationships among human communities and the ontological understandings of human existence? First, the Hobhousian approach queries the methodology of assigning primacy to

---

[37] Hobhouse, *Liberalism*, p. 124.   [38] Ibid., p. 167.

[39] S. Mulhall and A. Swift, *Liberals and Communitarians* (Oxford: Blackwell, 1992), pp. 290–4. See J. Raz, *The Morality of Freedom* (Oxford: Clarendon Press, 1986).

[40] M. Walzer, *Spheres of Justice* (Oxford: Blackwell, 1983), p. 10.

[41] For an excellent Italian instance of this perspective, see Carlo Rosselli, *Liberal Socialism* (Princeton: Princeton University Press, 1994).

one human attribute, as is the wont of many political philosophers. Second, the extolling of autonomy assigns priority to the analysis of individuals over the analysis of groups. Community is then either perceived as inimical to autonomy, or as a means to individual autonomy. But Hobhouse's social anthropology and his acceptance of non-voluntarist association pointed in a different direction. Autonomy was not a word Hobhouse used frequently. Even on a more generous interpretation of autonomy as self-fulfillment, or the pursuit of individual projects, and not just the condition of being subject to one's own will, the concept is unhelpful in a theory which categorically states that "the development which each man can achieve is conditioned in kind and degree by the development of others."[42] Indeed, even Hobhouse appealed to a supra-human evolutionary process whose design was a developmental harmony of life, and this was "the aim not of the human mind in particular, but of Mind as such."[43] Autonomy was thus limited by purposive laws of social development and the emergence of a shared conscious social intelligence.

Ritchie, with far greater Kantian roots than other new liberals, did address the notion of autonomy, which he saw as individual self-government in accordance with the dictates of his reason. However, the source of that reason was the issue at stake. Ritchie understood it as the result of training and discipline which must at first be given us by others. Character and circumstances were prior determinants of our motives and volitions. As he noted: "How often have measures of social reform been opposed on the ground that they weakened individual responsibility – as if men's characters were perfectly isolated phenomena, and not affected at every moment by their antecedents and surroundings!"[44]

The federal option

The twofold question of the relation of society to individuals and to groups was addressed by Hobson, employing his strong notion of community to develop the concept of federalism. In a central passage, Hobson declared that

the unity of this socio-industrial life is not a unity of mere fusion in which the individual virtually disappears, but a federal unity in which the rights and interests of the individual shall be conserved for him by the federation. The federal government, however, conserves these individual rights, not, as the individualist maintains, because it exists for no other purpose than to do so. It conserves them because it also recognises that an area of individual liberty is

---

[42] Hobhouse, *The Rational Good*, p. 90.
[43] Hobhouse, *Social Development*, p. 342.   [44] Ritchie, *Studies*, pp. 196–7.

conducive to the health of the collective life. Its federal nature rests on a recognition alike of individual and social ends, or, speaking more accurately, of social ends that are directly attained by social action and of those that are realised in individuals.[45]

Federalism, I submit, is a more appropriate term through which to address the specific features of new liberal ontology and ethics, both at individual and at group level, than the current reliance on conceptions of individual and group autonomy. Nevertheless, the latter still have to be addressed in any discussion of community. Ritchie had already criticized the notion of the "inviolable autonomy of nations"[46] and it needs to be understood that in the parlance of the times autonomy was frequently interchangeable with national self-determination. For Hobhouse, autonomy in the context of nationalities was not full independence, but being "a distinct constituent community."[47] Nations were based on history, sentiment, religion, race, or language and they were the viable macro-social unit. Consequently, when a smaller nation was incorporated into a larger one, a centrifugal force emerged, leading to division and to sectionalism, a situation which the majoritarian principle could not address. Unfortunately Hobhouse offered no clear solution to the tension between the right of the smaller national community to self-determination and the common responsibility for cooperation between a national majority and a national minority within the same state. "To find the place for national rights within the unity of the state," he wrote, "to give scope to national differences without destroying the organisation of a life which has somehow to be lived in common, is therefore the problem."[48] At best, he could argue that "the characteristic modern state ... exhibits the most complete reconciliation yet achieved on the large scale of social cooperation with the freedom and spontaneity of the component individuals, localities, and nationalities." That was due to the specific link between the state and its concomitant notion of group membership as citizenship, for "the principle of citizenship renders possible a form of union as vital, as organic, as the clan and as wide as the empire, while it adds a measure of freedom to the constituent parts and an elasticity to the whole which are peculiarly its own."[49]

Of greater interest in view of current concerns of scholarship is the internal conceptualization of whole–group, and of group–group, relationships. Indisputably, the nation was the overarching social group for the new liberals, and in that belief they merely inherited a nineteenth-

[45] Hobson, *Work and Wealth*, p. 304.   [46] Ritchie, *Studies*, p. 175.
[47] Hobhouse, *Social Development*, p. 297.
[48] L. T. Hobhouse, *Social Evolution and Political Theory* (New York: Columbia University Press, 1911), p. 146.
[49] Ibid, pp. 147–8.

century assumption. What, then, was the status of groups within the national framework? This is a question that has become central to the multicultural explorations of recent political theory. Those explorations still relate to the problem of group recognition in terms of autonomy, either by leaving groups as much as possible to their own devices, or by utilizing the cultural group as a crucial contributor to individual autonomy. Part of the problem is that contemporary theory has restricted its treatment of groups to those constituting the cultural identity of their members. By contrast, the new liberals would have enumerated additional substantive communal ends that extended from self-determination to the attainment of welfare. Whereas for many current theorists the right to a distinct identity is a defining feature of the good life, for the new liberals this had to be tempered by associated values such as cooperative human development. Even Kymlicka regards collective rights predominantly as those that entitle the collective to their *cultural* heritage.[50]

This raises a second concern. Kymlicka is concerned not only with choice in shaping the character of such a cultural community but, crucially, in a "context" of choice irrespective of the character of the community.[51] In his more recent work he has admittedly entertained weighty reservations about accommodating non-liberal minorities, arguing for a moral appeal to groups that do not respect the internal rights of their members to make and revise their choices. But, Kymlicka continues, "that does not mean that liberals can impose their principles on groups that do not share them."[52] Hence cultural communities are entitled to pursue practices that in themselves may be conservatively held and unconsciously or unreflectively endorsed, inasmuch as those practices are central to constituting their members' identity. However, the boundaries of liberalism are far from clear-cut. Liberal states do impose some of their practices on their members, such as free speech or the right to vote (individual members may not wish to take up those practices, but the rights to such practices are secured to them irrespective of whether they regard them as legitimate). The thin liberalism Kymlicka has assimilated from Rawls, modified by Kymlicka's inclusion within it of individual autonomy,[53] cannot be easily insulated from the interconnected configurations of broader, yet still fundamental, liberal concepts.[54] The new liberals realized full well that, with all its tolerance

---

[50] Kymlicka, *Liberalism, Community, and Culture*, p. 138.
[51] Ibid., pp. 166, 168, 172.
[52] W. Kymlicka, *Multicultural Citizenship* (Oxford: Clarendon Press, 1995), pp. 163–5.
[53] Ibid., pp. 160–3.
[54] Freeden, *Ideologies and Political Theory*, pp. 178ff.

and structural flexibility, liberalism was a competing *Weltanschauung* which required a wide range of moral positions, and those positions had to be translated into political action in order to survive the rivalry of ideological antagonists. Many current debates on community take the group on board simply in terms of the procedural granting of voice to the concerns of such a group, and only rarely, if at all, in terms of the substantive evaluation of the practices of the group. That is not an option that the new liberals would have encouraged, and the difference is, as ever, over the attributes and ends of the good life. Nor are the boundaries of coercion clear-cut. Kymlicka endorses speaking out against an illiberal practice. But that too may well be an exercise of considerable power.

There are two types of distinct non-rational ties that assist in consti-tuting communities: an accumulated cultural heritage that moulds understandings of a socially inherited collective identity; and affective relationships that bond a group into a sense of mutual obligation and of common ends. The new liberals could not accept the first unreflectively for fear of uncritically condoning tradition and custom. As for the second, the new liberals recognized that the non-rational, in Hobson's case even the irrational, had a place in social life,[55] but they also conceived of social evolution as transforming those non-rational emo-tions and instincts into purposive and systemic conduct. Hobson spoke for all new liberals when he proffered self-determination as the coordi-nation and cooperation of impulses and desires in conformity with a conscious plan.[56] Although both types suggested that groups could be based on non-voluntary membership, in terms of entry and exit alike, the new liberals took the discussion further. While they believed the main non-voluntary group to be the nation, grounded on both affective and instinctive ties, they also regarded the state as the rational agent of the nation-cum-community. In other words, the state was entrusted with the crucial function of enabling the transformation of a nation into a community, and the community ensured that the state was democrati-cally answerable to it.[57] Unlike other groups, to and from which entry and exit were not only possible, but ethically and politically funda-mental, the nation (seen as a natural grouping) and the community (seen as an inevitable evolutionary development) were thus elevated as an integrated entity to the status of ontological necessity.

[55] J. A. Hobson, "The Ethical Movement and the Natural Man," *Hibbert Journal*, 20 (1922), 667–79; J. A. Hobson, "Notes on Law and Order," *Nation*, October 24, and November 14, 1925.

[56] J. A. Hobson, *Problems of a New World* (London: Allen & Unwin, 1921), p. 252.

[57] Hobhouse, *Liberalism*, pp. 226–34. For Hobson's mature summing up, see J. A. Hobson, *Democracy and a Changing Civilization* (London: Bodley Head, 1934).

What the new liberals share with recent theorizing is the belief that groups are entitled to have their opportunities equalled in a society. They differ, however, in three major respects. First, over the nature of those opportunities; second, over the importance accorded to the internal purposive and democratic control of a group; and third, over the counter-claims of society, of the nation-cum-community, over the groups themselves. In this third dimension emerges another distinct contribution of the new liberals to conceptualizing community. When contemporary communitarians refer to cultural minorities, they focus on two aspects. First, they subscribe to a specific understanding of marginalized groups, one which concentrates mainly on the preservation of distinct community life-styles and practices, and tends to ignore alternative groupings in which members of a cultural group may be in an internally competitive, unequal relationship, say over questions of gender. Second, many contemporary communitarians underplay the multiple membership of individuals in cross-cutting groups, some of which promote practices of crucial importance to the goods their members require.[58] Some such groups are inimical to the concerns of non-group members; others are not. Thus, in group as class, one defining feature could be the desire to maintain power and hierarchy, or to gain as large a share as possible of available economic goods. For the new liberals, one facet of group conduct was precisely the pernicious aspect of group sectionalism as a central concern of liberalism. However, the inequality of groups in terms of their economic interests and opportunities is less pronounced in the particular ideology of egalitarianism contained in American political culture.

The other aspect of the new liberal attitude to groups was a recognition that some groups are significant in contributing to individual and social goods, but their mutual relationship – with a few notable exceptions[59] – is not one of equals. While Hobhouse is disappointing in his lack of any attempt to solve these problems, Hobson's notion of federalism was the linchpin of his structural solution, in its endeavor to balance potentially competing interests among groups. Hobson saw in each individual a unique personality, a member of a class or group, and a member of the wider community.[60] His democratic tendencies, notwithstanding his strong conception of organicism, allotted instinctive wisdom to the people, even in highly civilized communities. Hobson

[58] Walzer is an exception, arguing that tribalism can be transcended by multiple identities which divide passions. See M. Walzer, "The New Tribalism: Notes on a Difficult Problem," *Dissent* (Spring 1992), 164–71.
[59] Hobhouse's views on the rights of national groups to self-determination are one such instance.
[60] J. A. Hobson, *Towards Social Equality* (London: Oxford University Press, 1931), p. 5.

believed that the social attributes of human nature evoked a vital
communion of thought and feeling with race, society, even humanity.[61]
Among groups, federalism allowed for both autonomy and union[62] or,
we might argue, replaced these two limited concepts with a new one,
more subtle and dynamic. Neither individual nor social selves were
completely separate. Federal arrangements were predicated on a belief
in a broad area of mutual interest and common sympathy, which also
allowed for individual and group diversity in all areas not inimical to
that broad area. Federalism was equally emphatic in insisting that socio-
economic groupings require their own say, and that such groupings
impact upon the capacity for welfare, as distinct from the capacity to
choose one's identity and life-plans. That set of beliefs was so central to
the liberal tradition that its anemic American philosophical counterpart
must be seen as a somewhat different animal. In other words, federalism
eschews the introduction of a new *laissez-faire* legitimation of the quasi-
equal status and worth of different cultural groups under the umbrella
of group autonomy. Instead, it offers a mixture of integration and
separation which represents the manifold allegiances of individuals and
groups in society. Furthermore, it privileges a positive attitude to
cooperation and puts a premium on the development of individual and
social attributes as a hallmark of a liberalism in which welfare, liberty,
and sociability are mutually defining and constraining values, and all
three are conceived as goods to be pursued.

Conclusion

Contemporary philosophical liberalism is formulaic liberalism, all too
frequently sacrificing real-world complexity in the search for succinct
rules. The new liberals avoided that method, and one reason why they
did so was because they believed individuals to be in multiple, and
asymmetrical, relationships. The variety of human relationships per-
tained to the concurrent association of individual to individual, individual to group, and group to group. These nexuses were often, but not
always, encapsulated in rights. Some of them served to promote liberty,
some to promote welfare, and some to promote sociability, and the
balance among these was in continuous flux, rationally monitored by
responsible and critical individuals and groups. Revising one's ends was
never the sole argument for liberal rights, nor was it posited in a zero-
sum relationship with other liberal values which required rights protec-

---

[61] Hobson, *Work and Wealth*, pp. 355–6.
[62] Hobson, *Problems of a New World*, p. 253.

tion. That was the liberal logic emerging from the interpretative position of the new liberals.

The new liberal case-study reminds us that one of the features of liberalism is the dread of sectionalism, which is by definition the abandonment of the larger ethical purview. It attunes us to the fact that the mature liberal tradition has always sought to balance individual liberty and the requirements of community, not to support the one or the other. Indeed, the individualist–collectivist divide, that staple of late nineteenth-century analysis, had long been jettisoned by scholars as a false categorization, only to reappear recently under its current liberal–communitarian guise. The new liberalism reflected the sociological ontology of the times, cross-fertilized with developmental and welfare themes which have always been evident in the liberal tradition. It illustrates the polysemic range of the concept of community and the diverse ways in which it may be integrated with liberalism. It offers a more extensive notion of the political, with consequent benefits as well as pitfalls. It may, also, have been too optimistic to our tastes regarding the benevolence of the state, and too enamored of the promise of social harmony. Conversely, if – paradoxically – late twentieth-century approaches have something new to offer liberalism, it is the growing recognition that community has much to do with ties of emotion and sentiment, not merely with the consciousness of the purposive rational agent, be it individual or group.[63] This diachrony of horizons may, not least, enable us to put some of our own "self-evident" premises to the test in raising the question: what is liberalism?

[63] On this question, and its links with nationalism, see M. Freeden, "Is Nationalism a Distinct Ideology?," *Political Studies*, 46 (1998), 748–65.

2　T. H. Green on individual rights and the common good

Rex Martin

T. H. Green (1836–1882) developed a conception of individual rights as compatible with the common good. This conception, in the eyes of many, laid the foundations of the transition from the older, capital-"L" liberalism of nineteenth-century Britain to the "new" liberalism of twentieth-century democratic "welfare" states; and, by projection, to many of the social-service and interventionist policies of such states in the world today.[1]

　Green's theory of rights is set out in his posthumously published *Lectures on the Principles of Political Obligation*. It is, in my judgment, one of the finest books in the philosophy of rights written to date.[2] His

---

[1] The notion of a "new liberalism" refers (narrowly) to features of the program of the British Liberal Party, approximately in the period 1906–14. In a somewhat broader sense, as used here, it refers to a philosophical outlook found in a number of thinkers at or about the end of the nineteenth century (including many Idealist thinkers, centrally Green himself, as well as non-Idealists like Hobhouse and Dewey). For discussion, see Andrew Vincent and Raymond Plant, *Philosophy, Politics and Citizenship: The Life and Thought of the British Idealists* (Oxford: Blackwell, 1984); and the very interesting chapter (ch. 33, "Liberalism Modernized") in George H. Sabine's masterful book, *A History of Political Thought*, 4th edn, as revised by T. L. Thorson (Hinsdale, IL: Dryden Press, 1973).

[2] A brief word about Green's principal writings is in order here. The *Works of Thomas Hill Green* was edited by R. L. Nettleship, in three volumes (London: Longmans, Green, 1885–8; subsequently reprinted). These volumes contain almost everything of note except Green's *Prolegomena to Ethics*, virtually completed before his death in 1882 and published separately in 1883.

　Peter Nicholson has recently edited a five-volume *Collected Works of T. H. Green* (Bristol: Thoemmes Press, 1997). The first three volumes comprise Nettleship's edition of the *Works* (including Nettleship's long memoir of Green in vol. III, plus some appendix material added by Nicholson). The fourth volume is Green's *Prolegomena* (again with some appendix material added by Nicholson), and the fifth volume is a miscellany of published and unpublished items (including many of Green's letters), edited and introduced by Nicholson; it concludes with several useful bibliographies.

　Green's "Lectures on the Principles of Political Obligation" first appeared in print in *Works* vol. II (1886) and were reprinted as a separate book (1895), with a preface and a brief appendix by Bernard Bosanquet; an introduction by A. D. Lindsay was added in 1941. This book was still in print up through the 1970s (London: Longmans, Green, 1963; Ann Arbor: University of Michigan Press, 1967).

　A new version has subsequently appeared: T. H. Green, *Lectures on the Principles of*

theory emphasized two principal elements: (i) the requirement of social recognition and (ii) the idea of a common good. Since Green's account is bipolar, in the way just described, there is a potential tension in his overall theory.[3] Let me expand on this, briefly.

Either one of the two principal elements could plausibly be said to exist in the absence of the other. And where this happens (or could happen), does the element that stands alone lose all claim to the status of a right? This is not an easy question to answer. Suffice it to say that there is something perplexing in these borderline cases, where one element is present but not the other (for example, where slaves can be understood to have a common interest with free persons but where the institution of slavery constitutes a barrier to the social and legal recognition of this fact and to the treatment of slaves as persons). An attempted resolution of this potential source of confusion, in Green's theory, is one of the principal concerns in the present chapter.

It is not, however, my first order of business. I want instead to concentrate attention initially on Green's idea of social recognition. It is a difficult and very controversial idea, especially Green's claim that such recognition is necessary to any right properly understood.[4] And, in so

Political Obligation and Other Writings, Paul Harris and John Morrow, eds. (Cambridge University Press, 1986). This is now the definitive version. It takes account of Green's unpublished papers (on deposit in the library of his college, Balliol, Oxford) and indicates variants, etc. between the subsequent edited versions and the original unpublished lectures.

In the present chapter, I will typically cite from Green's "Lectures on the Principles of Political Obligation" (hereafter, Green, "Political Obligation") by section numbers; these numbers were introduced by Nettleship and are still conventionally used. All page references (where such are found) are from the Harris and Morrow edition.

[3] This particular tension in Green's thought (further described in n. 14 below) has been widely commented on, and I can pretend to no originality in descrying it.

Studies worth noting of Green on rights are Melvin Richter, *The Politics of Conscience: T. H. Green and His Age* (Cambridge, MA: Harvard University Press, 1964), esp. pp. 233–53, also pp. 262–5; Gerald N. Matross, "T. H. Green and the Concept of Rights," Ph.D. thesis, University of Kansas (1972), esp. chs. 3–6; Ann R. Cacoullos, *Thomas Hill Green: Philosopher of Rights* (New York: Twayne, 1974), esp. chs. 5–8; I. M. Greengarten, *Thomas Hill Green and the Development of Liberal-Democratic Thought* (University of Toronto Press, 1981), esp. ch. 4; Geoffrey Thomas, *The Moral Philosophy of T. H. Green* (Oxford University Press, 1987), esp. ch. 8, sect. 9, pp. 351–6; Peter Nicholson, *The Political Philosophy of the British Idealists: Selected Studies* (Cambridge University Press, 1990), pp. 83–95; Colin Tyler, *Thomas Hill Green (1836–1882) and the Philosophical Foundations of Politics: An Internal Critique* (Lampeter, UK: Edwin Mellen Press, 1997), esp. chs. 3 and 5. For an accessible brief account of Green's main views, in the context of his time, and for some additional bibliographical citations, see Mark Francis and John Morrow, *A History of English Political Thought in the Nineteenth Century* (London: Duckworth, 1994), ch. 13.

[4] "The right to the possession of them, if properly so called, would not be a mere power, but a power recognised by a society as one which should exist. The recognition of a power, in some way or another, as that which should be, is always necessary to render it a right" (Green, "Political Obligation," sect. 23, p. 45). This emphasis on the role of

focusing, I want to suggest (as a first stage towards the projected resolution) that Green's account of common good can perhaps be best understood as an outgrowth, of sorts, of his idea of social recognition.

The chapter falls, quite naturally then, into three main sections. The first is concerned with social recognition and the second develops Green's doctrine of common good. In the final section, there is a reflection on and assessment of the project of reconciliation I've undertaken on Green's behalf. In the end, as I have indicated, we must try to find some device for integrating the two main elements in his theory of rights more fully.

Social recognition

By social recognition, Green seemed to have in mind something like the following: an authoritative acknowledgment or affirmation within a society that a certain way of acting, or way of being treated, was desirable or should be permitted, together with appropriate steps taken to promote and maintain that way. Such a way of acting (or way of being acted toward) was thus said to be established or made secure. Social recognition, then, has the force of a guarantee of sorts to the individual that a certain pattern of activity is to be accredited and maintained socially. Since Green tended to focus, almost exclusively, on this first aspect of social recognition (that is, on the aspect of authoritative acknowledgment or accreditation) my discussion will follow his lead by emphasizing it throughout.

Green used the idea of social recognition and the claim that it was a feature of any right in his powerful critique of the natural rights theory of Hobbes, Spinoza, and Locke. For these thinkers had alleged that rights held good in a state of nature – a state which, almost by definition,

---

social recognition lies behind Green's notorious remark that "rights are made by recognition. There is no right but thinking makes it so . . ." (ibid., sect. 136, p. 106; see also sect. 41, p. 38). Note also sects. 23–6, 31, 99, 103, 113, 116, 121, 139, 142, 144–5, 148, 208.

In the sentences cited from sect. 136 (above) the phrase "but thinking makes it so" was enframed in single quotation marks by Nettleship, Green's editor, probably because Green was in effect borrowing these words from Shakespeare (specifically from *Hamlet*, act II, scene ii, line 250, where Hamlet says to Rosencrantz and Guildenstern, "for there is nothing either good or bad, but thinking makes it so"). The inverted commas (the single quotation marks) are not in Green's Balliol manuscript, however, as I found upon checking; and Harris and Morrow quite properly omit the quotation marks in their edition of Green's "Political Obligation" (see p. vii of that edition for the principles they followed).

I must say I miss Nettleship's inverted commas; they added a nice touch (of distancing, of tongue-in-cheek) to Green's remark. I'm indebted to George Smith for providing me with the *Hamlet* citation.

lacked devices for registering social agreement – and thus held good even in the absence of such agreement; this was part of the force, for them, of calling such rights *natural* rights.

It is useful to note at the very outset that Green did not argue directly for social recognition, and its essential status, and then use that argument against the classical natural rights theorists – that is, against Hobbes, Spinoza, Locke, and Rousseau. Rather, he regarded the notion of social recognition as, itself, a quite plausible philosophical explication of the very ideas he was criticizing. Thus, Green could be taken as holding an idea about rights (i.e., his insistence on the need for social recognition) which actually absorbed and was built up out of materials initially present in the earlier natural rights tradition.

Green's notion of social recognition was developed dialectically out of his careful attention to the theory of natural rights (where such rights were understood as rights of individuals that held good in a state of nature). Thus he was able, by what amounted to an internal critique of the natural rights tradition, to reach his own distinctive idea that all rights (including even natural rights) involve social recognition. And the criticism he developed of that tradition, since it represented a line of thought internal to natural rights theory, was for that very reason inescapable for its practitioners.

It might seem arbitrary for Green to have grouped so many different thinkers together in a single tradition. His procedure, though, was considerably more sophisticated than that. He saw the natural rights doctrine, in its classical seventeenth- and eighteenth-century phases, as itself a developmental thing.

He noted that Hobbes and Spinoza, in his view the two originating theorists in the natural rights tradition, had several important points in common. For each emphasized the need for all persons to act in concert (for Spinoza by combining; for Hobbes by each one's "standing aside" from or "laying down" the exercise of their natural rights, thereby waiving that right, permanently but conditionally). The result of this acting in concert, for each theorist, is the achievement of the civil condition. And there, paradigmatically, a single governmental agent acts for the multitude of persons, making them a single, collective body.

The gravamen of Green's objection to both Hobbes and Spinoza becomes, then, to show that this coming together, this concerted act (as a crucial point of consensus or common action within the so-called state of nature), creates a condition which is integral to the existence of rights and without which – as, for example, when persons are detached or separated from one another, except for occasions of conflict, in a presocial state of nature – rights would be impossible.

Here Green's main focus of attack, against both Hobbes and Spinoza, is their identification of rights, that is, natural rights, with natural powers. And one way to take his point, then, is to say that for Hobbes and Spinoza rights are *conceptually* the same as natural powers. Green attempts to show that this is not so: that a right is not simply a power, not simply a physical capacity (to act and affect others) and nothing else.

The main line of Green's argument here can be put briefly. Both Hobbes and Spinoza were willing to speak of one's natural liberty or power to do anything (that is, anything one is physically able to do) as a natural right. Green says of rights so conceived that it would follow that the rightholder is in no way inhibited with respect to the same right assumed to exist in the case of other people. Indeed, where a right is nothing but a natural power (a physical capacity to do something and then its doing), the responsive conduct of people was in no way normatively directed by such rights. Just as the rightholder could (normatively) do anything that the holder was physically able to do, so all other individuals could in anticipation or in response do literally anything, presumably in virtue of *their* natural right. The point is that no person – no second party – is afforded any positive normative direction on how that person is supposed to act in virtue of the natural liberty rights possessed by others. (Nor is any given by such duties as might exist in the state of nature.)

We conclude, then, that for Hobbes at least, a right *qua* right involves, can involve, no normative constraint on the behavior of others. For if Hobbes had *conceived* rights differently, as always involving second-party obligations or directions of some sort, he would simply have been unable to talk in the way that he did of rights in a state of nature.

But we should also note that this was an account of natural rights with which Hobbes was not satisfied. Otherwise, he would not have supported a doctrine of standing aside, of not exercising one's natural rights, as his preferred alternative. Thus, Hobbes argued instead that persons as subjects of government should waive their natural rights to do anything and defer to the *sovereign's* exercise of natural rights.

If we take this as Hobbes' preferred account of natural rights then a natural right so conceived (as the sovereign's power to do anything) is not simply a natural power. It is, rather, a power acknowledged by others, deferred to by them, and thereby determinative of their conduct. Here *natural right* refers to powers that have taken on a moral and a social dimension. By standing aside and deferring, the subjects have become *normatively* restricted by the sovereign's act: they are both normatively unable to resist it and normatively required to comply with it.

Now, when we consider that, for Hobbes, the sovereign's natural right has the character it does have in civil society *only* because the subjects have a duty (to conform) attached to that right, then it becomes imperative to say that the sovereign's right is always paired with such obligations. Accordingly, Hobbes could never contend about rights that duties or other normative directions were not implied – contend, that is, that there are no corresponding duties or even that such duties were necessarily omitted – if he was to have the theory of the natural right of the sovereign in civil society which he had espoused. This point is strong enough, then, to allow Green's argument to go through that rights could not be identified *conceptually* with mere natural powers. And we reach Green's conclusion that, even on the view developed by Hobbes and Spinoza, rights were not mere natural powers but, instead, had normative force (in particular, as involving duties and other kinds of normative direction of second parties).

Behind this shift of the concept of rights in a normative direction lies, as we have seen, the notion of concerted action, of consensus (of "consent," if you will, in one of its older, now obsolete senses). Hobbesian subjects, by standing aside, waived their natural rights to do anything and deferred to the sovereign in the sovereign's exercise of this selfsame right; in so doing they limited their own conduct with respect to the sovereign's acts and undertook to be guided by those acts.

Consent so understood, not contract, is the mediating notion that stands between rights (so called) in the state of nature and those in civil society. The crucial point is not that any one subject consents but that *all* do; each one consents; they act in concert here. Thus, the sovereign's right – the only right the exercise of which plays a significant role in the normal course of civil society – depends on mutual acknowledgment, of its priority and directive character on the part of the subjects severally. Green's main point here is that the sovereign's will, understood as the exercise of a right, then sets a standard for the conduct of the subjects (in particular, in specifying duties and other kinds of normative direction for their conduct).

Locke starts where Hobbes and Spinoza leave off. For Locke is one of the first philosophers to make the point that rights necessarily imply duties, or, if not imply, that all rights necessarily involve the normative direction of the conduct of second parties (that is, of persons other than a given rightholder). This feature, the correlation of rights with duties, even in the state of nature, was one that Green especially commended in

Locke's theory. And it is the point on which Locke, at least as a state-of-nature theorist of rights, chiefly differs from Hobbes and Spinoza.[5]

The difference here reflects fundamentally differing views about the concept of rights. It is a difference which occurred at the very time at which that concept was being molded, largely indirectly through talk of natural rights, by the founding theorists of the philosophy of rights. It is interesting to note, then, that the tradition of rights discourse has by and large followed Locke rather than Hobbes or Spinoza – influenced, no doubt, by Green and Bradley as well – for there has developed a consensus that rights always involve normative directions for conduct incumbent on second parties.[6]

Now the important question, in Green's view, becomes to ask what is involved in such normative direction, that is, in being obligated or being normatively directed, on the side of second parties. According to Green, a person's being normatively directed – being under obligation – necessarily involves that person's being conscious of such direction.[7] And the appropriate consciousness is, of course, one of affirmation, commitment to that direction. If the appropriate consciousness does not exist in the case of given individuals, then there would at least have to be a real possibility for persons in a particular society, including those on whom the obligations fell, to acknowledge such obligations by the lights they had (by reference to standards of morality actively involved in that society). For obligations that cannot be acknowledged in a given society, or that cannot be shown to follow, discursively, from accredited principles of conduct which are at least reflectively available to persons in that society, cannot be regarded as proper obligations which normatively bind conduct in that society.[8] One cannot have an obligation of which one literally cannot be aware. A person's action cannot be determined by duty (or obligation) if it is not possible for that person even to be

---

[5] Ibid., sect. 57.

[6] The point that rights and duties are logical correlatives, at least in that rights always entail the existence of duties (or as he sometimes puts it "obligations") on the part of second parties, is often made by Green. See, for example, ibid., sects. 8, 10, 21; also sect. 30.

[7] Ibid., sects. 54–5, 57; also sects. 143–4. The conclusion (as given here) and much of the argument that follows in this paragraph are Green's.

[8] A technical point. Green (in line with Kant) distinguished moral duties from normative obligations. Moral duties have to be done with a certain motivation and, hence, cannot be coerced or enforced. But obligations "as part of the 'jus naturae' correlative to rights" are "outward acts, of which the performance or omission can and should be enforced" (ibid., sect. 10, p. 17; see also sect. 14). Though it is common nowadays to talk of rights as correlated with *duties* (as I noted earlier), I have here followed the letter of Green's distinction by referring to the normative element correlated with a right as an obligation. I should add that Green does not himself religiously follow that letter at every point in his lectures.

aware of the obligation. Or not possible for them to see and take on board that the obligation is binding for them and others. And these things are no less true in the state of nature than in any other society.[9]

Rights are normative or, as Green called them, "ideal" entities.[10] A right is properly conceived, on the one side, as a claim that a certain capacity to act, a power or way of acting should be engaged in – or could be, without blame – and, on the other, as the securing of this claimed way of acting to the rightholder by the obligations and appropriate attendant actions of others.[11]

Without an appropriate awareness of obligation on the part of second parties, there could be no normative direction of their conduct. And without awareness that the way of acting should be, or could be, engaged in and that the conduct of others was limited so as to allow it, there could be no normative direction respecting the rightholder's conduct or of those who endorsed the claim on the holder's behalf.

One might say, then, that affirmative awareness or acknowledgment must come from both sides, from both parties, in the case of a right. Rights involve a giving of normative direction, on the one side, and a taking of such direction, on the other. Without such mutual recognition, rights would be mere powers or ways of acting/ways of being treated which lacked normative force and, thus, necessarily failed to constitute rights.

Where a right is itself general, as a right of many people, or where it constrains generally, then the mutual recognition involved must be a genuine *social* recognition. Social recognition – an appropriate awareness on all sides – is an ingredient of any general right properly so called. On this basis, Green was able to repudiate the foundational conception of

[9] In Green's view both Locke and Rousseau were committed to viewing the state of nature as itself a society of sorts. (See ibid., sects. 54–5; also sect. 52.)

[10] Ibid., sects. 38, 136.

[11] Ibid., sects. 23–5. Green habitually associates rights with certain *liberties* to do or have or, as he put it, "freedom of action and acquisition" (ibid., sects. 105, p. 84, 114, p. 90; also sect. 186, p. 144). Such a view of rights, though widespread, is too narrow. One would also have to include, among the main objects of rights, avoidances of injury at the hands of others and, more controversially, the provision of positive services by others (e.g., education or social security benefits).

I think Green's theory (and the Idealists more generally) would have trouble accommodating this last point, concerned with so-called welfare rights. For they had no serviceable theory of justice to provide content and direction for the development of a coherent theory of welfare rights, or for provisions of welfare *by the body politic* that go beyond rights.

For a sketch of a theory of justice based on Green, which might mark a jumping-off point to confront the criticism just made, see Avital Simhony's papers, "On Forcing Individuals to be Free: T. H. Green's Liberal Theory of Positive Freedom," *Political Studies*, 39 (1991), 303–20, at 315–20; and "T. H. Green's Theory of the Morally Justified Society," *History of Political Thought*, 10 (1989), 481–98, at 481–8.

rights – that isolated individuals in a state of nature have inherent rights – which had formed the starting point for theoretical reflection in the natural rights tradition.

Communitarian thinkers in our own time have advanced the notion of a "social thesis." At its simplest, the thesis denies that individuals are wholly formed "atoms" (monads in the real world, as it were) that can and do exist without society. Clearly, Green would agree with the "social thesis" on this point. But the holders of the "social thesis" also urge that many of the values of traditional individualism (self-determination, for example) can only be exercised and, more to the point, can only flourish in a certain kind of society, one with something of a communitarian or common good ethos.[12] Whether Green concurs in this second feature of the "social thesis" – and whether, if he does, his overall theory can measure up to it – is, of course, something we will have to see. We turn to such matters in the next two sections.

Common good

As we noted at the very beginning, Green makes two claims that concern us here. One involves the concept of a right; the other specifies the feature which justifies the most important kind of right, that is, universal rights. We discussed the first claim in the previous section. Let us turn to the second one now.

Universal rights are divided by Green into two main sorts: the natural and the civil. For each is in some sense a universal right. Clearly, natural rights, as normally understood, are rights of all persons. Active civil rights, as Green used that term, are political rights universal within a given society.[13] They are ways of acting, or ways of being treated, that are specifically recognized and affirmed in law for each and all the citizens there (or, in the limiting case, for all individual persons there) and are actively promoted.

[12] For general discussion of the "social thesis," see Will Kymlicka, *Contemporary Political Philosophy: An Introduction* (Oxford: Clarendon Press, 1990), ch. 6, esp. pp. 216–30. For an account of the "social thesis" developed specifically as a critique of rights theories (in particular, theories of the "primacy of rights"), see Charles Taylor, *Philosophy and the Human Sciences: Philosophical Papers 2* (Cambridge University Press, 1985), ch. 7. For a somewhat more nuanced statement of these views, see Charles Taylor, "Cross-Purposes: The Liberal–Communitarian Debate," in Nancy Rosenblum (ed.), *Liberalism and the Moral Life* (Cambridge, MA: Harvard University Press, 1989), pp. 159–82.

[13] See, for instance, Green, "Political Obligation," sect. 24. It is clear that both natural rights and civil rights are special cases of what were called general rights in the previous section: they are rights of all people (of all citizens) and, in some important cases (e.g., the right to life), they constrain generally (all other people or all other citizens), either directly or through the mediation of public law.

All universal political rights are important rights and all reflect a high level of social commitment. But not all can be justified as natural rights (as what we today call "human rights"). Nonetheless, all can be justified in a distinctive way – in accordance with one and the same pattern.

The background supposition here is that all rights (be they natural rights or simply civil ones) are, in some way, beneficial to the right-holder. Thus, all proper civil rights (all political rights universal within a given society), if true to this supposition of benefit, should identify specific ways of acting, or of being treated, that are of benefit to each and all of the citizens (or to each and all of the persons there). For these claimed ways of acting or of being treated are, arguably, part of the "good" of each person or instrumental to it.

Where this requirement (of mutual and general benefit) holds good in a given case, then, what is, legally speaking, a civil right is a way of acting (or of being treated) that is correctly understood to be in every-body's interest; or would be so understood upon reflection (and given time and experience). All active civil rights could be regarded as justified insofar as they actually do identify and sustain ways of acting, or ways of being acted toward, that satisfy the criterion of mutual perceived benefit.

For the ground of any such political arrangement is that identifying and sustaining these particular ways of acting (or of being treated) is, arguably, in the interest of everybody, of each and all the citizens. All could claim it for themselves individually and acknowledge it for everyone else on that basis. A way of acting (or of being treated) so secured, through some such form of mutual acknowledgment of interest or benefit, is *justified* as a civil right.

One might say, in sum, that social recognition identifies a feature of all rights (even of those "established" rights which, though we might doubt their justification, do appear to be, in a sense at least, rights properly so called).[14] Social recognition, then, belongs to the *definition*

---

[14] Thus Green is even willing to say: "An intentional violation of a right must be punished, whether the right violated is one that should be a right or no, on the principle that social wellbeing suffers more from violation of any established right, whatever the nature of the right, than from the establishment as a right of a power which should not be so established . . ." (ibid., sect. 189, p. 146; see also sect. 144).

It is evident, then, that Green countenances *as a right* any established right, any way of acting that is socially affirmed and to which obligations of second parties have been attached (for example, by law or convention) and conformed to. It is, of course, plausible to say of some such ways of acting that they should *not* be socially recognized (see ibid., sects. 185, 187) and of some such ways of acting not socially recognized that they *should* be (see ibid., sects. 9, 144). Green did not, for the most part, however, call these latter ways of acting rights (i.e., those that should be socially recognized but were not). For they were not rights in any full sense.

of rights, to the concept of rights, whereas the notion of mutual perceived benefit (of a common good so understood) belongs to a quite different dimension, to the dimension of *justifying* something as a right. Or at least it belongs to the justification of the most important kind of political right, the civil right – one that is universal within a particular body politic.

Even where a degree of official or social recognition exists in a particular body politic, there can in a given case be no such thing as a fully *justified* universal political right without the element of a mutual and general good – that is, without an identifiable (and reflectively available) interest on the part of each and everyone within a given society that certain identical ways of acting (or of being treated) be acknowledged and maintained there.

Thus, by *justified* I mean simply that such a right actually fulfills the idea relied on in the case of any civil right. The presumption of mutual perceived benefit has been cashed in here. The presumption holds good: what is, legally speaking, a civil right is in practice a way of acting (or of being treated) that is correctly understood to be in everybody's interest. Hence a justified civil right is simply a universal political right that, in satisfying the criterion of mutual perceived benefit, meets the justifying standard for all civil rights.

The leading ideas in Green's account (as presented in this section) are that civil rights are justified by the fact of mutual perceived benefit and that such benefit refers to interests each citizen has in the establishment, within the society, of certain ways of acting or of being treated, ways that are identically the same for all.[15] And the essential sense of what Green capaciously calls "common good" is captured, for purposes of the *justification* of civil rights, by what I have been describing as mutual perceived benefit.

Assessment and conclusion

Of course, there are other senses of common good which Green some-times uses (especially those related to individual human perfection or to

---

[15] See, for these two points, ibid., sects. 29 and 217; also sects. 25–7, 30, 38–9, 41, 99, 114, 121, 143–4, 151, 206, 208, 216.

What I call here mutual perceived benefit (or, sometimes, mutual and general benefit) has much likeness, I suspect, with the idea of "Humanistic social ethics," as presented in A. J. M. Milne, "The Common Good and Rights in T. H. Green's Ethical and Political Theory," in Andrew Vincent (ed.), *The Philosophy of T. H. Green*, Avebury Series in Philosophy (Aldershot, UK: Gower, 1986), pp. 62–75. See also Matross, "Green and the Concept of Rights", chs. 4–6; and Avital Simhony, "T. H. Green: The Common Good Society," *History of Political Thought*, 14 (1993), 225–47, in particular, pp. 237–47.

the moral perfection of society).[16] And there are, for Green, linkages of common good with metaphysical principles such as the eternal consciousness[17] or with corporate entities such as organized society, in particular the state.[18] Affirmation of these other senses or of these linkages goes beyond what is required for the justification of rights. As regards the justification of rights we require only the one sense, of mutual perceived benefit. Here each individual has a notion of his or her interests and of what ways of acting (or of being treated) might contribute to those interests – in the situation where those ways are identical ones for each and all.

Admittedly, as Green points out, this awareness of interests and ways of acting/ways of being treated depends, further, on an ideal of one's (not yet realized) self. If we move our focus to this particular dimension, a mutual good can be said to exist where each individual conceives him or herself and others as having (some) identical traits of character, at the point of full self-realization. But since Green typically talks here of rights as establishing *conditions* for such self-realization, it appears that his emphasis, when discussing rights and their justification in this context, is on an identity of such means and not of the ends *per se* (as given in the notion of the traits of a fully realized self).[19] That is, his emphasis is on justified rights as established ways of acting/ways of being treated, identical for each and all, and, secondarily, on establishing the conditions for such ways to be exercised. Thus, my discussion of common good here has been restricted to the notion of identical ways of acting/ways of being treated – as giving the one, necessary rights-justifying conception of mutual perceived benefit in Green's theory.

Thomas Hurka takes exception to my use of mutual perceived benefit as the principal justifying ground for civil rights, and, by implication, takes exception to it as a helpful way of explicating Green's notion of common good.[20] Hurka's point is to distinguish a "parallel" sense of

[16] On individual human perfection, see Green, "Political Obligation," sects. 6–7, 19, 21, 23; on social perfection, see sect. 186. For a subtle and careful statement of the common good motif in its relation to individual human perfection, see Nicholson, *Political Philosophy of the British Idealists*, ch. 2.
[17] Green, "Political Obligation," sect. 131. Eternal consciousness is discussed by Green at considerable length in his *Prolegomena to Ethics*, book I, in Nicholson, *Collected Works of Green*, vol. IV, pp. 13–89. There it is treated as an epistemological notion that has metaphysical and even moral implications; for discussion, see Thomas, *Moral Philosophy of Green*, ch. 3, esp. pp. 141–5, 148; also p. 14.
[18] For example, in Green, "Political Obligation," sect. 99. The state is very important to my account of Green and I will have more to say about it later in the present section.
[19] Ibid., sects. 20–1, 23, 25, 29.
[20] See his review of my book *System of Rights* (Oxford: Clarendon Press, 1993) in *Mind*, 104 (1995), 178–82. I base my remark here also on conversations we have had, in person and by e-mail.

mutual benefit (where person a's having a right R benefits person a, and person b's having that same right R benefits person b, etc.) and a "reciprocal" or "shared" sense (where person a's having a right R benefits both person a and all other persons, and person b's having that same right R benefits both person b and all other persons, etc.). Hurka's claim is that what I call mutual perceived benefit is a case of "parallel" benefit but that only "shared" benefit can justify civil rights. I accept Hurka's location of mutual perceived benefit with the notion of "parallel" benefits, but I nonetheless think that mutual perceived benefit, so conceived, can ground an adequate justification of civil rights And I do think it affords an adequate and proper interpretation of Green's notion of common good in the context envisioned, that of justifying rights.

Let me briefly elaborate my claim that mutual perceived benefit, understood as "parallel" benefits, can justify civil rights. Here the parallel benefit in question is that the same way of acting or the same way of being treated is beneficial for each and every one of the right-holders (= all citizens or all persons within a given body politic), beneficial in the sense that that way is a means to or a part of some good, some interest of the holders. That is, person a's having a right R benefits person a, and person b's having that same right R benefits person b, and so on.

The claim here is not that these persons are benefited on every single occasion that the right is exercised (by themselves or by someone else), or benefited in precisely the same way, or benefited equally (as regards the result of so acting or so being treated). Nor is the claim made that everyone is benefited maximally, let alone that anyone is, by being in a situation where identical ways of acting/being treated are established in law for each and all.

Though we might grant all the things just said in the previous paragraph, it is, nonetheless, the case that these legally established ways of acting/being treated (identical for each and all) are regarded by everyone as beneficial. People see these ways as means to or part of things they regard as valuable, and they would rather have these ways available than not. Indeed, each would rather have these ways available than not, even on the condition that this same way is available to others – in fact, to everyone. Here everyone's having the same right R benefits (in the manner just described) everyone, person a and person b and so on, down the line. It must be this way for those civil rights that have been justified by the relevant standard, by satisfying the test of mutual and general benefit.

The test here is not the same as Hurka's idea of "shared" benefit, where person a's having a right R benefits both person a and all other persons. For nothing like this would follow, as to mutual and general benefit, simply from *a*'s having a right that benefits *a*, or from *b*'s having a similar one. Rather, it's from the fact that *everyone* has the same right(s) that this mutual and general benefit arises. Legally established ways of acting/ways of being treated, identically the same for everyone, are justified, then, when they actually are beneficial (in parallel fashion) for each and all.

I think Hurka's version ("shared" benefit) is too strong a notion to be typically found in the real social world. For it is unlikely we will find, for a given way of acting or of being treated, that in being beneficial for person *a* it will also be beneficial for all others. It is likely to be so only if that same way of acting/way of being treated is extended to each and all. Hurka's notion of "shared" benefit carries with it a whiff of the very ideas, that the good of each includes within it the good of all others (or is non-competitive with the good of others or is the same good for everyone), that critics of Green have seized on time and again.[21]

There is, nonetheless, an account of reciprocity that is appropriate to Green's theory and I want briefly to turn to that now. We start with the obvious point that sometimes a particular way of acting or of being treated – the same way in each case – can be a beneficial thing for a large number of people. It would be likely, then (where this was so), that when someone perceived that it was a good for them, they would also perceive that it was a good for others as well. Now, such ways have to be sustained in practice; they do not just happen. They have to be accomplished and maintained through some sort of effort and choice. Typically, they are sustained through joint effort.

The citizens or lifelong members of a given system of civil rights have pooled their efforts to achieve a common set of values or norms for conduct in their society, as given (especially) in the civil rights laws that constitute or are among the main rules in this particular system of rights. The texture of any such body politic is spelled out not only in the specific list of civil rights that all enjoy but also in the normative directives imposed on the conduct of every person – but variously – by those rights. Thus, persons who are citizens or lifelong members of that particular society are rightholders there and have made their contribution to that society and to its system of rights, when they've acted in character as typical citizens, through their conduct in conforming to law. It is *their* system, for they have contributed to it in this way. Its

---

[21] These criticisms are identified and expanded upon in John Horton, *Political Obligation* (Atlantic Highlands, NJ: Humanities Press, 1992), ch. 3, pp. 70–9, 177. See also Nicholson, *Political Philosophy of the British Idealists*, ch. 2, sects. 2–4, where these criticisms are identified and a careful attempt at answering them is made.

flourishing is the work of their hands and of others like them. A system of rights so understood is always the work of its citizens or lifelong members; they are its primary beneficiaries but they are also its primary progenitors.

Some features of that particular system, indeed, may well be unique. And the citizens have accorded a sort of preference to the achievement of this precise set of rights. They have put an emphasis on the achievement of these legally secured ways of acting or of being treated, ways that are in the interest of each and all. And they have established a priority of determinate universal rights – certainly of basic rights – in that society over certain other options.[22] Thus, in these ways, a kind of reciprocity and a *social* sense of common good – an active concern for the good of each as connected with the good of all – comes to characterize the conduct and ultimately the attitudes of typical citizens in a particular system of civil rights.

Just as it is important to distinguish Green's account here from Hurka's notion of shared benefit, it is also important to distinguish it sharply from self-interest-based accounts of the sort associated with David Gauthier. Green's account bears none of the background features characteristic of Gauthier's. In Green's account there is no notion of individual endowments and individual productivity as conceivably independent of society, no notion of individuals as rational utility maximizers (who are then enticed away from straightforward maximization of their own good by the realization that such a strategy, in the context of rational bargaining, would prove to be suboptimal). Green's moral psychology is quite different as well, relying as it does on the notion that others are not mere *means* to one's own good but, rather, are fellow citizens who share identical goods (ways of acting/being treated) with us, under conditions of reciprocity.[23] Most important here, the crucial

---

[22] The priority I have primarily in view is a priority of basic rights over (i) any common good that serves the social or corporate good but not necessarily the good of each individually (e.g., national defense) and over (ii) majority decisions that serve the good of some individuals but not all, and may even be injurious to some (e.g., a particular tax code as regards allowable credits, deductions, exemptions, etc.).

I should add that the notion of a basic right has not, up to this point, been defined. What I have in mind are, paradigmatically, those civil rights (such as the right of habeas corpus) that have been identified and established by democratic decision, and exhibit a very high level of social consensus, have survived the self-correcting processes of the democratic institutions, and now enjoy explicit endorsement by various of the checking devices (such as judicial review). I will turn to the issue of democratic institutions in the next part of this assessment.

[23] See here, in particular, sects. 199–200 of Green's *Prolegomena* in Nicholson (ed.), *Collected Works of Green*, vol. IV, pp. 210–12. I am indebted to the editors of the present volume for raising the query about Gauthier and for calling my attention to these sections of the *Prolegomena*.

account of reciprocity in Green's theory is not reached or justified by rational choice strategies. Indeed, one of the main criticisms leveled against Gauthier's own account of "moral bargaining" is that rational maximizing strategies could never reach the goal of mutually optimal "constrained maximization" or, if they did, such strategies would continue to operate so as to undermine and make unstable that very goal.[24]

Green's theory – unlumbered with the Gauthierian baggage of atomistic individualism, non-cooperative bargaining strategies, and maximization of rational self-interest – appeals directly to the idea that some ways of acting/being treated are mutually beneficial, if engaged in by everyone. And Green then deepens this account, in the ways I have indicated, by showing that reciprocity is required to make that idea work. Recognition of this fact in turn generates an abiding and reflective commitment, presumably a widespread one, existing on many sides, to a sense of one's own good as a *social* good, fully realizable only in a certain kind of society.

I want to continue now the particular line of thought implicated in this very last point, but I will return to the theme of reciprocity again, at the very end of the chapter.

Green argues that, though rights may arise, indeed do arise, in the social relations that persons have with one another (and are sustained there through the sort of reciprocity I have been describing), a certain overarching political arrangement is required as well. This arrangement is the state (as Green calls it). "The state is [for the citizen] the complex of those social relations out of which rights arise, so far as those rights have come to be regulated and harmonised according to a general law, which is recognised by a certain multitude of persons, and [behind] which there is sufficient power to secure [such rights] against violation from without and from within." Elsewhere Green speaks of the state as being peculiarly concerned with "sustaining, securing, and completing" rights.[25] The state exists, in short, to formulate, maintain, and harmonize legal rights, in particular civil rights (those that are universal within

---

[24] Gauthier's well-known views, always elegantly expressed, are set forth in his book *Morals by Agreement* (Oxford: Clarendon Press, 1986). Some of the background to these views is provided in a collection of his essays, curiously entitled *Moral Dealing: Contract, Ethics, and Reason* (Ithaca, NY: Cornell University Press, 1990); Gauthier's concerns about his own theory (along the lines just sketched) are set out in the last essay in that collection. Criticisms of Gauthier's views are plentiful. Some of the best spell out the points presented here; a useful compendium of such criticisms is found in Peter Vallentyne (ed.), *Contractarianism and Rational Choice: Essays on David Gauthier's Morals by Agreement* (Cambridge University Press, 1991).

[25] See Green, "Political Obligation," sects. 141, 134 (pp. 110, 104), respectively, for the passages quoted; see also sects. 138, 142, 143.

a given society). The question naturally arises, then, as to what particular institutional processes, if any, are apt in the production of civil rights – that is, in their formulation especially but also in their maintenance and harmonization. This question arises naturally, I say, but Green did not put that question directly, to himself or his auditors. The failure to ask and attempt to answer this particular question is, in my view, the most central failure of Green's theory of rights. However, an answer could be suggested that is not uncongenial to Green's overall view. Let me turn to it now.

Active civil rights, as was just said, require an agency to formulate and maintain and harmonize them. More specifically, they require an agency to identify and establish ways of acting, or ways of being treated, that can reasonably be supposed to be in everyone's interest. It could be argued that democratic institutions – universal franchise (on a one-person, one-vote basis), contested voting, and majority rule – can effectively perform this job and thus provide the setting required by civil rights. For it could be claimed that democratic procedures are a stable and relatively reliable way of identifying, and then implementing, laws and policies that serve interests common to all the voters or to a large number of them, presumably at least a majority.

Admittedly, an argument would be required to show that democratic institutions have a special affinity for civil rights and would accord them the sort of priority I mentioned above (in the discussion of reciprocity). But such an argument could, I think, be set out. The upshot, then, were such an argument accomplished, would be that the setting required by civil rights could be provided by democratic majority-rule government. Democracy, in its turn, needs a suitable justification and this can best be provided by giving preference to policies that serve the interests of each and all and by avoiding policies that override these interests. And such a preference would include, as a proper subset, universal political (or civil) rights.

Thus, what were initially two quite independent elements – civil rights and democratic procedures – have been systematically brought together and connected to one another, by the line of argument just sketched. Our two key notions (accredited civil rights – of individual persons – and justified democratic government) are mutually supportive of one another. Thus, they can form the central undergirding of a distinctive political system, one in which civil rights are accorded priority. This priority does not arise from the idea of universal rights, as one might have initially supposed, but, rather, from the idea of democratic institutions, as suitably justified. Perhaps it would be clearer, though, to say that this priority arises from the connection and grounding of each of the two key elements in the same justificatory pattern, in the idea of mutual and general benefit.

Green did believe that the operation of democratic institutions afforded a certain authority to the laws produced.[26] But he did not suggest that democracy bore any special relationship to civil rights, such that bringing these two ideas together (in the way just described) could provide any sort of closure – a needed closure, I would add – to his idea of a sustainable system of civil rights.

With this point made, we have reached the end of a rather long argument. What conclusions can we draw here, then?

It is often alleged that societies in which civil rights are given priority (or, even, emphasis) are overcommitted to values such as personal autonomy and the rights of single individuals; accordingly, it is further alleged, such societies at heart are atomistic, lacking in cohesion, and afford no sense of community or of a common good to their members, at least not to those who are clear-headed. The members, then, can have no reasonable sense of identification with or allegiance to an archetypically rights-focused society. Or, to put the point more precisely, the sense of commitment of persons there is wholly instrumental; it does not go beyond treating such a society and the other members (beyond a small circle of family, friends, and associates) as merely a viable means to the self-interest and personal aggrandizement of the various particular individuals who make it up. Clearly, then, there is no sense in which the body politic or the well-being of its members overall could be an end in itself or a good *per se* to the individuals involved.

But I have argued that civil rights (the fundamental sort of right in a society like this) are justified there in a characteristic way, by reference to the standard of mutual perceived benefit. It follows that the members (the citizens), insofar as they have civil rights, must have upon reflection a sense of common good (given that some of the important goods of person *a* are also goods of person *b*, and so on round the ring) and that this sense is, in fact, identical (to that degree) for each and all. And it can be shown, in a fashion acceptable to each, that persons in such a society must or should give priority to civil rights and thereby restrain

---

[26] See, for example, ibid., sect. 100. Green was an enthusiastic supporter of the tendency towards democracy that could be descried in the governmental institutions of the USA, in particular, and also of Britain. He supported the extension of the franchise in the direction of one person/one vote. So, as I say, the turn to democratic institutions here would not be uncongenial to Green. For further discussion see Sandra M. Den Otter, *British Idealism and Social Explanation: A Study in Late Victorian Thought* (Oxford: Clarendon Press, 1996), pp. 164–5, and Nicholson, "Introduction," *Collected Works of Green*, vol. V, pp. xxiv–xxv.

self-seeking and the deployment of rights for mere partial or "factional" advantage.

Moreover, I think it could be shown, in view of this pattern of justification, that the members will have a characteristic allegiance to such a society (and an obligation to obey many of its laws). This allegiance and its attendant duty are not modeled on voluntary obligations and, in an interesting and recognizable way, are specific to that one particular society (or community) of people with which the members' lot in life has been cast.

People have this allegiance – a sense of affiliation and a sense of being especially open to the claims made on them by fellow citizens (two wholly appropriate attitudes to have, I would add) – because the scheme of political benefits they and others participate in is a reciprocal one. Reciprocity here grounds the allegiance, the sense of identification I have just described, that typical citizens have towards a particular body politic.[27]

Thus, a political system in which civil rights have priority in the public domain (over rights that are not universal within the society and over other normative considerations which are not rights) is not essentially atomistic. Nor is it antithetical to many of the traditional values associated with communitarianism, to theories of common good, or to republican civic virtue.

The points just made merit emphasis. It is often alleged, in naive or polemical versions of communitarianism, that the culture of community is radically distinct from and cannot be embraced by the culture of rights. Rights cannot comport with the common good, for rights are always radically individualistic, anti-social artifacts. They spring from a different and alien soil, the competitive marketplace of civil society (in Marx's well-known critique of rights) or the barren wastes of the state of nature (in Bentham's).[28]

We have here a radical oversimplification. Green's theory of a system of civil rights (rights of individuals), if grounded in democratic institutions and norms and embedded in the practices and attitudes of reciprocity (like Rawls' more recent theory of political liberalism), stakes out a middle ground. It is a middle ground between devil-take-the-hindmost atomistic individualism, on the one hand, and the celebration

---

[27] The three previous paragraphs as well as the one that follows are drawn, with revisions, from my chapter, "Civil Rights and the U.S. Constitution," in Gary C. Bryner and A. Don Sorenson (eds.), *The Bill of Rights: A Bicentennial Assessment*, ©Brigham Young University (Albany: State University of New York Press, 1994), pp. 27–62.

[28] For sample criticisms of natural rights by these two thinkers, and for helpful general commentaries on them, see Jeremy Waldron (ed.), *Nonsense Upon Stilts: Bentham, Burke, and Marx on the Rights of Man* (London: Methuen, 1987).

of community as an overarching value in and of itself (without undue concern for the question of what goods the community invests in and for what people), on the other. Green's vision of the good society, because its theory of rights is not individualistic in the unattractive way deplored by communitarianism and because it is democratic and depends on reciprocity and engenders allegiance to a particular kind of body politic (and, within that kind, to particular ongoing societies), can avail itself of the resources of a robust sense of the common good.[29]

It is in the notion of an institutionally justified right of each and all – a *democratically* justified right, in a system of rights that require reciprocity – that we find Green's basis for reconciling the two main elements in his own account of rights, the elements of social recognition and common good. That notion provides the basis for Green's "new liberal" conception of individual rights as compatible with the common good.[30]

[29] For a helpful and up-to-date survey of the liberal–communitarian debate, see Stephen Mulhall and Adam Swift (eds.), *Liberals and Communitarians*, 2nd edn (Oxford: Blackwell, 1996). Their book takes as its focus the theories of John Rawls, as developed in his two magisterial books, *A Theory of Justice* (Cambridge, MA: Harvard University Press, 1971) and *Political Liberalism* (New York: Columbia University Press, 1993). In addition, the paperback version of Rawls, *Political Liberalism* (1996) should be consulted; it incorporates a new, second introduction (specific to the paperback) and adds a new ninth chapter.

For Green's own emphasis on the appropriateness of the notion of community in any sound theory of rights, see "Political Obligation," sect. 39. This section occurs as part of Green's discussion of Spinoza's theory of rights, but it reflects, I think, with suitable modification, Green's overall view. I am indebted to Will Sweet for drawing this section to my attention, as bearing on the discussion of the paragraph to which this note is attached.

[30] The present chapter is based on two papers I have delivered: one at a meeting of the American Political Science Association, in Chicago, in September 1995; the other at a meeting of the Canadian Maritain Association, held in conjunction with the sessions of the Canadian Congress of the Social Sciences and Humanities, in Ottawa, in May 1998. One motivation I had in writing these papers and in expanding on them for the present volume is a dissatisfaction, at two points in particular, with the now prevailing accounts of Green's thought: (i) with the account offered of the relation of recognition and common good in Green's theory of rights (in Thomas) and (ii) with the account of common good (both there and in Nicholson). For further discussion see my review (in *International Studies in Philosophy*, 24 [1992], 143–5) of Thomas' book, *Moral Philosophy of Green*.

In writing the present chapter I have drawn, sometimes verbatim, on my paper "Green on Natural Rights in Hobbes, Spinoza and Locke," in Vincent, *The Philosophy of T. H. Green*, pp. 104–26, esp. pp. 105–11, and on my book *System of Rights*.

3   T. H. Green's complex common good: between liberalism and communitarianism

Avital Simhony

Introductory

One major way of capturing the liberal–communitarian debate is in terms of Sandel's dichotomous classification of "politics of rights" as opposed to "politics of the common good." Liberal politics of rights is premised on the Kantian claim that the right is prior to the good. Communitarians question that claim and ground the politics of the common good in a conception of the good life while claiming Hegel and Aristotle as their intellectual resources. According to this classification liberals fail to (and indeed cannot) recognize a genuine shared common good.

In a vigorous response to communitarian criticism Holmes argues that liberals hold "an emphatic conception of the common good."[1] Because they are pluralists, liberals, he holds, do not provide a definition of "the good life" as opposed to "the bad life"; but they do provide an obligatory distinction between "right action" and "wrong action": "Rightness ... defines the liberal conception of the common good."[2] Though pronounced in response to communitarian criticism, that liberal conception of the common good is not entirely new.[3]

Interestingly, Taylor makes a similar claim from a communitarian-republican standpoint. He recognizes that because "[t]he ethic central to liberal society is ethic of the right, rather than the good," "procedural liberalism" cannot recognize "a socially endorsed conception of the good;"[4] but liberalism can and does endorse a conception of common good in terms of the right.[5]

---

[1] Stephen Holmes, *The Anatomy of Antiliberalism* (Cambridge, MA: Harvard University Press, 1993), p. 200; see also pp. 237–40.

[2] Ibid., p. 200.

[3] See, for example, S. I. Benn and R. S. Peters, *The Principles of Political Thought* (New York: The Free Press, 1959), pp. 318–21; B. J. Diggs, "The Common Good as Reason for Action," *Ethics*, 83 (1972–3), 283–93.

[4] Charles Taylor, "Cross-Purposes: The Liberal–Communitarian Debate," in N. Rosenblum (ed.), *Liberalism and the Moral Life* (Cambridge, MA: Harvard University Press, 1989), pp. 164, 165, respectively.

[5] Ibid., p. 172.

The liberal–communitarian dualism is, therefore, no longer between politics of rights and politics of the common good, but rather between two rival, liberal and communitarian-republican, conceptions of the common good. Let us call them "rightness-common good" and "goodness-common good," respectively. That classification, however, retains and indeed is premised on the rival ethical perspectives of the right and the good where liberal rightness-common good is not, and communitarian-republican goodness-common good is, premised on a conception of the good life.

The idea of the common good is central to Green's liberalism; indeed with Green that idea entered modern liberal thinking. Though liberal, Green's common good is goodness- rather than rightness-common good, which seems to place it with the communitarian-republican common good. Yet, the way justice and rights are constitutive of Green's common good is a clear point of difference with the communitarian-republican common good. Green, I suggest, defends what may be described as complex common good. The complexity of the common good reveals itself in one's inability to place it neatly in the rightness-common good and goodness-common good classification, the dualism of which it defies and transcends. To appreciate that claim is to see how, for Green, though the right is derivative from the good, which is primary, the right is, nevertheless, constitutive of the good and is necessary for its realization. Herein lies the complexity of the common good, which is further exhibited in the way Green appeals to both Kant and Aristotle (and Hegel too) as complementary resources of his common good project. The complexity of his common good may be seen, therefore, as an attempt to forge a third way which escapes the said dualisms.

Two claims propel my exploration of Green's common good. One claim concerns the liberal–communitarian debate; the other, the liberal tradition. My first claim is that Green's common good clearly shows that the relationship between communitarianism (and republicanism) and liberalism is not, and cannot be, one of opposition; rather, opposition obtains between communitarianism and individualism, but the latter is not the same as liberalism.[6] Green's connection of liberalism with the common good reflects his deliberate effort to rid liberalism of its

---

[6] This claim informs major contemporary writings, e.g., W. Kymlicka, *Liberalism, Community and Culture* (Oxford University Press, 1989); S. Macedo, *Liberal Virtues. Citizenship, Virtue, and Community in Liberal Constitutionalism* (Oxford: Clarendon Press, 1990). Of particular interest are the deliberate attempts at reconciliation by Richard Dagger, *Civic Virtues: Rights, Citizenship and Republican Liberalism* (Oxford: University Press, 1997), and Joseph Raz, *The Morality of Freedom* (Oxford: Clarendon Press, 1986).

association with self-centered individualism from within a liberal framework. My second claim concerns the liberal tradition.

Liberal tradition can embrace, consistently and cheerfully, Green's goodness-common good which is immune to traditional liberal anxieties, not least because rightness-common good is internal to it. To sustain that claim is to take seriously a current liberal claim, partly made in response to communitarian criticism, that liberals need to tap the richness of liberal tradition. This is just what this chapter intends to do, thereby highlighting his triple contribution to our appreciation of the liberal tradition. First, again, Green's goodness-common good is consistently liberal (much as perfectionist liberalism is). Second, Green's common good argument does not dispense with the language of interest, but transforms it, such that the idea of social interest rather than public interest is essential to the common good project; hence, the latter can be profitably situated within modern liberals' attempt to revise the relation between liberalism and self-interest. Third, Green's common good project extends the concerns of liberal theory by insisting on giving institutional effect to the moral requiredness of *joint* self-realization.

The chapter has four sections. The first introduces the common good as the good society which is grounded in an ethic of joint self-realization. I then proceed, in the following two sections, to explore the Kantian, Hegelian, and Aristotelian resources which give form and content to the common good conception of the good society. The final section focuses on justice and citizenship as the positive expressions of the complexity of the common good. The chapter concludes by briefly diffusing liberal anxieties about the commonness of the good.

Introducing the common good

There is no doubt that the idea of the common good is the central concept of Green's thought. Doubts, however, abound as to the nature and role of that concept. What is necessary, I believe, is to reconstruct the common good from within Green's own thought, since though nowhere does he provide a full account of the common good, that concept does not float free of the context of his ethical writings. The result of my reconstruction is an understanding of the common good as an ethic of joint realizability which is ethic of a certain kind of social life: co-operative individual-developing social life or harmonious individual-realizing sociability. The common good emerges as an ideal of the good society: a community of mutually developing individuals, the moral requiredness of which justifies the construction of social order in terms of both justice and citizenship. My reconstruction of the common good is twofold. I first analyze the two components of "common good," and then see how the latter transcends the dichotomy of egoism and altruism.

The good in "common good" is self-realization, self-development, abiding self-satisfaction, or the perfecting of human character. By self-realization Green means, in Aristotelian fashion, exercising one's human capacities. The common good, then, is common self-realization. But how is self-realization common? What does "common" in "common good" mean? I suggest three related senses of "common" without appreciation of which Green's common good cannot be fully apprehended: "mutual," "universal," and "distributive."

The primary sense of "common" is, I believe, "mutual," or "joint" as opposed to "separate" or "private."[7] It can be gleaned from the contrast, foundational to Green's common good project, between common and private good.[8] Enjoying private good consists in "separating . . . instead of uniting,"[9] and may be described as "separate satisfiability" in that the end (good) one pursues is logically independent of the ends of other individuals and hence can be enjoyed without other individuals. Each person desires and pursues it as *own*-good and not as *good*.

Self-realization, by contrast, is mutual good: no one can achieve self-realization in separation from and independently of others; one's development is dependent on and is reciprocal with others'. As Hobhouse puts it: "the development that each man can achieve is conditioned in kind and degree by the development of others."[10] This claim presupposes a view of shared social life: "In thinking of ultimate good he thinks of it indeed necessarily as perfection for himself . . . But he cannot think of himself as satisfied in any life other than a social life . . . in which . . . all men . . . shall participate."[11] "All" alludes to the inclusive and distributive nature of the common good.

"Common" is "universal" as opposed to "particular" or "exclusive." The good as self-realization equally relates to all human beings in virtue

---

[7] What I describe as mutual good, Philip Pettit describes as "interactive good" in "Liberal/Communitarian: MacIntyre's Mesmeric Dichotomy," in John Horton and Susan Mendus (eds.), *After MacIntyre* (Cambridge: Polity Press, 1994), pp. 176–24.

[8] "Lectures on the Philosophy of Kant, II. The Metaphysics of Ethics," in R. L. Nettleship (ed.), *Works of Thomas Hill Green* (London, 1906), vol. II, sects. 107–8, 118, 123 (hereafter, "Kant"); "Popular Philosophy and Its Relation to Life," in *Works of Thomas Hill Green*, vol. III; "Introductions to Hume's 'Treatise of Human Nature.' II. Introduction to the Moral Part of Hume's 'Treatise,'" *Works of Thomas Hill Green*, vol. I, sects. 16–18, 21–4 (hereafter, "Hume").

[9] "Kant," sect. 118.

[10] L. T. Hobhouse, *The Rational Good* (London: Allen & Unwin, 1921), p. 90.

[11] T. H. Green, *Prolegomena to Ethics*, ed. A. C. Bradley (Oxford: Clarendon Press, 1883; 5th edn., 1907), sect. 370; see also sect. 288 (hereafter, *Prolegomena*).

of "unfulfilled possibilities of the rational nature common to all men," and "not merely ... [of] the members of a particular community."[12] Importantly, therefore, the good society is premised on the moral equality of individuals which renders it an inclusive, rather than an exclusionary, ideal. It is also distributive.

"Common" in "common good" is "distributive" as opposed to "collective." "Common" may mean two things: the good in question may pertain either to society as a whole (collective sense), or to each of its members individually (distributive sense).[13] The good society is "common" in the distributive sense, such that justice, as we shall see, is constitutive of it. The distributive nature of the common good may be seen in two ways. For Green the good does pertain to society as a whole which is, strictly speaking, the collective sense; but he employs "society as a whole" distributively, meaning each and every member of society individually, though jointly and not separately.[14] Alternatively, Green insists, "[o]ur ultimate standard of worth is an ideal of *personal* worth. All other values are relative to value for, of, or in a person."[15] The good, then, pertains to each member of society individually though not separately: "it is only in the *inter*course of men ... that the capacity [for self-realization] is actualised and that we really live as persons."[16]

The second element in my reconstruction of the common good is that as mutual good or an ethic of joint self-realizability, Green intends the common good to escape the dualism of egoism and altruism, self-love and benevolence. Instead, the common good ethic forges a non-dichotomous moral framework which aims to occupy a moral terrain of human connectedness where one's good and the good of others are intertwined, where one's fundamental interest in one's own development is not pitted against one's interest in the development of others.

[12] The two quotations are from ibid., sect. 207.
[13] Roger Scruton, "common good," in his *Dictionary of Political Thought* (London: Macmillan, 1982), p. 77. See also Alan Gewirth, *The Community of Rights* (Chicago University Press, 1996), p. 94.
[14] "Lectures on the Principles of Political Obligation," in T. H. Green, *Lectures on the Principles of Political Obligation and Other Writings*, Paul Harris and John Morrow, eds. (Cambridge University Press, 1986), sects. 132, 142 (hereafter, "Political Obligation"); "Lecture on 'Liberal Legislation and the Freedom of Contract,'" in T. H. Green, *Lectures on the Principles of Political Obligation and Other Writings*, p. 199; see also below, section entitled "The complementary argument."
[15] *Prolegomena*, sect. 184; see also "On Different Senses of 'Freedom' as Applied to Will and to the Moral Progress of Man," in T. H. Green, *Lectures on the Principles of Political Obligation and Other Writings*, sect. 6; "Political Obligation," sects. 23, 25.
[16] *Prolegomena*, sect. 183, emphasis added; see also sects. 184, 288, and my "Idealist Organicism: Beyond Holism and Individualism," *History of Political Thought*, 12 (1991), 514–35.

Such social connectedness does not give rise to rival egoist and altruist interests, but rather to social interest which escapes that rivalry. Social interest is central to the common good in the same way that selfish (egoist) interest is essential to private good. That contrast may be best appreciated as that between two conceptions of social life: common society vs. private society. Green's common good aims at rejecting private society as the ethical basis of liberalism.

According to the idea of private society, individuals enter into social relations only to meet their egoistic needs. Individuals have interests in others, but only as a means to the satisfaction of these narrowly self-centered needs. It is in this way that, for Green, private good is inextricably bound up with selfishness: "selfishness ... [is] the direction of a man's dominant interests to an object private to himself, a good in which others cannot share."[17] To be selfish or egoist is, as Bradley holds, to think only of oneself. As Rawls explains, "an egoist is someone committed to the point of view of his own interests. His final ends are related to himself."[18] For Rawls, the problem with the egoist is that he lacks the settled desire to take up the standpoint of justice. Without forcing any comparison with Rawls,[19] Green may be said to have a similar complaint taken from the common good vantage point: the egoist lacks the settled desire to take up the standpoint of the common good society (which embraces the standpoint of justice but also that of citizenship), without which its justification and viability are put in jeopardy. The problem of private society, therefore, is the problem of egoism (or selfish interest). Insofar as egoist interest is the primary basis of judgment and action, egoism cannot be the basis of common society because it cannot be the basis of individual-developing sociability. Being an egoist is inconsistent with the reasons and motivation that the standpoint of sociability requires. Social interest is.

"The man cannot contemplate himself as in a better state ... without contemplating others, not merely as a means to that better state, but as sharing it with him."[20] This is what Green describes as "distinctive social interest." "Distinctive" means that to have social interest is to have intrinsic rather than instrumental interest in others. It means that social relations with others are not simply of derivative interest, as

---

[17] "Kant," sect. 123.
[18] John Rawls, *A Theory of Justice* (Cambridge, MA: Harvard University Press, 1971), p. 568.
[19] A comparison, however, is likely to be intriguing, as Gerald F. Gaus, *Modern Liberal Theory of Man* (London: Croom Helm, 1983) suggests.
[20] *Prolegomena*, sect. 199; see also sects. 234–6, 239, 242–3, 253; "Political Obligation," sect. 248.

means to egoistic gratification, but of direct interest to us. Such interest is premised on seeing others as our "alter ego"[21] and, therefore, internal to our own life. Hence, "distinctive social interest" also means interest which is neither merely selfish nor purely altruistic, but mutual:[22] it is other-regarding without being self-forgetful or selfless.

Two points follow. Nicholson is quite right to insist on keeping apart Green's idea of the common good and the idea of public interest.[23] This claim, however, is fully consistent with my insistence that the common good and social interest are inextricably bound up. For social interest is not public interest. Green rids the idea of interest of its selfish, competitive, materialist, and maximizing associations (all connected with public interest), much as he rids the idea of rights of its atomist connection. That he does not abandon the language of interests situates him firmly within modern liberal tradition. In particular, his idea of social interest ought to be appreciated against a sustained attempt by modern liberals to rid liberalism of its association with self-centered individualism.

The second point concerns communitarian criticism of liberalism. Communitarians object to the way, as they allege, liberals see society as nothing more than a cooperative venture for the pursuit of individual advantage, as an essential private association formed by individuals whose essential interests are defined independently of, and in a sense prior to, the community of which they are members. Green's common good ethic of joint realizability aims at rejecting just such an idea of private society as the ethical core of liberalism. Kant, I suggest, is essential to such a project, but it is not immediately obvious how, since, whereas Green defends goodness-common good, Kant defends rightness-common good; hence, the reversal argument to which I now turn.

The reversal argument: the relevance of Kant

The reversal argument reverses the relationship between the good and the right such that the good precedes the right but the right, though derivative of the good, is internal to it and is essential to its realization. This is how Kantian rightness-common good is essential to Green's goodness-common good: Kantian rightness (common good) is constitutive of and is essential to the realization of Green's goodness-common good. I proceed in two steps: first, I look at the reversal itself which, I

---

[21] *Prolegomena*, sects. 191, 200.
[22] Compare Green's interchangeable use of social and mutual recognition to explain rights, e.g. "Political Obligation," sects. 25–6, 136, 139.
[23] Peter Nicholson, *The Political Philosophy of the British Idealists* (Cambridge University Press, 1990), pp. 62–4.

claim, Green pursues from within Kant's own resources; second, I show how, once the right–good relationship is reversed, the right is, nevertheless, essential to the common good project.

First step: the primacy of the good

A typical statement of the reversal argument is found in Green's revision of "Kant's statement, 'everything in nature works according to laws; *the distinction of a rational being is the faculty of acting according to the consciousness of laws ...*.'" Green's revision reads: "Everything in nature works so as to yield certain results according to law; *the distinction of a rational, or free, being, is that he acts*, not so as to yield certain results, but from consciousness of ends in attaining which he may satisfy himself, *out of which arises the consciousness of laws according to which they are to be attained*." This revision rests on Green's claim that "[a]ction according to the consciousness of laws clearly presupposes the consciousness of ends to be attained by conformity to these laws."[24] Thus, consciousness of ends precedes consciousness of laws, conformity to which realizes the end. Consciousness of laws (right) arises out of consciousness of ends (good), but adhering to those laws (right) is essential to attaining the ends (good).

Green's reversal argument is employed from Kant's own resources. In particular he makes use of the teleological nature of Kant's philosophy. To the standard Hegelian-communitarian criticism that Kant's notion of "duty for duty's sake" reduces itself to a duty to do nothing, Green answers:

when Kant excludes all reference to an object, of which the reality is desired, from the law of which the mere idea determines the *good will*, he means all reference to an object *other than* that of which the presentation ipso facto constitutes the moral law. That in that law, the willing obedience to which characterises a *good will*, there is implied some relation to an object, and that this object moves the will in the right sort of obedience to the law, appears from *his account of man as an absolute end*, on which he founds the second statement of the categorical imperative.[25]

Green's answer, then, is that Kantian duty is inseparable from realizing the "self as an absolute end" for "man in his rational nature is an absolute end,"[26] which, in turn, is bound up with the idea of the good will. The good will is a "desire determined not merely by ... *any* conception of the self as an absolute end, but by a *true* conception of the

[24] The three quotations are from "Kant," sect. 84, emphasis added.
[25] Ibid. sect. 111, emphasis added.
[26] Ibid. sects. 118, 112, respectively.

self as an absolute end";[27] thus, consciousness of "absolute good" – the good will – "carries with it the idea of a law," that is "as having a claim on me, ..." In other words, conforming to "a universally binding law of conduct ... the rule of conduct ... upon which the good man acts ... bears an authority derived from an ideal of absolute good."[28] The problem with Kant, therefore, is not that he lacks a view of the end or good; the problem is that his view of the end is lacking. Mending that lack is the concern of the complementary argument, to which I shall turn once the second step of the reversal argument is completed.

Second step: the constitutive role of the right

The reversal of the good–right relationship understood, the task now is to appreciate the constitutive role Kantian rightness-common good plays in Green's goodness-common good. The essential text for that purpose is that which supports Green's claim that Kantian reason "gives us the idea of a common good."[29] How does reason give us the idea of a common good? It does so, negatively, because non-egoist reason rejects the idea of private society; and, positively, because that rejection pre-supposes a positive ideal of moral community which lies at the heart of the common good society, a society which is realizable through Kantian rightness.

Kantian reason rejects the idea of private society. Recall that the common good may be seen as a view of social life in contradistinction to egoism-based private society. Egoism cannot justify common good society because the egoist's desires are for things for him. For Kant, however, "the moral faculty is a faculty of 'categorical' imperative, namely pure practical reason, which is not egoistic but universalizing";[30] hence, "[s]uch conformity [to universal law] on the part of everyone else I must desire in desiring it for myself, and everyone else in desiring it for himself must desire it for me." Universalizing reason is non-egoist in that it guides one's actions such that they are not concerned only with oneself. "My own reason" is not personal, "but is, to speak metaphorically, an inlet which the general will of humanity can enter and enable the individual to control personal needs and desires."[31] Hence: "It is in *my own person* that I seek to realise it [the end] but in so doing I am realising it for the *benefit of everyone else* ..." Universalizing reason, in its

[27] Ibid. sect. 115.　　[28] Ibid. sects. 111, 125, respectively.
[29] Ibid. sect. 107, from which also the two next Green quotations are taken.
[30] W. K. Frankena, "Sidgwick and the History of Ethical Dualism," in B. Schultz (ed.), *Essays on Henry Sidgwick* (Cambridge University Press, 1991), p. 191.
[31] H. B. Acton, *Kant's Moral Philosophy* (London: Macmillan, 1970), p. 41.

reciprocal capability, rules out egoism. This is in form Green's idea of the common good as mutual good and this is how reason "unites us."

Rejecting egoism-based private society presupposes a positive ideal of a community (kingdom of ends) of mutually respecting persons each recognizing the others as equal members of one community. That ideal of community is both constitutive of Green's common good society and essential to its realization. It is constitutive of Green's common good society in that the latter is a "society of equals" in which each member respects and is respected by all other members. This is what Greek ethics did not recognize, that is the universality of "the principle that humanity in the person of every one is to treated always as an end, never merely as a means . . ."[32]

Kantian moral community is essential to the realization of the common good society. To see this is to see how justice-as-fairness is internal to the common good project. In the Kantian ideal community, no one would be required to do anything which he would not think it reasonable for everyone to do. Thus, Kant holds that "no one is bound to refrain from encroaching upon the possession of another man if the latter does not in equal measure guarantee that the same kind of restraint will be exercised with regard to him."[33] This is moral rightness which, according to Holmes, is "the ethical center of liberalism." This ethical center generates, for Kant, obligation of reciprocity.[34] And some such obligation justifies the structural requirement, grounded in the common good ethic, for mutually assured self-realization without which the common good project cannot be realized. How so?

That Kant's community of ends structures the common good society has consequences for the sort of claims that members of common good society can make on one another. Of particular importance is the claim for self-realization. Since self-realization consists in exercising distinctive human capacities, and since the common good society is concerned with the self-realization of all its members, members can expect their society to enable and maintain the exercise of such capacities. But since the basis of the claim to self-realization is the claim to having the status of an equal member in the community, to claim self-realization for oneself is to recognize the perfectly reciprocal and equally legitimate claims to self-realization by others. Accordingly, the good society is a "social union, in which the claims of all are acknowledged by the loyal

---

[32] *Prolegomena*, sect. 267; see also sect. 280.
[33] Quoted in Jeffrie G. Murphy, *Kant: The Philosophy of Right* (Macon, GA: Mercer University Press, 1994), p. 115.
[34] Ibid., p. 121.

citizen as the measure of what he may claim for himself ...," and, therefore, rests on "[the] recognition of reciprocal claims."[35]

Now, since self-realization is an exercise-conception, one's claim to self-realization for oneself is a claim to be secured the conditions for self-realization, among which rights are of particular importance; hence "on the part of every person ... the claim ... to rights on his own part is co-ordinate with his recognition of rights on the part of others."[36] Thus, justice is the impartial maintenance of a system of rights as well as distributive justice, with regard to which Green goes beyond Kant, who regarded the state as a just protector of rights.[37] The point to stress now is that Kantian rightness is essential to realizing the common good society.

The complementary argument

Now that the reversal of the relations between the good and the right has been accomplished, the complementary argument comes into play. Why so? Because, as we have just seen, Kant's ideal of moral community structures the common good society; hence, Green does not seek to displace Kantian argument, but rather to mend it by complementing it. A useful entry into the complementary argument is Norman's claim that Kant fails to refute egoism. I said that Kant's ruling out egoism structures Green's common good society by rejecting private society and justifying the community of ends as a positive ideal of a community of equals. Norman's criticism might jeopardize Green's reliance on Kant. Seeing how it does not is doubly helpful: it helps explain how Green's common good is liberal in a complex way; also, since Norman's criticism is of communitarian nature, the complementary argument shows how Green's Kant is immune to such criticism while being essential to Green's liberalism.

Norman claims that Kant fails to provide a refutation of egoism because his universalizing reason is consistent with justifying a world of self-respecting egoists.[38] Without a shift from universality as impersonality to universality as impartiality Kant cannot refute egoism. That shift, however, cannot be achieved as long as the universalizability principle is grounded in purely formal rationality. Rather, "we have to start ... with the idea of the individual as a social being involved in

---

[35] *Prolegomena*, sects. 283, 216, respectively.
[36] "Political Obligation," sect. 26; see also sect. 139.
[37] Murphy, *Kant: The Philosophy of Right*, pp. 124, 125; see also p. 125, n. 26.
[38] Richard Norman, *The Moral Philosophers. An Introduction to Ethics* (Oxford University Press, 1983), p. 119.

relations which carry with them commitments to others."[39] Norman's criticism recalls the communitarian claim that Kant conceives rationality in purely procedural terms and considers the agent in abstraction from any concrete historical, social, or political context.

My response to Norman's criticism is that Kant's problem is not a problem for Green's Kant. It is not, because, much like Norman, Green starts "with the idea of the individual as a social being." The self, Green insists, "is not an abstract or empty self," but "a determinate self,"[40] namely the social self. Norman's understanding of the social self as relational is based on Bradley. Unlike Norman, though, Green may be said to take two routes to the social individual: the "relational self" route, which is not surprising given the Bradley connection, and the self as a "subject of interests" route, which is surprising unless we appreciate the role of the language of interest in Green's common good argument, as I claim we should. The essential point, however, is that both routes aim to achieve that which Norman's single route does: the appreciation of the social nature of the individual provides refutation of egoism by "revealing the inadequacy of the dichotomy between egoism and altruism."[41] Further, the two routes reveal, respectively, the Hegelian and Aristotelian complementing of Kant. I shall consider the Hegelian route first.

The complementary argument: Hegelian route

Green, like Bradley, holds that the self is not "an abstract empty self" since it "is from the first" a self "existing in manifold relations to nature and other persons" and "these relations form the reality of the self."[42] Intriguingly, however, this account of the relational self is, for Green, "the germ of what Kant calls ... 'kingdom of ends.'"[43] It becomes less intriguing, however, if we give that claim a Hegelian twist, as Green does. The Hegelian twist complements Kant in two ways: first, Kant's community of ends is grounded in the Hegelian community of mutual recognition; second, the Kantian ideal is socially situated.

Green grounds the Kantian community of rights (mutual respect for persons) in the Hegelian-inspired community of mutual recognition.[44] In such a community each person finds his identity as a free individual through relations with others. Similarly, Green holds that such a

---

[39] Ibid., p. 156.
[40] *Prolegomena*, sect. 199, and "Kant," sect. 118, respectively; see also "Kant," sect. 124.
[41] Norman, *The Moral Philosophers*, pp. 156–7.
[42] "Kant," sect. 124.   [43] Ibid.
[44] "Fragments on Moral and Political Philosophy," in T. H. Green, *Lectures on the Principles of Political Obligation and Other Writings*, p. 312.

community of mutual recognition is essential to sustain a Kantian community of reciprocal respect, for "it is only in the intercourse of men, each recognised by each as an end, not merely a means, and thus having reciprocal claims, that the capacity is actualised and that we really live as persons"; hence, mutual recognition is the sphere of the individual's "*realised* possibility."[45] This sphere, therefore, "must be a social life, in which all men freely and consciously co-operate, since otherwise the possibilities of their nature, as agents who are ends to themselves, could not be realised in it."[46]

Membership in shared cooperative social life is, to borrow from Raz's relevant anti-individualist argument, a "collective good,"[47] namely it is constitutive of the very possibility of individuals becoming self-realizing persons. In other words, such membership is the normative source both of one's pursuit of valuable goals and of one's obligation to others and service to one's community. This non-confrontational view of morality which propels Green's common good calls into question the whole opposition between the individual and community in a way that transcends the terms of debate between liberals and communitarians.

This is abundantly clear from the way Green revises the link forged by Kant between respect for persons and the separateness of individuals. Whereas Kantian subjects are conceived of as selves equal by virtue of exclusion of difference, for Hegel each self is for the other a means through which each mediates itself with itself. In this reciprocal process subjects recognize themselves as mutually recognizing one another. This process produces a subject which is relational at its core. This is, Green believes, how moral philosophy regards the individual, that is "as related to himself in relation to others – as through relation to others gaining realization of the relation to himself, which is otherwise merely formal."[48] Relational social ontology informs the common good society, which is not just a collection of individuals, although neither is it a mere collectivity above and beyond individuals.

The second Hegelian complementing of Kant is seen by appreciating how the Kantian community of ends takes shape in actual social

---

[45] *Prolegomena*, sect. 183, emphasis in original; see also sect. 288.
[46] Ibid., sect. 288.
[47] Raz, *The Morality of Freedom*, pp. 189–90, 203–7.
[48] "Fragments on Moral and Political Philosophy," p. 310. See also, "Political Obligation," sect. 138; *Prolegomena*, sect. 216; "The Philosophy of Aristotle," in *Works of Thomas Hill Green*, vol. III, pp. 60–71; "Popular Philosophy," pp. 112–13, 116–20, 123–4. For the Hegelian twist of Kant, to which Green clearly subscribes, see E. Caird, *The Critical Philosophy of Immanuel Kant*, 2nd edn. (Glasgow: James Maclehose & Sons, 1893), vol. II, pp. 328–50, 554–66, 570–3.

institutions. This Hegelian argument is important to Green's interpretation of Kant:

> The mistake of those who deny the a priori character of such "intuitions" of the conscience as that represented by Kant's formula [i.e. respect for persons], does not lie in a history of the intuitions, but in ignoring the immanent operation of ideas of the reason in the process of social organisation, upon which the intuitions as in the individual depend.[49]

For Green, then, the Kantian principle of humanity takes shape in concrete social institutions because they "are, so to speak, the form and body of reason, as practical in men."[50] Hence, the social practices which embody "reciprocal rights and obligations" educate individuals such that "we are conscious of ourselves and others as ourselves," and hence treat others as an "alter ego."[51] Though the "articulation, and application to the particulars of life, of that principle of an absolute value in the human person as such, of a like claim to consideration in all men, which is implied in the law and conventional morality is in fact partial and inconsistent," it nevertheless is essential in establishing "practice of justice"[52] which is, in turn, essential to the realization of the common good society. Essential also is the practice of virtue which connects Kant with Aristotle.

The complementary argument: Aristotelian route

Recall that the result of the reversal argument was to show that the problem with Kant was not that he lacks a view of the good, for the good consists of the good will, but that his view of the good is lacking. This is because the good will "may be taken to mean a will presented by some abstract idea of goodness or of moral law."[53] The charge of abstraction, recall, propels Norman's claim that Kant fails to refute egoism. "But it is not thus that we understand the good will," Green would retort.

How, then, does he understand the good will? "When we speak of the formation of such will [the good will] ... we understand it, not as determined merely by an abstract idea of law, but as implying (what in fact it must imply) a whole world of beneficent social activities ..."[54] The reference to beneficence is significant not only because it overcomes Kantian abstract reason by connecting the good will with social activities, but also because that connection is distinctively Aristotelian. The

---

[49] *Prolegomena*, sect. 215.
[50] Ibid., sect. 205; see also sects. 204, 216–17.
[51] Ibid., sects. 204, 200, respectively; see also sect. 201.
[52] Ibid., sect. 215.   [53] Ibid., sect. 247; see also sect. 266.
[54] Ibid., sect. 288; see also sect. 247 where Green connects the good will with virtues explicitly.

capacity of beneficence is one of Aristotle's definitions of virtue, as Green well recognizes when he states: "Virtue was ... a faculty of beneficence,"[55] citing Aristotle's *Rhetoric*'s definition of virtue. The beneficence definition of virtue exposes the connection of virtue with fine action.

Fine activity contrasts with "acting for the sake of either expedience or extrinsic pleasure. It is the end of virtue, but an immanent end ..."[56] Fine activity, then, cannot be selfish activity as Irwin establishes by reference to Aristotle's beneficence definition of virtue. All virtues aim at the fine; the fine is both intrinsically good and praiseworthy; hence concern for the fine is contrasted with narrow and exclusive concern for one's own interest; therefore actions display great virtues (which are for the sake of the fine) insofar as they especially benefit others.[57]

The connection between virtue and fine activity reveals the distinctive nature of virtuous activity as mutually beneficial. Green intends the practice of virtue to occupy the ethical terrain of shared social relations which the dualism between self-love and benevolence squeezes out of consideration. Such dualism is invalidated by the Aristotelian account of self-love: "correct self-love does not allow selfishness."[58] If "correct self-love" is, in the first place, unselfish, the dualism of self-love and benevolence is excluded: "the Aristotelian self-lover does not suffer from the kind of self-love we normally condemn: He does not suffer from excessive self-concern or think himself better than others."[59] Such self-centered self-love may characterize Hobbes' idea of self-love but not Aristotle's.

This reading of Aristotle should be seen as a resource for Green's revision and retention of the language of interest as essential, rather than hostile, to the language of the common good. Recall that the problem with the good will is Kant's "too abstract view of the *interest* on which he held that goodness must depend." A similar language of interest Green employs with regard to Aristotle who, Green claims, "[o]nce and for all ... conceived and expressed the conception of a free or pure morality, as resting on ... *disinterested interest in the good*."[60] That claim – having an "interest in the development of our faculties"[61] – is foundational to the

---

[55] Ibid., sect. 248.
[56] Nancy Sherman, *The Fabric of Character* (Oxford: Clarendon Press, 1989), p. 114.
[57] T. H. Irwin, "Eminent Victorians and Greek Ethics. Green, Sidgwick and Aristotle's *Ethics*," in Schultz, *Essays on Henry Sidgwick*, p. 296.
[58] T. H. Irwin, *Aristotle's First Principles* (Oxford University Press, 1988), sect. 208, p. 390.
[59] Marcia L. Homiak, "Virtue and Self-Love in Aristotle's *Ethics*," *Canadian Journal of Philosophy*, 11 (1981), 639.
[60] *Prolegomena*, sect. 253, emphasis added.
[61] Ibid., sect. 234; see also sects. 247, 255.

common good project. For Aristotle to complement Kant is, therefore, to give content to the abstract interest in the good. This Aristotelian virtues do, since, following Aristotle, Green regards "the several virtues as so many applications of that interest to the main relations of life." And virtues do so not as external means to the good of self-realization; rather, following Aristotle again, Green views "the good itself not as anything external to the capacities virtuously exercised in its own pursuit but as their full realisation."[62] Because the human good, for Aristotle, consists in virtuous activity, this closes the gap between what is in one's interest and the life of virtue. Green views such an "interest in the development of our faculties" as "a governing interest"[63] which is "not in abstraction from other interests, but as an organising influence upon and among them," and "must be active in every character" which pursues perfection, thereby giving reality to the Kantian "true conception of the self as an absolute end." It is, therefore, appropriate to describe that self as a "subject of interests"[64] which Green does. It is in this way that the language of interest is not hostile, but indeed essential, to the language of the common good.

Let me conclude with that claim by drawing attention to two points. One point is that to make this claim is to go against the standard view that pits the idea of the common good against the idea of self-interest. This is a version of the dualism of morality and self-interest. For Green the common good is itself a resolution of such dualism. From the point of view of the common good, the tension is not between common good and interest as such, but between common good and selfish interest. The second point is that the connection between social interest and the common good gains special importance if we are to be able properly to situate Green in liberal tradition. Here's why. Not appreciating the importance of social interest to the common good runs the risk of excluding Green as a fully paid-up liberal. For one thing, the idea of the goodness-common good has not played a central role in liberal thinking; indeed, it has been associated with non-liberal and even anti-liberal trends of thought.[65] For another, the language of interest is essential to liberalism. Freeden claims that the idea of general interest is one of the core concepts of liberalism, and that the full core is essential to the identity of any liberal tradition: "Remove one [concept of the core] and we are looking at a borderline case."[66] Seeing how Green employs

---

[62] Ibid., sect. 253 for both quotations.
[63] Ibid., sect. 247; see also sects. 252, 255.   [64] "Hume," sect. 4.
[65] Holmes, *The Anatomy of Antiliberalism*, pp. 198–9.
[66] Michael Freeden, "The Family of Liberalisms: A Morphological Analysis," in James Meadowcroft (ed.), *The Liberal Political Tradition. Contemporary Reappraisals* (Cheltenham, UK: Edward Elgar, 1996), pp. 14–39; see also p. 16.

"general interest" in terms of "social interest" rather than "public interest" shows that he is not. It also shows Green's contribution to modern liberal effort to revise liberalism's link with the idea of self-interest.

A final word: for Green to speak of Aristotelian Kant is equally to speak of Kantian Aristotle. Ritchie put the point well: "If we are to connect him [Green] with any particular names of philosophers, it would be least misleading to say that he corrected Kant by Aristotle and Aristotle by Kant."[67] Perhaps the main Kantian correction of Aristotle concerns universality. Whereas Green finds room in the Kantian ethic of rules for the Aristotelian idea of character, the Kantian claim that all moral agents are ends in themselves creates the possibility of universality of character.[68] Though there are some current attempts to reconcile Kantian and Aristotelian ethics in a similar vein,[69] it is nevertheless the case that contemporary moral and political discourse views them as rival dualistic perspectives, as the liberal–communitarian debate amply shows. Green's refusal to subscribe to that dualism reveals the complexity of his common good. This is the focus of the final section.

Complex common good: justice and citizenship

That Green's project of the common good draws on both Kantian and Aristotelian (and Hegelian) resources reveals its complexity and is the source of our inability to place the common good neatly in either of the classifications of liberal or communitarian/republican. These classifications are grounded in the divide between rightness- and goodness-common good, ethics of right vs. ethics of good, and politics of rights vs. politics of common good. Green's common good defies and transcends these dualisms. This is how the complexity of the common good reveals itself negatively. But how does it reveal itself positively? It does so in the ideas of justice and citizenship as the affirmative implementation of the good society. This is the focus of the final section. I shall conclude it by looking briefly at liberal anxieties about the "commonness" of the good, which I shall find to be unfounded, and then briefly commenting on Green's extension of liberal concerns, the locus of which, I hold, lies in the ethic of the common good.

---

[67] D. G. Ritchie, *The Principle of State Interference: Four Essays on the Political Philosophy of Mr. Herbert Spencer, J. S. Mill, and T. H. Green* (London, 1891), p. 139.

[68] For example, *Prolegomena*, sect. 267.

[69] Roger Crisp (ed.), *How Should One Live? Essays on Virtues* (Oxford: Clarendon Press, 1996).

Justice and citizenship

The claim that justice and citizenship are mutually supportive and essential for a viable good community reveals the complexity of the common good positively. The essential point is this: the common good as an ethic of joint self-realization requires that both justice and citizenship will structure the social order. Both, that is, are justified by, and are derived from, one ethical foundation of individual-developing sociability.

Citizenship, for Green, is captured by the idea of "rendering service to the state,"[70] where the state is understood widely as the entire political community or scheme of social relations.[71] To render service to the state is to act as a member: "He [Aristotle] regards the state ... as a society of which life is maintained by what its members do for the sake of maintaining it."[72] It is, unsurprisingly, on this Aristotelian ground that Green's common good meets communitarian/republican common good.

This is especially evident in relation to Taylor's discussion of communitarian/republican common good.[73] Green, like Taylor, views the relationship between the individual member and the political community in terms of identification which is properly understood neither in terms of enlightened self-interest nor abstract altruism.[74] This is Green's point that Aristotle's view of the state has "[n]o need to dwell on benevolence as a balance of selfishness."[75] For the state is not viewed instrumentally but as a system of institutions and arrangements which are expressive and enhancing of the joint realizability of individuals as a common enterprise in which all share and which is, therefore, intrinsically valuable. Further, Taylor's distinction between two models of a citizen's dignity highlights Green's own understanding of citizenship. Taylor distinguishes between the liberal model of equal rights and treatment and the republican model of participatory self-rule, as well as making the claim that the viability of liberal rightness-common good is put in jeopardy insofar as it adopts the former model.[76] In a similar vein Green insists on "active interest in the service of the state ... [which] can hardly arise while the individual's relation to the state is that of a passive recipient of protection in the exercise of his rights of person and property,"[77] which, much like Taylor, he describes as (intelligent) patriotism.

[70] *Prolegomena*, sect. 263.   [71] Ibid., sect. 264.
[72] "Political Obligation," sect. 38.
[73] Taylor, "Cross-Purposes: The Liberal–Communitarian Debate."
[74] Ibid., pp. 160–70.
[75] Quoted in Irwin, "Eminent Victorians and Greek Ethics," pp. 309–10, n. 33.
[76] Taylor, "Cross-Purposes: The Liberal–Communitarian Debate," pp. 178–9.
[77] "Political Obligation," sect. 122.

Against this basic accord, two points of difference are important. One point is that Green's "active service in the interest of the state" is not the same as Taylor's participatory self-rule account of citizenship, insofar as the latter is the same as participating in political decision-making.[78] To be sure, Green recognizes the need of the active citizen "to have a share, direct or indirect, by himself as a member or by voting for the members of supreme or provincial assemblies, in making and maintaining the laws which he obeys."[79] But the activity of Green's citizen is not as strictly political as that; rather, it embraces activities of "mutual helpfulness" in the "maintenance and furtherance of a free society,"[80] which may be described as "obligation of support." Moreover, it is telling that Green concedes "a lowering of civil vitality" in the modern state, but endorses "the price of having recognised the claim to citizenship as the claim of *all* men."[81] This shows that Green would refuse to see Taylor's two models of citizen dignity as two rival and mutually exclusive perspectives. Hence, my second point.

This is that the requiredness of citizenship is justified only in a just state: "It is the fault of the state if this conception ['of a common good maintained by law'] fails to make him a loyal citizen, if not an intelligent patriot. It is a sign that the state is not a true state; that it is not fulfilling its primary function of maintaining law equally in the interest of all ..."[82] Setting aside for a moment the important point regarding the "primary function" of the state, the essential point is that rendering service to the state, though required by the common good, is inseparable from, and is reciprocal with, the state rendering service to its members: "the function of society being the development of persons, the realisation of the human spirit in society can only be attained according to the measure in which its function is fulfilled."[83] But how is that function to be fulfilled? By establishing and maintaining "a society of men really free ... 'really free,' in the sense of being enabled to make the most of their capabilities ..."[84] The obligation of supporting a free society depends on the obligation of society to enable freedom for all. Consequently, as the above quotation suggests, the "primary function" of the state is that of "maintaining law equally in the interest of all." Therefore, the "active interest in the service of the state" on the side of its members is normatively inseparable from, and is reciprocal with, the state acting

[78] Taylor, "Cross-Purposes: The Liberal–Communitarian Debate," p. 170.
[79] "Political Obligation," sect. 122.
[80] Ibid., sect. 248. This wider understanding of citizenship probably applies to Taylor's citizen too, but he is insufficiently clear on that issue.
[81] Ibid., sect. 119, emphasis added; see also sect. 258.
[82] Ibid., sect. 121.   [83] *Prolegomena*, sect. 191; see also sect. 184.
[84] "Political Obligation," sect. 248.

"equally in the interest of all." Because the state fulfills its "primary function," and hence service to its members, individual members come to value it for itself and not as a mere instrument. They can identify themselves with their society because it embodies the ideal of joint self-realization whose value and requiredness they support. The individual comes to identify with his political community "as the condition of the maintenance of those rights and interests, common to himself with his neighbours, which he understands."[85]

The "primary function" of the state, then, may be described as justice, and is twofold. One aspect is that of maintaining law equally in the interest of all by upholding "equal rights":[86] "maintaining the rights of its members as a whole or a system, in such a way that none gains at the expense of another (none has any power guaranteed to him through another's being deprived of that power)."[87] The second aspect is distributive justice, the importance of which is clearly implicit in Green's claim that "[t]he justice of punishment depends on the justice of the general system of rights ... on the question whether the social organisation in which a criminal has lived and acted has given him a fair chance of not being a criminal."[88] The point is that the state's "primary function" embraces securing its members a "real opportunity for self-development" with a special emphasis on "the less favoured members of society."[89]

Justice is constitutive of the very possibility of realizing the common good and, indeed, may be best understood as giving effect to the "distributive" sense of "common" without which the "joint" sense of "common" remains unfulfilled. Securing a real opportunity for self-development for all with a special emphasis on the worse-off members of society illustrates that the good of the common good society is understood in terms of benefit to each and every member of society, not separately but jointly. As Hobhouse puts it relevantly, "the good of society is bound up with the recognition of the rights of its members."[90] And the good of the common good society is joint or mutual good, such that no member (or group of members) can enjoy their good at the expense or loss of others' real opportunity. This, Green holds, is just what utilitarianism leads to; hence, from the standpoint of the common good, it is not only the utilitarian hedonist good which is unacceptable,

---

[85] Ibid., sect. 121.   [86] *Prolegomena*, sect. 258.
[87] "Political Obligation," sect. 132.   [88] Ibid., sect. 189.
[89] *Prolegomena*, sect. 245.
[90] L. T. Hobhouse, *The Elements of Social Justice* (London: Allen & Unwin, 1922), p. 40, note.

but also objectionable is the utilitarian principle of moral rightness.[91] It is in this way that rightness (as twofold justice), though being derived from the good which precedes it, is nevertheless internal to the common good project such that justice is essential to the realization of the common good society.

That normative reciprocity of justice and citizenship is an ethical requirement of the common good creates a distinctive justificatory sequence of twofold significance. First, this justificatory sequence suggests that communitarians who tend to emphasize one-sidedly the obligation of support run the risk of endorsing unjust communities as worthy of support.[92] The point cannot be overstated that the just society is internal to the common good society, which is unrealizable without justice. Second, the obligation of support is an obligation of reciprocity (or of mutual service). Insofar as the just state maintains a system of law and rights equally in the interest of all, and secures a real opportunity of self-development with emphasis on the worse-off, then supporting the state is mutual support: supporting oneself and others at the same time. Put differently, rendering service to the just state is mutual service to oneself and others because a just state serves everyone.

Liberal anxieties and extending liberal concerns

Certain issues never go away. Liberal anxieties about Green's liberalism are a case in point. Space does not allow discussing them in detail nor is there a pressing need to do so since many of the criticisms have been sufficiently shown to be groundless.[93] I shall, therefore, focus on the liberal anxiety that the commonness of the (common) good is exclusionary and suppressive of diversity and difference. The commonness of Green's common good is, I claim, immune to this liberal charge. For one thing, "common" is not collective but distributive, as is evident from the centrality of justice to the common good project; for another, Green does not believe that there is a single correct path to the good life. The good as self-realization is multi-pathed. Since the former point ought to be clear by now, I shall focus briefly on the latter.

Two points need attention. First, what is singlular is the form not the substance of self-realization.[94] The form consists in realizing one's capacities. To do that, one pursues "dominant interests" (or life-plans)

---

[91] *Prolegomena*, sect. 214, and, for Green's relationship with utilitarianism, Avital Simhony, "Was T. H. Green a Utilitarian?" *Utilitas*, 7 (1995), 122–44.

[92] Gewirth makes this criticism explicit, *Community of Rights*, pp. 86–7. See also Dagger, *Civic Virtues*, ch. 7, esp. pp. 114–15.

[93] Nicholson, *The Political Philosophy of the British Idealists*, pp. 83–95.

[94] *Prolegomena*, sect. 283; "Kant," sect. 118.

which give effect to one's conception of oneself; "dominant interests" are the substance of self-realization of which there is a "great variety."[95] Personal pursuits of dominant interests depend on the available stock of social forms, and therefore there are as many possible pursuits as one's society may offer. To be sure, not all pursuits are self-realizing. For one thing, like Raz,[96] Green holds that self-realization is achieved only in valuable pursuits; however, there is a "great variety" of these (as I have just explained), and there is certainly no single path. What valuable pursuits clearly exclude is habitual pleasure-seeking: the voluptuary is not self-realizing. Further, no one can achieve self-realization by exploiting, oppressing, or degrading others. Thus, though both constraints restrict self-realization, they do not reduce it to a single-pathed good.

The second point is that the good is *self*-realization; it can be achieved only by one's own effort. As Green famously claims, "[n]o one can convey a good character to another. Everyone must make his character for himself. All that one man can do to make another better is to remove obstacles, and supply conditions favourable to the formation of a good character."[97] Though he is indebted to Aristotle's understanding of self-realization, Green parts way inasmuch as he denies that it is the role of the state to legislate self-realization. This is abundantly clear from his view of punishment.[98] Though the ultimate end of the state is moral, its primary goal in punishing is the maintenance of rights. Thus, "it is the business of the state, not indeed directly to promote moral goodness . . . but to maintain the conditions without which a free exercise of the human faculties is impossible."[99] This is how justice is internal to the common good project.

A final point. Freeden claims that "Green's importance lies in his input into modern liberal thinking about rights." Specifically, "[r]ights were . . . moral claims for self-development but extended the concerns of liberal theory by their equal emphasis on the development of others."[100] It is extending the concerns of liberal theory that I wish to comment on, and this is not by rejecting Freeden's claim; rather, I suggest that to fully appreciate his claim is to appreciate the common good ethics of joint self-development as the proper locus of that extension. Recall my claim

---

[95] "Kant," sect. 123; see also *Prolegomena*, sects. 283, 234.
[96] Raz, *Morality of Freedom*, pp. 378–81.
[97] *Prolegomena*, sect. 332.
[98] "Political Obligation," sects. 204–6; see also *Prolegomena*, sect. 332; "Liberal Legislation," p. 202.
[99] "Liberal Legislation," p. 202.
[100] Michael Freeden, *Rights* (Minneapolis: University of Minnesota Press, 1991), pp. 22, 21, respectively.

regarding "mutually assured self-realization": one's claim for self-realization for oneself is reciprocal with the equally legitimate claim of others for self-realization. The normative requiredness of this claim is grounded in the ethic of mutual or joint self-realization. This is the ethic of the common good in which, therefore, we should, ultimately, locate Green's extension of the concerns of liberal theory.

4   Private property, liberal subjects, and the state

John Morrow

Despite the significant and much discussed differences between Rawls' and Nozick's accounts of property rights, these thinkers' property theories have at least two common features. First, in sharp contrast to many other statements of liberal political theory, neither Rawls nor Nozick make individual rights to private property a necessary requirement of a just society. It has been observed that private property rights occupy a contingent position in Rawls' scheme of things, while Nozick makes them a matter of historical accident rather than a moral necessity.[1] Second, both of these writers think that entitlements can be treated in purely individualistic terms. Although Nozick's claim that just holdings are products of transactions determined solely by rightholders reflects this perspective most clearly, it is also present in Rawls' account of the original position. Rawls holds that objects are available for distribution in this situation because individuals have no legitimate claims upon them: they do not deserve them. An implication of this argument is that if individuals *did* deserve these possessions, they would not be available for distribution. People either deserve things, in which case their hold upon them would be as tenacious as that of Nozick's bearers of natural rights, or they are not deserved at all and thus fall into a common pool whence they can be doled out on the basis of an acceptable principle of distribution.[2]

The new liberal thinkers who will be discussed here (T. H. Green, Bernard Bosanquet, L. T. Hobhouse, and J. A. Hobson) argued that some form of private property is a necessary condition for liberal subjects. However, they do not see these rights as purely private claims. For these writers, private property rights depend on individuals' em-

---

[1] Brian M. Barry, *The Liberal Theory of Justice: A Critical Examination of* A Theory of Justice *by John Rawls* (Oxford: Clarendon Press, 1973), p. 166; Jeremy Waldron, *The Right to Private Property* (Oxford: Clarendon Press, 1988), p. 291.
[2] Robert Nozick, *Anarchy, State, and Utopia* (Oxford: Blackwell, 1974), pp. 167–74; John Rawls, *A Theory of Justice* (Oxford University Press, 1972), pp. 103–4.

92

beddedness within a community. Moreover, they argue that entitlements are not fully explicable by reference either to what individuals have done, as in Rawls' theory, or to their position in a chain of past transactions, as they are in Nozick's account. New liberals thought that liberal subjects should possess private property because it is a basic precondition of individuals' self-development within their community: property rights are morally significant in relation to what individuals may do with them in the future, as well as for what they have done in the past.

In contrast to the abstract cast of many recent treatments of private property rights, those advanced by new liberals focused upon concrete issues of public contention and were meant to provide a basis for policy-making. New liberals thought that state action could secure substantive rights to private property for all members of the community and would thus give reality to the idea of a liberal subject.

Rights, individuality, and the common good

New liberals claimed that rights are recognized and enforced because they promote a common, rather than a purely individual, conception of the good. This claim is part of a broader argument that individuals' consciousness, their understanding of right action, and the institutional framework in which they act are explicable in terms of the community to which they belong. Individuals are "encumbered" rather than "un-encumbered" beings. However, the new liberals did not regard this inheritance as fixed. Whether conceived in idealistic or in quasi-biological terms, communities were thought to have dynamic potentialities that can be realized by the self-determined action of individuals. Prompted by reflection upon the fruits of human experience encapsulated in customary practice, recorded in literary, philosophical, and religious sources, or derived from evolutionary analysis, individuals create a community that embodies refined expressions of the values current in the world into which they are born.

This conception of community incorporates a prospective focus and a concern with individual autonomy that are characteristic of progressive and libertarian tendencies in nineteenth-century liberalism. But while new liberals endorsed the conventional view that rights secured liberties for individuals, they insisted that they were recognized and upheld in the interests of both the individual and the community. As Green put it, "[t]he capacity . . . on the part of the individual of conceiving a good as the same for himself and others, and of being determined to action by that conception, is the foundation of rights; and rights are the condition of that capacity being realised."[3] By contrast with those modern libertarians who treat rights as "natural" attributes of individuals that have implications for other human beings but are not determined by reference to them, new liberals tied them to a common rather than a purely personal idea of the good.

In addition, however, the new liberals' position pointed to a convergence of the "good" and the "right" and thus avoided the tendency to dichotomize these values that has been a feature of the contemporary debate between liberals and their communitarian critics. For Green and later new liberals, rights were recognized as such because they provided opportunities for individuals freely to pursue a common good which also constituted their personal good. Green, for example, relates good actions to human perfection, but he insists that they must be motivated by individuals' desire for perfection, not by extraneous considerations such as a wish to gain rewards or avoid sanctions: "the actions which *ought* to be done ... are actions expressive of a good will, in the sense that they represent a character of which the dominant interest is in conduct contributory to the perfection of mankind."[4] Freedom and morality are inextricable: since moral actions are done for the sake of their goodness, they are free in the "positive" sense that they advance the rational goal of personal development.[5] Rights "guarantee" that individuals will be insulated from interference by others; they also ensure that they have opportunities for freely choosing to act in ways that conform with their understanding of the requirements of the good.[6]

Although new liberal accounts of rights generally followed the pattern established by Green, particular formulations varied. Bosanquet thought of a community as the focal point, the correlating and organising center, of a "general will" that has the common good as its object. The general will is a product of the particular wills or "minds" of the individuals who belong to the community, and its creative and progressive capabilities reflect the moral quality of its constituent elements.[7]

[3] T. H. Green, "Lectures on the Principles of Political Obligation," in T. H. Green, *Lectures on the Principles of Political Obligation and Other Writings*, ed. Paul Harris and John Morrow (Cambridge University Press, 1986), p. 28. For recent discussions of Idealist views on rights see Sandra Den Otter, *British Idealism and Social Explanation. A Study in Late Victorian Thought* (Oxford: Clarendon Press, 1996), pp. 160–3, and William Sweet, *Idealism and Rights* (Lanham, MD: University Press of America, 1997).

[4] T. H. Green, *Prolegomena to Ethics*, ed. A. C. Bradley, 3rd edn. (Oxford: Clarendon Press, 1890), p. 317.

[5] T. H. Green, "Lecture on 'Liberal Legislation and the Freedom of Contract,'" in Green, *Lectures on the Principles of Political Obligation and Other Writings*, pp. 199–200.

[6] Green, "Political Obligation," pp. 27–8; Avital Simhony, "Beyond Negative and Positive Freedom. T. H. Green's View of Freedom," *Political Theory*, 21 (1993), 28–54.

[7] Peter P. Nicholson, *The Political Philosophy of the British Idealists: Selected Studies* (Cambridge University Press, 1990), pp. 208–10.

Moralized human beings realize themselves by making the common good their object, and acting in ways that utilize the opportunities open to them for pursuing it. Moral beings are self-directing agents: rights are powers secured to them in order to make free action possible. Bosanquet thought that since moral actions are free, they are a product of the "mind" or "character" of actors, but he understood this in social rather than individualistic terms: the "promotion of character" is the criterion of the "socialisation of will."[8] Bosanquet observed that complex modern societies contain a large number of socially significant positions, and that those who occupy them are endowed with a variety of different rights. However, these distinctions are merely functional elaborations set within social and political structures that rest upon the citizen body as a whole. All adults capable of being members of the community occupy a "position" in it, and all should possess the rights necessary to make it possible for them to contribute to the common good.[9]

Hobhouse's account of rights reflects his view that the common good harmonizes the aspirations and interests of individuals with those of their community.[10] The development of personality was an essential element in harmony, and Hobhouse thought that this made individual rights a moral necessity. He stressed, however, that the development of personality must be seen in relation to the common good. "[Rights] are the conditions of personal development. But personality is itself an element in the common good, and that is why its rights have moral validity."[11] But although rights may have to be adjusted from time to time in order to ensure harmony, Hobhouse made it clear that they are not contingent, or even derivative of the common good. The good conditions all rights, but the role ascribed to free action makes rights of some kind a moral necessity.[12]

Hobhouse's appeal to the "principle of harmony" allowed him to treat community as an embodiment of the collective aspirations of individuals without taking the illiberal step of seeing it as a discrete and real entity that could require individuals to sacrifice their interests to it. An "ideal society" is "a whole which lives and flourishes by the harmonious

---

[8] Bernard Bosanquet, *The Social Criterion: or, How to Judge of Proposed Social Reforms* (Edinburgh: William Blackwood & Sons, 1907), p. 8.

[9] Bernard Bosanquet, *The Philosophical Theory of the State* (London: Macmillan, 1899), p. 211.

[10] Stefan Collini, *Liberalism and Sociology: L. T. Hobhouse and Political Argument in England, 1880–1914* (Cambridge University Press, 1979), pp. 125–9.

[11] L. T. Hobhouse, *The Elements of Social Justice* (London: Allen & Unwin, 1922), pp. 40–1.

[12] Hobhouse, *Elements of Social Justice*, pp. 42–3; cf. David Weinstein, "The New Liberalism of L. T. Hobhouse and the Reenvisioning of Nineteenth-Century Utilitarianism," *Journal of the History of Ideas*, 57 (1996), 504.

growth of its parts, each of which in developing on its own lines and in accordance with its own nature tends on the whole to further the development of the others."[13] Sacrifice of individual interests is only necessary because harmony has been imperfectly realized.

Hobson's belief in the explanatory value of the idea of a social organism led him to emphasize the distinctness of social groupings far more than Hobhouse. He argued that communities are organic entities with psycho-physical structures and a common consciousness.[14] They are directed by common social, or "general," wills that cannot be reduced to the wills of their individual members, and have to be seen as the product of a "social mind." Hobson's claim that legitimate governments upheld individual rights because they recognize that "an area of individual liberty is conducive to the health of the collective life"[15] evoked an instrumental image of individuality, one that highlighted an unresolved tension on the question of whether the community or individuals had moral priority.[16] But like Green, Bosanquet, and Hobhouse, Hobson thought that the progressive development of society depended upon the free action of individuals, and that rights were necessary to facilitate it. This theme was prominent in *The Crisis of Liberalism* (1909) where it served to distinguish new liberalism from state socialism.[17]

Green's rationale for private property

The new liberals believed that while rights were essential for liberal subjects, their content had to be determined by reference to the common good. This belief played a central role in their property theory. Once again, Green established a pattern of argument that was adopted by later thinkers. Having first related appropriation to the free action of rational beings, he then explained why it was endowed with the status of a right. These arguments established a rationale of the right to private property against which particular right claims should be evaluated. They would also be useful in determining the most effective ways of

---

[13] L. T. Hobhouse, *Liberalism* (London: Butterworth, 1911), p. 136.
[14] Michael Freeden, *The New Liberalism: An Ideology of Social Reform* (Oxford: Clarendon Press, 1978), p. 106.
[15] J. A. Hobson, *Work and Wealth: A Human Valuation* (New York: Macmillan, 1914), p. 304.
[16] Freeden, *The New Liberalism*, pp. 110–11; see also John Allet, *The New Liberalism: The Political Economy of J. A. Hobson* (University of Toronto Press, 1981), pp. 202–6.
[17] J. A. Hobson, *The Crisis of Liberalism. New Issues in Democracy*, P. F. Clarke, ed. (New York: Barnes & Noble, 1973), pp. 93, 97, 173.

ensuring that liberal subjects are equipped to contribute freely to the common good.

Green's property theory hinges upon the claim that human appropriation (as opposed to that of animals) is distinguished by being linked to a capacity to conceive of a future condition of well-being and to realize that certain possessions can be integrated in the pursuit of this condition. If rational agents are to pursue the good freely, and to order their lives so as to facilitate it, appropriations must be "permanent," or secure, and they must be under the control of the appropriator. They thus become "a sort of extension of the man's organs – the constant apparatus through which he gives reality to his ideas and wishes."[18]

Green's argument goes beyond the conventional claim that the possession of property insulates the rightholder from the coercive influence of others, and incorporates the Hegelian idea that property is "realized will." Property is both an "expression of will," and a means for future expression, that make it possible for individuals to develop and maintain the capacities that are necessary if they are to be autonomous persons.[19] In Green's formulation, however, acquisition is related to a conception of rights that is inseparable from membership of a community:

[J]ust as the recognised interests of a society constitute for each member of it the right to free life ... so it constitutes the right to the instruments of such a life, making each regard the possession of them by the other as for the common good, and thus through the medium first of custom, then of law, securing them to each.[20]

Thus, unlike Rawls and Nozick, Green regards private rights to property as a necessary feature of a just community. When this requirement is set in the context of his account of the relationship between free action, property rights, and the pursuit of the common good, it means that a morally acceptable property regime must do the following: allow individuals full rights in legitimate property-holdings; disallow right claims which prevent some members of the community from acquiring private property; and modify existing rights if they are not compatible with the rationale of property.

Green's account of the rationale of property points to the need for a "full liberal right."[21] Society itself has "a common interest in the free play of the powers of all" and in the development of "free morality," or

---

[18] Green, "Political Obligation," pp. 164, 165.
[19] See Alan Patten, "Hegel's Justification of Private Property," *History of Political Thought*, 16 (1995), 576–600.
[20] Green, "Political Obligation," p. 168.
[21] See Gerald F. Gaus, "Property Rights and Freedom," in Ellen Frankel Paul, Fred D. Miller, Jr., and Jeffrey Paul (eds.), *Property Rights* (Cambridge University Press, 1994), pp. 213–14.

"a certain behaviour of men determined by an understanding of moral relations and by the value which they set on them as understood." Consequently, Green regarded limited rights (such as those he identified with the "clan system") as inappropriate for beings who had developed a capacity for rational reflection and for self-willed action directed towards a common good. Green thought that in modern Western communities the rationale of property could best be satisfied by "freedom of trade." Free trade opens up the prospect of "the more complete adaptation of nature to the service of man by the free effort of individuals," and it requires the recognition of full property rights in both the means and fruits of production.[22] At the same time, however, Green insisted that since property rights are essential for liberal subjects, *all* individuals must have genuine possibilities of acquiring ethically significant possessions. Everyone "should be secured by society in the power of getting and keeping the means of realising a will, which in possibility is a will directed to a social good."[23]

But while Green's understanding of the relationship between freedom and morality endowed private property rights with great moral significance, he did not, as is the case with some modern libertarians, regard liberty and property as equivalent terms. Moral freedom was the end towards which property was a means,[24] and the character of this end meant that Green's conception of property was neither exclusive nor individualistic. Although Green thought that the acquisition and disposal of property lost any moral value if it was not "expressive of a good will" *of an individual*[25] his understanding of "a good will" meant that, unlike many contemporary liberals, his preference for free market exchanges did not rest on a conception of the unencumbered self.[26] Nor did it mean that ethically significant property had to take the form of the ownership and control of productive capital. Green thought that ownership of permanent personal effects, dwelling places, or shares in cooperative stores or benefit societies, fulfilled the moral purpose of property. Property rights of this kind were a consequence of rational action in the past, and they made it possible for individuals to exercise a socially significant form of rational freedom in the future.[27] The rationale of property pointed to a functional threshold, not the remorse-

[22] Green, "Political Obligation," pp. 168, 169, 172.
[23] Ibid., pp. 170–1.
[24] Ibid., p. 169; cf. the characterization of some modern liberal views by Gaus, "Property Rights and Freedom," p. 225.
[25] Green, *Prolegomena*, pp. 317, 193.
[26] Cf. Allen E. Buchanan, "Assessing the Communitarian Critique of Liberalism," *Ethics*, 99 (1989), 866.
[27] Green, "Political Obligation," p. 175.

less accumulation that C. B. Macpherson identified with "possessive individualism."[28]

But if Green's claim concerning the moral potentialities of freedom of trade were to be sustained, he had to show that the inequalities resulting from market transactions did not undermine the rationale of property. He first argued that there was nothing objectionable in unequal possession *per se* because it merely reflected the differing capacities of human beings and was necessary if individuals were to fulfil a range of different, socially beneficial, functions. A more fundamental issue concerned the possibility that capitalism prevented some sections of the community from acquiring ethically significant amounts and forms of property. Green acknowledged that although the economic expansion engendered by free trade made ethically significant property a real possibility for all members of a modern community, these potentialities had not been realized in modern societies. However, he insisted that this outcome was not inherent to market systems. In the British case, for example, it resulted from the continuing effects of "feudal" ideas, institutions, and practices that prevented sections of the lower classes from acting as free and rational beings.[29]

Some of these historical problems – the results of grossly inadequate educational provisions, social stratification, and politically enshrined privilege – were being addressed by legislative initiatives promoted by "advanced" liberals such as Green. Others, however, were being perpetuated by claims that the exercise of property rights should not be regulated by the state. In response to these claims Green insisted that when the exercise or possession of property rights impeded the acquisition of property by others, state interference was necessary to sustain liberal subjects in their pursuit of the common good and was justified by reference to it.

As noted above, Green did not think that this stricture could be applied to most forms of property in a free-market economy. However, he argued that under existing conditions of popular ignorance and urban overcrowding, the state ought to regulate contractual relationships between landlord and tenants. He also thought that the finite

---

[28] C. B. Macpherson, *The Life and Times of Liberal Democracy* (Oxford University Press, 1977) and *Property: Critical and Mainstream Positions* (University of Toronto Press, 1978); cf. John Morrow, "Property and Personal Development: An Interpretation of T. H. Green's Political Philosophy," *Politics*, 18 (1973), 84–92; Colin Tyler, "Context, Capitalism and the Natural Right to Property in the Thought of Thomas Hill Green," in Iain Hampsher-Monk and Jeffrey Stanyer (eds.), *Contemporary Political Studies*, 3 vols. (Glasgow: Political Studies Association of the United Kingdom, 1996), vol. III, pp. 1406–14.
[29] Green, "Political Obligation," pp. 171, 170, 177–8.

nature of landed property meant that it should be subject to state regulation to ensure that land was not used or transmitted in ways that prevented it being effectively utilized for the common good. Large landed estates were bastions of class interest, and primogeniture and other restrictions on bequests that were used to maintain them were an abuse of the rights of one set of proprietors at the cost of others and of society as a whole. Measures such as these discriminated against women[30] and prevented owners of property from disposing of it in ways which reflected their judgment on the needs and moral worth of their children. Green also opposed tenancy agreements that reserved game rights to landlords. These agreements were a consequence of class power and they interfered with the effective cultivation of land by tenant farmers. In countries such as Ireland, where the population was heavily reliant upon landed property and prospects of economic expansion seemed limited, the need for state regulation of property rights was particularly pressing. At a minimum, tenants should be secure in their holdings and should be entitled to compensation for improvements they made to the land they rented. Once the unjust rights of landlords had been discounted, Green hoped a system of peasant proprietorship would emerge that would reflect the common interests of members of the Irish rural community.[31]

Measures of this kind were designed to address situations that were marred by class legislation, or by an absence of legislation that buttressed *de facto* class power. In these cases, Green's objective was to facilitate the pursuit of the common good by ensuring that putative property rights were brought into line with the rationale of property. But in addition to preventing morally significant abuses of property rights, Green also thought that the rationale of property raised questions about its more positive application to the common good. For most of the population, participation in conventional processes of production and exchange ensured that entitlements would reflect a rough equivalence between dessert and contributions to social benefit. The same point might also hold for inherited property, but that would depend upon how it was used. In this case, Green emphasized the importance of voluntary service. However, he also thought that it was legitimate for the state to tax inherited wealth and to apply the proceeds to the provision of services (such as mass education) that would contribute to the common good.[32]

---

[30] For an account of Green's feminist interests, see Olive Anderson, "The Feminism of T. H. Green: A Late Victorian Success Story?," *History of Political Thought*, 12 (1991), 671–93.
[31] Green, "Political Obligation," pp. 176–8; Green, "Liberal Legislation," pp. 202–9.
[32] Green, "Political Obligation," p. 173.

In this, as in other cases, the needs of the community had to be balanced against the moral benefit of leaving individuals free of interference. In any case, moralized individuals would not regard taxation of inherited wealth as an imposition. It might, for example, be seen as a way of coordinating individual conduct so that it contributes to the common good, for, as Green points out in another context, "though the law with its penal sanctions still continues, it is not felt as a law, as an enforcement of action by penalties, at all."[33]

Property and moral individuality in Bosanquet's philosophy

Green's property theory was part of a more general attempt to show that the policies being promoted by "advanced" liberals were practical expressions of theoretical developments that were necessary to further the liberal cause.[34] Liberalism needed to advance beyond the salutary, but one-sided, juxtapositioning of individualism with the illiberal demands of a society dominated by class interests and buttressed by theologically rationalized notions of hierarchy and subordination. From the late 1880s, partly as a result of Green's efforts, ideas of an active state promoting a positive conception of freedom gained a strong foothold within liberal circles.[35] This development, and the closely related revival of socialism as an intellectual and political force, extended the parameters of non-individualistic political thinking to an extent that Green could not have envisaged. Furthermore, disruptions to economic development, and growing alarm at the moral and political implications of apparently endemic poverty among numerically significant and visible sections of the urban working classes, encouraged advanced liberals and parliamentary socialists to promote measures that foreshadowed the emergence of a welfare state.[36] The effects of these developments are apparent in the writings of Bosanquet. Although Bosanquet's treatment of the rationale of private property consciously echoed that of Green,[37] he was not primarily concerned with establishing the liberal credentials of a socially embedded conception of property. Rather, he sought to

[33] Ibid., p. 162.
[34] See Green, "Liberal Legislation," and the extensive collection of speeches in T. H. Green, *The Collected Works of T. H. Green*, 5 vols., ed. Peter Nicholson (Bristol: Thoemmes Press, 1997), vol. V.
[35] See Michael Bentley, *The Climax of Liberal Politics: British Liberalism in Theory and Practice* (London: Edward Arnold, 1987).
[36] See Jose Harris, "Political Thought and the Welfare State 1870–1960: An Intellectual Framework for British Social Policy," *Past and Present*, 135 (1992), 116–41.
[37] Bernard Bosanquet, "The Principle of Private Property," Bernard Bosanquet (ed.), *Aspects of the Social Problem* (London: Macmillan, 1895), pp. 309, 311.

warn his contemporaries of the dangers of adopting policies that failed
to recognize the necessary relationship between liberal subjects, community, and morally significant property rights. In discussing these
matters, Bosanquet focused on the connection between the personal
qualities that were called into play and developed in the process of
acquisition, and the attributes required by individuals whose moral wills
constituted particular elements of the general will. He contended that
contemporary welfare proposals threatened to undermine the moral will
of individuals, and compromise both the general will and the common
good that was its object.

For Bosanquet, as for Green, property rights rested on the recognition
of the relationship between the possession of material resources and
contributions to the common good: this is why property is a *right*, that
is, a socially recognized claim that is upheld by the state. Bosanquet's
statement of this position emphasized the connection between the
general will and viable individual wills possessing the capacity for free,
rational action. Private property rights are necessary for rational individuality because they embody "the unity of life in its external or
material form." They result from "past dealing with the material world,
and the possibility of future dealing with it. Property made it possible for
individuals to be in 'contact with something which in the external world
is the definite material representation' of themselves."[38] The retrospective basis of entitlements is significant because moral wills that advance
the common good are a product of past action expressive of the same
tendency.

Like Hegel, to whom he seems to have been deeply indebted for his
understanding of the importance of private property and self-maintenance, Bosanquet did not discount the damage done to individuals
and to society by extreme poverty.[39] He was, however, at the forefront
of a long-running battle to resist what he regarded as the morally
dehabilitating effects of indiscriminate private and public charity.[40]
Traditional philanthropy and the state provision of individual and
family support, old age pensions, and even free meals for school-
children, threatened to reduce large sections of the working classes to a
"childish" condition of dependency on "miraculous" external sources
that were unrelated to their own actions, or to their internal moral

[38] Ibid., pp. 311, 313.
[39] See G. W. F. Hegel, *Philosophy of Right*, trans. T. M. Knox (Oxford University Press, 1973), pp. 148–9.
[40] See A. M. MacBriar, *An Edwardian Mixed Doubles: The Bosanquets versus the Webbs. A Study of British Social Policy, 1880-1929* (Oxford: Clarendon Press, 1987) and Andrew Vincent and Raymond Plant, *Philosophy, Politics and Citizenship: Idealism and the Welfare State* (Oxford: Blackwell, 1984), pp. 94–114.

qualities.[41] Like indiscriminate private charity, state welfare provisions undermined the moral solidity of individual wills. Recipients could not become full members of the community because they were not self-sustaining particular embodiments of the general will. There was, Bosanquet argued, a paradoxical convergence between abstract individualism and the assumptions underlying modern socialism: both ignored the relationship between the will of individuals and the system of ideas that made up the "social mind." Conventional individualists treated property as a purely personal matter, and socialists tacitly endorsed the same position by promoting policies that divorced the idea of community from the moral attributes of its members.[42]

Bosanquet's opposition to state welfare, and his profound dismay when confronted by pauperism in London, led him at times to adopt the harsh language of contemporary "Social Darwinism," and to endorse the penal views of poor relief that were associated with the 1834 Poor Law. It is important to bear in mind, however, that for Bosanquet the key issue was individuals' capacity to be full members of their community, not the economic costs of dependency or worries about biological degeneracy. In dealing with this theme he advanced beyond the stance taken by those who adopted a conventionally "conservative" position on social policy.[43]

For example, Bosanquet's opposition to welfare proposals reflected his belief that social wholes are not abstract entities. To the contrary, they are based upon developed individual wills, and are built up through forms of intermediary social interaction and identification in families, neighborhoods, and institutions such as trade organizations.[44] State provision of welfare weakens these forms of association by undermining the moral character of their members, and thus inhibits the emergence

[41] Bernard Bosanquet, "Socialism and Natural Selection," in Bosanquet, *Aspects of the Social Problem*, pp. 302–7.

[42] Bernard Bosanquet, "The Antithesis Between Individualism and Socialism Philosophically Considered," in Bernard Bosanquet, *The Civilization of Christendom and Other Studies* (London: Swan Sonnenschein, 1893), p. 330.

[43] On Bosanquet's relationship with contemporary Social Darwinism, see Greta Jones, *Social Darwinism and English Thought* (Brighton: Harvester Press, 1981), p. 51, and for examples of harsher statements of his position, see Bernard Bosanquet, *"In Darkest England": On the Wrong Track* (London: Swan Sonnenschein, 1891). The line taken here reflects the influence of the sensitive approach to the complexities of Bosanquet's position taken by Nicholson, *The Political Philosophy*, pp. 205–21; cf. James Meadowcroft, *Conceptualizing the State. Innovation and Dispute in British Political Thought, 1880–1914* (Oxford: Clarendon Press, 1995), pp. 129–32, and John Morrow, "Liberalism and British Idealist Political Philosophy: A Reassessment," *History of Political Thought*, 5 (1984), 101–3 which focus on the conservative aspects of Bosanquet's views on social policy.

[44] See John Morrow, "Community and Class in Bosanquet's 'New State,'" *History of Political Thought*, 21, (2000), 485–99.

of a concrete general will. Bosanquet's remarks on the effect of welfare on the family should be seen in this context. He regarded this institution as one element in a complex network that made up the community, as part of the framework that made individuals embedded beings. Moreover, Bosanquet stressed the participatory requirements of community membership and argued that some types of participation were morally problematic in advanced capitalist societies. In particular, the relationship between property rights, control, and efficiency became tenuous in large-scale enterprises with diffuse ownership.

This issue was of great importance for Bosanquet because he thought that productive activity was central to individuals' engagement with their community: it was both the avenue through which the actions of individuals produced the material basis of the common good, and the means through which particular interests were related to a wider and more complex whole. A person's economic occupation takes the man or woman beyond the family and the neighborhood; and for the same reason takes him [*sic*] deeper into himself. He acquires in it a complex of qualities and capacities which put a special point upon the general need of making a livelihood for the support of his household. In principle, his individual service *is* the social mind, as it takes, in his consciousness, the shape demanded by the logic of the social whole.[45] Among this "complex of qualities" were those stimulated by the qualitative potentialities of labor. Work need not be prompted solely by economic or physical necessity because it also provided scope for satisfying humans' esthetic and technological aspirations.[46]

In common with Green, Bosanquet argued that the social basis of property rights meant that particular rights could be modified or abolished if they inhibited the acquisition of property or the free action of other members of the community. He also thought that in very populous countries there may be grounds for curtailing private rights to landed property.[47] For the most part, however, Bosanquet believed that a free market would provide an effective means for individuals to acquire ethically significant property rights and to exercise them in ways that created the material requirements of the common good. This claim

---

[45] Bosanquet, *Philosophical Theory*, p. 313.
[46] Bernard Bosanquet, "Individual and Social Reform," *Time*, 19 (1888), 316–17; Bernard Bosanquet, "Three Lectures on Social Ideals," in Bosanquet, *Social and International Ideals. Being Studies in Patriotism* (London: Macmillan, 1917), p. 247. Originally Bosanquet's views on labor were influenced by John Ruskin and William Morris; later he drew on aspects of Georges Sorel's more technocratic ethos. The first of these sets of influences is discussed by Vincent and Plant, *Philosophy, Politics and Citizenship*, pp. 120–1.
[47] Bosanquet, "Individual and Social Reform," p. 318.

rested on the assumption that the relationship between individual action and the realization of social goals would be closest where individuals, either separately or in partnership, owned and controlled instruments of production, and Bosanquet recognized that in modern economic systems there was a tendency for ownership to be divorced from effective control or participation. While acknowledging this difficulty, Bosanquet rejected contemporary claims that social efficiency justified state control of large enterprises. Even if one accepted the putative benefits of social ownership – the reduction of mismanagement, the creation of a larger pool of social wealth, and the reduction of harsh terms of employment – it was neither economically nor ethically acceptable. In the first place, state ownership would not bridge the gulf between ownership and management. If productive resources belonged to society as a whole, ownership would be even more diffuse than in joint-stock companies. Furthermore, any softening effects of social ownership would be purchased at a high cost. In an argument that foreshadowed Hayek's defense of free markets' capacity to signal demand and prompt efficient production,[48] Bosanquet speculated that an efficient system of socially directed production and distribution must either replicate the directive forces of what he called "economic efficiency," or rely on draconian supervision by public agencies. Bosanquet doubted whether the second of these strategies would actually work. In any case, it would conflict with the rationale of property and be self-defeating: individual contributions to the common good would not arise from free action. Finally, state ownership severed "ownership for production" from "ownership for consumption" because individual property rights would be restricted to objects of consumption. This arrangement would impede economic efficiency by inhibiting the sort of risk-taking that produces innovation; it would also be morally problematic because it limited the quality and range of will that could be expressed through property. "The idea of property as earmarked for mere consumption, and as incapable of being transformed into employers' capital by a resolution of the will ... [is] a very serious matter for the *moral* of the community."[49]

In light of the last of these considerations, Bosanquet argued for the retention of private ownership rights in productive resources, even when these took the diverse and generalized form of stock investment in large enterprises. While recognizing the conventional outcome of Bosanquet's consideration of this issue, it is important to note that he offered more innovative solutions to the problems caused by the separation of property

---

[48] See F. A. Hayek, *Law, Legislation and Liberty*, 3 vols. (London: Routledge & Kegan Paul, 1982), vol. II, pp. 107ff.
[49] Bosanquet, "Three Lectures," p. 224.

rights from participation in production. Bosanquet not only supported cooperative ownership, he also argued that in some circumstances it was desirable for producers to have control over the productive resources of large-scale, joint-stock enterprises.[50] While the characteristics of complex industrial societies appeared to make the relationship between morality, private property, and the individual's free realization of community problematic, these difficulties could be overcome by identifying relationships between free individuals and the material dimensions of the common good which embodied the moral point of property rights.

Hobhouse and Hobson on liberal individuality and the social dimensions of production

The idea that moralized liberal subjects freely created their community continued to play an important role in Hobson's and Hobhouse's understanding of the rationale of private property rights. In particular, both of these writers made it clear that private property of some kind was necessary if individuals were to be both liberal subjects and embedded members of their community. Hobhouse's statement of this position echoed Green's formulation: "Property is ... an integral element in an ordered life of purposeful activity. It is, at bottom for the same reason, an integral element in a free life."[51] When claiming that an insistence on the importance of private property rights distinguished "social" liberalism from state socialism, Hobhouse reiterated a position that had already been articulated by Hobson.

In *The Social Problem* (1901) Hobson argued that liberty specified "a special sphere of activity, a scope of life and work, which is apportioned to the individual," and the right to private property provided the means through which freedom could be exercised.[52] Hobson signaled his wish

---

[50] These possibilities are explored in Bernard Bosanquet, "Two Modern Philanthropists," in Bernard Bosanquet, *Essays and Addresses* (London: Swan Sonnenschein, 1889), pp. 17–21 and Bosanquet, "Three Lectures." In these essays Bosanquet drew upon examples of mutualism in France and Guild Socialism in Britain. He also argued that there were points of importance to be gained from Georges Sorel's account of syndicalism in *Reflections on Violence* (1908). Bosanquet reviewed T. E. Hulme's translation of this work (1912); see Bosanquet, "Reflections on Violence," in Bosanquet, *Social and International Ideals*, pp. 183–8. For a discussion of this material, see Morrow, "Community and Class."

[51] L. T. Hobhouse, "The Historical Evolution of Property in Fact and in Idea," *Property, its Rights and its Duties* [ed. Charles Gore] (London: Macmillan, 1913), p. 9. This statement suggests that when Hobhouse wrote that we "must not assume any of the rights of property as axiomatic" (Hobhouse, *Liberalism*, p. 100) he was referring to particular claims, not to property rights as such.

[52] J. A. Hobson, *The Social Problem. Life and Work* (London: James Nesbit, 1901), pp. 96–7.

to connect his claims about individual property with the liberal tradition by ascribing it the status of a "natural right." He thought that this term was appropriate not because such rights were non-social, but because they were essential to human life: they secured the means for free action, and they also provided the basis for life-sustaining labor and incentives to engage in it.[53] Unlike some modern libertarians who treat property rights in ways that divorce them from fundamental human purposes,[54] Hobson and other new liberals insisted that they must be tied directly to a conception of these purposes that locates liberal subjects within communities.

But while Hobson and Hobhouse shared Green's and Bosanquet's general perspective on property rights, they maintained that modern economic systems gave rise to patterns of distribution that were incompatible with the rationale of property, prevented many individuals from taking their place within the community, and inhibited the progressive realization of the common good. Free-market capitalism was characterized by injustice, by inefficient labor and misdirected effort.[55] Moreover, Hobson refused to accept that poverty, itself a source of social inefficiency, could be explained adequately by reference to the personal failings of the poor. Poverty had structural rather than personal causes. The lower classes were denied access to land and industrial capital and were thus forced to sell their labor at a price that made it difficult for them to purchase the necessaries of life. These problems were compounded by cyclical trends in developed economies that made periodic unemployment an unavoidable, rather than an accidental, feature of working-class existence.[56] In these circumstances it was quite wrong to treat "character" as an independent variable, or to expect that the free market could be relied upon to provide the property rights necessary if liberal subjects were to pursue effectively the common good.[57]

This line of argument, one that reflected Hobson's professional interest in economics, was absorbed by Hobhouse, but he reformulated it in a way that corresponded to conventional liberal concerns about class power. He argued that in "developed society" there had been a shift from "property for use" to a situation where increasing discrepan-

[53] Ibid., pp. 102–5.
[54] See Mark Francis, "Human Rights and Libertarians," *Australian Journal of Politics and History*, 29 (1983), 465–7.
[55] Hobson, *The Social Problem*, pp. 106, 113–14; J. A. Hobson, *The Industrial System. An Inquiry into Earned and Unearned Income*, 2nd edn. (London: Longmans, Green, 1910), p. 331.
[56] J. A. Hobson, *Problems of Poverty. An Inquiry into the Industrial Condition of the Poor*, 2nd edn. (London: Methuen, 1906), pp. 166–8, 205.
[57] Hobson, *The Crisis*, p. 165.

cies in property-holding meant that it became a means through which some sections of the population exerted power over others.[58] When the liberty of property-holders compromised that of other sections of the population the liberal ideal of free subjects pursuing a common good could not be realized.

Hobson and Hobhouse's response to the failings of the market was to argue for systems of state regulation that fostered efficiency, and promoted justice by ensuring that all members of the population were able to possess the amount and types of property necessary for full membership of the community. These provisions fell into two distinct categories, one relating to those who through age or disability were unable to labor, the other to the appropriate remuneration of wage-earners.[59] Individuals in the first category were to be provided by state or local government agencies with the material resources necessary to sustain social membership and avoid marginalization. As members of the community, the recipients of such aid were entitled to it. Personal charity was a way of providing comforts and expressing affection; it was not a substitute for the duty owed by society to those who were unable to support themselves: "The task of palliating or of healing social sores should be left to society; it is her duty, and she should learn to do it."[60] But while the provision of such support was a social duty, it should not be confused with the entitlements acquired by labor since these were a consequence of the services that individuals performed for society through their engagement in productive activities.

Because property rights were conditioned by the common good, they could only be acquired through socially beneficial actions. On the one hand, this specification provided the basis for a critique of what Hobhouse termed "functionless wealth" acquired though "socially useless or injurious labour."[61] More positively, however, the relationship between individual labor and the common good had important implications for determining levels of remuneration.

Both Hobson and Hobhouse argued in favor of a "social minimum" for the least capable workers, and for income levels for the more capable that were determined by the needs of society. Hobson's statement of the first of these issues stressed the importance of sustaining a workforce that was both able and willing to labor effectively. He argued that

---

[58] Hobhouse, "The Historical Evolution," pp. 9–10; Hobhouse, *Elements of Social Justice*, pp. 157–8.
[59] See Gerald F. Gaus, *The Modern Liberal Theory of Man* (London: Croom Helm, 1983), pp. 243–4.
[60] Hobson, *The Social Problem*, p. 163.
[61] Hobhouse, *Elements of Social Justice*, p. 133.

because labor was social it was not possible to motivate individuals by rewarding them on the basis of their individual effort. But while rewards could not be effectively related to "social utility," "needs" could: "Only by satisfaction of genuine needs can an individual be kept in a position to serve society by efficient labour 'according to his powers.'" [62] Seen in this light, individual entitlements had a purely instrumental character, but Hobson maintained that in order to satisfy social requirements they also had to correspond with the aspirations of individuals and take account of their distinctive characteristics:

On the physical side there exists a sharp separability of the individual, both in work and in consumption; and this character, or aspect, demands economic recognition through property. The same ... must be said of the will, or moral character; that, too, requires in varying degrees, to be stimulated by an acknowledgement of a separate property. [63]

Hobhouse's defence of a social minimum also related remuneration to the common good, but it did so in a way that reflected his formulation of this end in terms of harmony. "Civic efficiency" required that wage-earners received enough to sustain their health, develop and exercise their faculties, and experience family life. This, Hobhouse argued, "is the lowest standard required to harmonise the interests of the worker and the community, for without it the producer does not secure the elementary and essential conditions of a good life." [64]

A social minimum for non-producers, and the related adjustment of more than minimal earned income to stimulate socially beneficial production, could only be achieved if the market was regulated by socially responsible agencies. Hobson and Hobhouse argued that transfers of wealth required to satisfy these conditions did not infringe the property rights of individuals. This point was made quite clear by Hobson when he rejected the idea that legitimate taxation was a necessary, but regrettable, imposition on the property rights of individuals. To the contrary, taxation was "a process by which society acting through the state takes income which *it has earned* through social work, and which it needs for social life." [65]

Hobson's understanding of taxation rested on a conception of property that recognized both individual and social entitlements, and reflected his view that society was a real entity with a psycho-physical basis and a real will. This argument drew upon earlier claims about the extra-individual sources of the increase in land values resulting from location and marginal utility that were associated in the 1870s with Henry

[62] Hobson, *The Social Problem*, p. 162.   [63] Ibid., p. 156.
[64] Hobhouse, *Elements of Social Justice*, p. 134.
[65] Hobson, *The Industrial System*, p. 223; emphasis added.

George. It also echoed socialist arguments concerning the role that social factors played in both production and exchange.[66]

Thus while Green and Bosanquet thought that value was created by individuals within the context of a community, Hobson and Hobhouse's understanding of both the community and modern economies led them to ascribe a direct productive role to social forces and to use this as the grounds for recognizing forms of social property. As Hobson put it, society was a creator of values and had "some rights of property" in its product.[67] These rights could be applied to the realization of social goals, either by funding public goods, or by ensuring that individuals were able to possess sufficient resources to take their place within society. Such measures were not redistributive, and nor did they rely upon a conception of welfare rights as a charge upon the property of other members of the community.[68] "Social property" does not belong to particular individuals, and is therefore available for the realization of social purposes.

Conclusion

New liberal property theory exemplifies the thesis of this collection of essays. Its conceptions of property rights underline the distinctively liberal character of new liberal doctrine, and they reveal some of the complexities of a liberal conception of common good. Taken together, these ideas give rise to an embedded conception of individuality, one that lies at the heart of the public policy focus of this form of non-individualistic liberalism.

New Liberals regard private property as an essential feature of morally progressive societies because it sustains liberal subjects. As noted above, however, new liberal theory gave rise to divergent views on the relationship between acquisition and moral personality. Green, Hobhouse, and Hobson focused on the idea that acquisition was a *means to* moral personality, while Bosanquet stressed that the process through which property was acquired was also *constitutive of* moral personality. For this reason, he argued that moral development would be impeded if individuals acquired property through means that were not related directly to their prevailing understanding of social roles and responsibilities.

[66] J. A. Hobson, "The Influence of Henry George in England," *Fortnightly Review*, 62 (1897), 835–44; see Freeden, *The New Liberalism*, p. 43.

[67] Hobson, *The Social Problem*, p. 146; see also Hobhouse, *Liberalism*, pp. 188–9 and *Elements of Social Justice*, pp. 161–75.

[68] This formulation comes from Loren E. Lomasky, *Persons, Rights and the Moral Community* (Oxford University Press, 1987).

These differences in perspective had an important bearing on the policy implications that Bosanquet and other new liberals drew from their theories of property. It is important to note, however, that they did not affect the new liberals' endorsement of the idea that accounts of property must relate the liberty of individuals to the pursuit of a common good. For these thinkers control over property was a way of securing to individuals the means necessary for acting freely on the basis of their conception of the good. At a more fundamental level, private property was seen as something that was necessary for the formation and exercise of the moral will of individuals, for the development of "character." Character in this sense was not an abstract personal quality; rather, it referred to the type of personality that was capable of conceiving and pursuing an ideal of personal good that was understood in relation to a common good.

The new liberal thinkers considered here differed in their view of the objects that should be the subject of rights claims, with both Hobhouse and Hobson restricting ownership within much tighter limits than those envisaged by either Green or Bosanquet. For all these thinkers, however, private property rights were regarded as a central element in a liberal theory of society and the state. They provided a means through which the realization of shared objectives could reflect the rationally formed preferences of individual members of society, and their free pursuit of them. The advancement of social objectives was thus tied to the enhancement of the moral and rational capacities of individuals. On the one hand, this perspective eschewed the abstract conception of individuals to which modern communitarians have drawn attention. On the other hand, however, it remained firmly anchored (as new liberals often pointed out) to ideas about the value of individuals that are distinctive marks of a liberal perspective.

New liberal property theory had a number of implications for the relationship between individual action and a common good. At one level, private property made it possible for self-directed individuals to contribute to the material well-being of their community. For new liberals, however, the good was primarily an ethical, rather than an economic, idea. From the point of view of the individual, property rights were significant for moral, and hence free, action, and for the development of moral personality that resulted from attempts to enhance the common good. From a societal perspective, the development and exercise of the moral character of its members was the means through which a progressive community was conceptualized and brought into being. In more advanced stages of individual and social development, a community was distinguished from its predecessors by its willingness to recognize the distinctive characteristics of its members, and by its determination to make property and other rights substantive and universal rather than merely formal and restricted. For their part, members of advanced liberal societies are freely and self-consciously committed to it. This means, for example, that they regarded their property rights as legitimately subject to adjustment and coordination to ensure that they were compatible with the common good.

Since new liberals charged the state with upholding rights, their property theory provided the basis for many of their forays into the field of public policy. In this as in other respects, the state was thought to embody the community's view of the relationship between the good of individuals and that of their fellows, and had the means to determine and uphold rights. All the writers considered here insisted that the state was entitled to play a regulatory role – a point that was made quite clear in the title given to Green's lecture on this topic: "The Right of the State in Regard to Property" – although there were significant variations in their views of what sort of regulation was necessary. These variations were influenced by contextual considerations, as seen, for example, in the contrast between Green's focus upon anti-social right claims made on behalf of the landed classes, and Hobhouse's and Hobson's concentration upon commercial, financial, and manufacturing capitalism. Underlying these differing perspectives, however, was a common commitment to the idea that property rights were of simultaneous and corresponding significance both to individuals and to the communities to which they belonged. The common good was furthered through the exercise of rights, but so too was the good of individual rightholders.

The common good was the good of all members of a community, and this meant that the new liberal justifications for the regulation of property rights were accompanied by critiques of those features of modern social and political life that inhibited their acquisition and exercise. This issue lay behind Green's analysis of the implications of "freedom of trade" and Hobhouse's and Hobson's critique of this tendency in nineteenth-century liberal politics. It was also central to Bosanquet's response to state welfare. Recipients of welfare faced no formal or informal external impediments to acquiring and exercising property rights, but they were unlikely to develop the personal attitudes or the standing in relation to their families or local communities that would enable them to grasp and pursue the common good.

The divergence between Bosanquet's position and that of his new liberal contemporaries raises questions about the source of entitlements. Bosanquet's opposition to welfare proposals rested on an assumption that entitlements were a manifestation of the rational character of individuals. This assumption committed him to the view that resources that were not a product of particular individuals could not become their property. By contrast, Hobhouse's and Hobson's conception of social entitlements meant that liberal subjects could be sustained through possessions provided from social sources because these resources were a result of collective endeavor. As members of society, individuals could draw upon what they themselves had played a role in creating. In the conditions prevailing in turn-of-the-century Britain it was necessary for some sections of the population to be supported by socially created wealth so that they would be in a position to contribute to the further development of the common good.

The question whether Bosanquet's position could accommodate welfare rights is difficult to answer. His endorsement of free markets was always conditional upon them producing outcomes that were compatible with the rationale of property, and, as observed above, he countenanced a potentially significant departure from conventional views of full liberal rights to private property. Moreover, when defending inherited wealth Bosanquet modified the stringency of his specifications concerning the sources of ethically viable possessions. He argued that while doles were precarious and never formed a sufficient basis for rational action, inheritances fell under the control of beneficiaries and could serve as a starting point for morally significant action. This line of argument shifts the focus of Bosanquet's theory from a concern with the *source* of possessions towards an appreciation of the opportunities that they open up. Hobson pointed out that if the latter of these concerns was applied to the problem of welfare, the rationale of property would be satisfied by a system of income support that was generous and dependable.

Bosanquet does not seem to have responded to this suggestion, but if he had done so it is likely that his understanding of "character" would have led him to reject it. On this point, however, it is worth noting that both Hobhouse and Hobson were aware of the ethical and economic dangers of dependency. In their case, however, a belief in the social sources of value combined with a faith in the invigorating potentialities of full membership of the community for those who were presently marginal to it, allowed them to see dependency as a pathological aspect of unreformed society. Bosanquet's progressive conception of the state as an embodiment of a democratic citizenry, was, as Jose Harris has noted, a far cry from the seedy plutocracy of Edwardian Britain.[69] Despite this, however, he seems to have been unwilling to extend this

---

[69] Harris, "Political Thought and the Welfare State," 132.

vision to embrace the ideas about the full implications of embedded notions of liberal subjects that were advanced by some of his new liberal contemporaries. Hobson and Hobhouse extended the notion of embeddedness beyond culture and identity and incorporated within it at least some of the processes through which wealth was created. This move allowed them to argue that some income was not assignable to individuals. It could thus be used to support members of the community without damaging their status as liberal subjects and without compromising the integration of individuals in community that was the distinctive feature of the non-individualistic liberalism that they espoused.[70]

[70] In the last paragraph of his lecture on property, Green made reference to the idea of an "unearned increment" in the value of land that may relate to George's position. He argues, however, that "the relation between earned and unearned increments is so complicated, that a system of appropriating the latter to the state could scarcely be established without lessening the stimulus to the individual to make the most of the land, and thus ultimately lessening its serviceableness to society." (Green, "Political Obligation," p. 178.) Hobhouse and Hobson avoided the need for finely calculating the social element in wealth and tried to deal with the issue of incentives by relating income to social function.

5 Neutrality, perfectionism, and the new liberal conception of the state

James Meadowcroft

This chapter will consider the British new liberal theorist L. T. Hobhouse in light of three different sorts of assumption often made today about the character of liberal political argument. The first assumption is that liberals are "individualists."[1] An atomistic conception of society, an image of the human "self" abstracted from all social ties, and an affirmation of the ethical primacy of the individual are considered typical of liberalism. In short, liberals marginalize community, focusing almost exclusively on the rights of individuals and the autonomy of the individual moral agent. The second assumption is that liberalism can be identified with a straightforward affirmation of the virtues of the free market, private property, and self-help.[2] Liberals are held to resent government interference with economic processes, believing that people are entitled to rewards for effort and initiative, and that economic freedom is an essential component of individual liberty. The third assumption is that liberals are advocates of "state neutrality" – they believe that the state should in some sense remain "non-aligned" with respect to the competing conceptions of the "good life" manifest among its citizens.[3] To privilege ways of life selected by some individuals over those favored by others is to fail to treat all citizens equally, and so constitutes an illegitimate exercise of public authority.

The first of these claims about liberalism has a long-established pedigree and is encountered quite generally. The second is more typical

---

[1] Consider R. M. Unger, *Knowledge and Politics* (New York: Free Press, 1975); Amy Gutman, *Liberal Equality* (Cambridge University Press, 1980); Patrick Dunleavy and Brendan O'Leary, *Theories of the State* (London: Macmillan, 1987); and Michael Sandel, *Liberalism and the Limits of Justice* (Cambridge University Press, 1982).

[2] See, for example, R. C. Macridis, *Contemporary Political Ideologies* (Cambridge, MA: Winthrop Publishers, 1980); David G. Green, *The New Right* (Brighton: Wheatsheaf, 1987); and John Gray, *Liberalism* (Milton Keynes: Open University Press, 1986).

[3] Consider B. Ackerman, *Social Justice in the Liberal State* (New Haven: Yale University Press, 1980); R. Dworkin, "Liberalism," in S. Hampshire (ed.), *Public and Private Morality* (Cambridge University Press, 1978); R. E. Goodin and A. Reeve (eds.), *Liberal Neutrality* (London: Routledge, 1989); and Will Kymlicka *Contemporary Political Philosophy* (Oxford: Clarendon Press, 1990).

of European political exchange, and has acquired renewed currency with the application of the labels "economic liberal," "classical liberal," or simply "liberal" to supporters of recent political initiatives to "roll back" state interference with economic life. The third is a contemporary accretion, linked to academic debates about liberalism in the United States and Britain during the 1970s and 1980s. In this chapter I shall argue that despite their popularity these three characterizations cannot without difficulty be applied to Hobhouse; that Hobhouse's political theory is nevertheless recognizably liberal; and that in consequence, the descriptions cited above cannot be invoked as identifying traits of liberalism without careful qualification. While the discussion focuses on Hobhouse, its purpose is to raise more general issues about contemporary political theory and the character of liberal political argument.

Community, state activism, and pursuit of a common good

Even a cursory reading of Hobhouse's political writings suggests that he fits uncomfortably with the characterizations cited above. In the first place, Hobhouse cannot simply be described as an "individualist." As this term is applied to contemporary liberal theory, emphasis usually is placed on two dimensions: the ontological and the ethical. As ontological individualists, liberals are supposed to be committed to the idea that individuals are primary and society is derivative. The individual is conceived as existing prior to, or as abstracted from, social interaction. In the words of one critic, the liberal portrays the human "self" as an entity "unencumbered" by social determinations.[4] For its part, society is presented as a second-order phenomenon, resulting from an assemblage of preexisting units. As ethical individualists, liberals are held to attach value only to the claims of individuals. Individual rights are taken as absolute, as moral trumps grounded in the constitution of the rational subject. Rights maintain a ring fence around the individual protecting her from the intrusion of others. Furthermore, the self-reliant and self-supporting individual, free from outside entanglements and from dependence on public or private beneficence, appears as the ideal character type.

With respect to his understanding of the nature of the individual and of the social collectivity, Hobhouse explicitly argued that the individual was in an important sense a social product. Following thinkers such as T. H. Green and D. G. Ritchie, Hobhouse argued that "by language, by

---

4 Sandel, *Liberalism.*

training, by simply living with others, each of us absorbs into his system the social atmosphere that surrounds us."[5] Indeed, he insisted that were it possible to strip society away from the individual we would find that "his life" represented "something utterly different," in fact "a great deal of him would not exist at all."[6] In a parallel vein, Hobhouse argued that society could not be considered an assemblage of preconstituted individuals – instead it must form a more intimate moral union, simultaneously determining and being determined by the character of its constituent parts. Like many of his contemporaries, Hobhouse invoked organic imagery to capture the subtle mutualism of the individual/social bond.[7]

With respect to ethical principle, Hobhouse was prepared to consider the claims of collectivities. Rights did not spring from the individual as an abstract being, but were socially grounded – with each right finding its justification as a condition of social well-being. According to Hobhouse, there could be "no absolute or abstract rights of the individual independent of, and opposed to, the common welfare."[8] This was not to say that society should abrogate a right whenever its exercise might cause harm – for such a right might be essential to the long-term social good. What had to be assured was that the rights guaranteed to individuals were indeed those conducive to the common good. While Hobhouse valued the responsible individual, he spoke also of collective responsibility. He observed that on some dimensions the individual could only be truly self-determining by acting as part of a collectivity. Modern industrial conditions, for example, made it impossible for a workman to control the circumstances of his employment: a chance discovery, or a shift in buying patterns half a world away, could render his skills redundant. To the extent that macroeconomic conditions could be controlled, or their consequences mitigated, only society acting consciously through the state had the power, and therefore also the responsibility, to do so. Furthermore, according to Hobhouse, government action could embody moral purpose. In a democratic polity, when the majority consciously resolved to apply law and public administration to remedy some recognized social evil, then the action had "just as much moral value as though it were performed by the individuals themselves through the agency of voluntary association."[9] In other

---

[5] L. T. Hobhouse, *Liberalism*, reprint, with an Introduction by Alan Grimes (Oxford University Press, 1964), p. 68.
[6] Ibid., p. 67.
[7] See Michael Freeden, *The New Liberalism* (Oxford University Press, 1978), p. 105.
[8] L. T. Hobhouse, *Democracy and Reaction* (London: T. Fisher Unwin, 1904), p. 126.
[9] L. T. Hobhouse, *Social Evolution and Political Theory* (New York: Columbia University Press, 1911), p. 191.

words, Hobhouse was prepared to acknowledge an important role for the community.

So, in the senses in which the term is often applied to describe liberals today, Hobhouse was not an "individualist." Nor does he fit well with that other popular characterization of the liberal as an unambiguous supporter of private property and free markets, and an opponent of the activist state (sometimes also termed "political individualism"). With respect to property, Hobhouse argued that there could be no absolute right of the individual to "do what he would with his own." That which presently accrued to individuals as their property did so as the result of specific laws, laws which could be modified if the general interest so required. Furthermore, if individual property was considered essential to the growth of personality, then the social system must be so arranged that all citizens could have access to such property. And, if private property was important to individual growth, then "common property" was "equally of value for the development and expression of social life."[10] Following his new liberal collaborator J. A. Hobson, Hobhouse argued for the recognition of "social factors" in wealth creation. Production was a social process: it depended upon scientific, technical, and material resources accumulated over generations; it relied on cooperation and an elaborate division of labor; and it involved market exchange at prices based upon supply and demand, "the rates of which are determined by complex social forces."[11] Because society contributed to the productive process, it had an independent claim to some part of the product. Thus Hobhouse could argue that taxation did not represent the taking away from the individual of something he had created, but social reabsorption of a social product, which otherwise would be appropriated illegitimately by individuals.

With respect to markets, Hobhouse rejected the assumption that market-mediated bargains were necessarily free bargains. He suggested that wherever there was a substantial inequality of condition between the parties to a bargain, there was a danger that agreement was the product of coercion. Thus the appeal to "freedom of contract" could act as a cover for the exploitation of the weak by the powerful. In such circumstances the state was justified in curtailing the coercion of the stronger party by fixing the terms on which exchange could be conducted. Legislation establishing minimum wages, maximum hours of

---

[10] L. T. Hobhouse, "The Historical Evolution of Property, in Fact and in Idea," in Charles Gore (ed.), *Property, its Duties and Rights* (1913); and reprinted in *Sociology and Philosophy: A Centenary Collection of Essays and Articles*, with a preface by Sydney Caine and an introduction by Morris Ginsberg (London School of Economics, 1966), p. 105.

[11] Hobhouse, *Liberalism*, p. 109.

work, and safety standards for industrial laborers could be justified along these lines. Furthermore, Hobhouse noted that the choices made by individuals in a competitive market could generate outcomes opposed "to the interest of all considered collectively and permanently." Consumer preference for low prices, for example, could encourage producers to adopt practices damaging to their workers' health, and so it was up to the community acting collectively to circumscribe legally the parameters within which competition was permitted.

With respect to the activity of the state, Hobhouse argued that modern life was complex and dynamic, and subtle intervention was required to assure adequate conditions for individual flourishing and an optimal trajectory for social development. Typically, Hobhouse described the state's functions under two general headings: the application of force to regulate social conduct; and, the mobilization of governmental machinery and public resources for collective benefit. Coercion was necessary: first, to uphold rights and prevent any individual or group from injuring others or restricting their freedom; and second, to make effective the "general will" of the community in cases where collective action would otherwise be frustrated by recalcitrant individuals. With respect to the second kind of coercion, Hobhouse had in mind the community's use of law "to secure certain conditions ... necessary for the welfare of its members" which could "only be secured by an enforced uniformity."[12] Government imposition of minimum levels of quality in certain industries – necessary to prevent individual defection from a standard beneficial to the community as a whole – was a case in point. Of course, a great deal of government activity was non-coercive, representing rather the mobilization of social resources for social ends. No direct compulsion was involved in state-maintained libraries or museums, or in government-run hospitals or public transport, for citizens were free to use, or to abstain from using, these services as they saw fit. With respect to such non-coercive state action the problem was not one of "freedom, but of responsibility" – of determining which matters should be left to the individual and voluntary enterprise, and which should be organized on behalf of the collectivity by the state.[13]

This brings us to the third modern characterization of liberalism: as a doctrine which supports state "neutrality" with respect to competing conceptions of the good life. The idea is that individuals should be left free to determine what they value, and what kind of life they want to lead. The state's place is to maintain a framework of rights which allows

[12] Ibid., p. 78.   [13] Ibid., p. 82.

citizens equal opportunity to make these all-important choices. As among the various patterns of life open to individuals, however, the state must not play favourites. It must not penalize individuals for pursuing projects they regard as valuable, even though these ends may be considered trivial or misguided by government officials, prominent "experts," or the bulk of the citizenry. As one consistent advocate of "liberal neutrality" has argued with reference to governmental support for cultural activities (subsidizing theatre or museums, for example): "liberals believe that a state which intervenes in the cultural market place to encourage or discourage any particular way of life restricts people's self-determination."[14] Sometimes neutrality of this kind is described as "anti-perfectionism" – for the state is not entitled to act to encourage general adoption of any particular moral ideal. A link may also be made to affirming "the priority of the right over the good" – for the state's basic concern must be the provision of rights to individuals, not the pursuit of any particular understanding of the good.

Since Hobhouse was writing during the early decades of the twentieth century it is hardly surprising that his theory was not cast in the late twentieth-century idiom of "state neutrality," "anti-perfectionism," and "the priority of the right." Yet it is also true that the substance of his approach differed significantly from what liberal neutrality is now held to entail. For example, Hobhouse had no objection to spending public funds to provide services such as libraries, even though particular individuals (say, those who preferred gambling to literature) might complain that their conception of a good life was being slighted by the unfair expenditure of their taxes to make books available to readers. For the collectivity to expend public resources on objects deemed worthy by the majority was perfectly reasonable. There was no affront to the minority, provided there was no contemplation of compelling the minority to conform to majority tastes. The real problem was whether the majority was in fact pursuing elevated ends – and this was an issue for informed debate.

Hobhouse believed that the state should function to promote the good life – in particular, to further a common good of which each member of the community had some part. From such a perspective, insistence upon the "neutrality" of the state would have appeared misplaced, for the state could not be indifferent to the orientation which individuals gave to their lives, and its institutions and policy necessarily embodied a substantive (although imperfectly realized) conception of the good. The things individuals were permitted to do with and to one

---

[14] Kymlicka, *Contemporary Political Philosophy*, p. 217.

another, the authorized forms of property and marriage, the range of liberties and the pattern of social control, would always help or hinder the realization of particular individual and social ends. Similarly, talk of "the priority of the right" would have appeared misleading, for the right could not be ascertained without reference to the good, nor could maintenance of the right be delegated to the state while pursuit of the good was left to individual enterprise.[15] Individuals could, without reference to society, strive to accumulate personal "goods," but if one was concerned with the good as an ethical ideal, then this must be a good that was not only compatible with, but also contributory to, the good of others. Thus, some part of the true good was a collective good. In particular, participation in political life – taking responsibility for determining the laws under which the community would live – was in itself a part of the good life.[16]

The value of the individual, free enterprise, and a self-directed life

So far I have argued that Hobhouse's views do not correspond closely with three widely touted assumptions about what liberals believe. Nevertheless, it is my contention that Hobhouse is best understood as a liberal thinker. Thus I am suggesting that these disjunctions result more from the simplistic ways in which liberalism is often characterized, than from any particular failure of coherence or liberality in Hobhouse's theory. But if Hobhouse was a liberal thinker, how can this liberalism be appreciated? One way to answer this question is to return to the three issues we have been considering, for, while Hobhouse did not accept individualism, glorify the free market, private property, and the minimal state, or advocate state neutrality, neither did he embrace the anti-liberal conclusions with which straightforward rejection of these doctrines is sometimes associated.

Hobhouse was not an individualist, at least in the sense in which this term is usually applied, yet concern for the individual lay at the heart of his political philosophy. While he invoked organic imagery to express the intimate character of the moral bond between individual and society, he avoided any suggestion that society constituted a "physical organism" to

---

[15] Indeed Hobhouse explicitly argued that any approach to social ethics which did not base personal rights on the requirements of social welfare "must lead to an insoluble contradiction between what it is right to do and what it is good to do" (L. T. Hobhouse, *Government by the People* ([London: People's Suffrage Federation, 1910], p. 4).

[16] In *Liberalism*, Hobhouse wrote: "the democratic thesis is that ... the extension of intelligent interest in all manner of public things is in itself a good, and more than that, it is a condition qualifying other good things" (p. 118).

which individual lives (like cells in an animal body) were subordinate. Nor did society possess a "distinct personality separate from, and superior to, those of its members."[17] According to Hobhouse, the social whole was not a mysterious or transcendent power, but the members taken in their interconnections. If it was a mistake to so resolve society "into individuals so that the character of the life which they share in common is left out of account," it was equally wrong to elevate social life to something "other than what its members live in their dealings with one another."[18] In other words, neither individual nor society had ontological priority: any real individual was socially grounded; no society was more than the individuals taken in all their interrelationships.

Hobhouse also emphasized that society was composed "wholly of persons." The ethical significance of this statement was that any authentic common good must be (i) a good for individuals; and (ii) a good in which all individuals shared. In the first place, there was no happiness or pain except as experienced by individuals. Personality was ultimately individuated. Thus, the true welfare of a collectivity must be a welfare for the persons of which it was composed. According to Hobhouse, whenever "an organized society has a 'good' opposed to the summed up gain and loss of its component members, it is either that some of those alleged members are [being] treated merely as instruments external" to the community, "or that the good is a false good, cheating even those that partake of it."[19] Second, since all individuals were equally persons, the common good must accommodate the good of each and every individual. To deny any individual equal opportunity for self-expansion would be to fail to take seriously the claims of personality. In other words, a good society was one which maximized equally distributed opportunities for the growth of personality.

Hobhouse believed that each human being had a unique identity, the ability to realize a distinctive set of achievements, and potential to make a specific contribution to the communal life. Basic to his understanding of "personality" was the notion of rational self-guidance – as contrasted with individual subordination to impulse or to external coercion. Hence the importance of liberty. Without free choice there could be no self-determination along rational lines. Freedom was essential to the growth of personality; it was vital to the unfettered exercise of feeling, will, intellect, and ethical spirit; it was "the condition of mental and moral

---

[17] Ibid., p. 68.
[18] L. T. Hobhouse, *The Metaphysical Theory of the State* (London: Allen & Unwin, 1918), p. 133.
[19] Ibid., p. 131.

expansion."[20] The individual, and freedom for the individual, were therefore at the heart of Hobhouse's ethical preoccupations.

Let us turn next to the issues of property, markets, and state action. We have seen that Hobhouse made property rights relative to social welfare; but this did not mean that he rejected private ownership. The realities of advanced industrial production made it impossible for each producer individually to own the implements with which they worked. But individuals must at least be guaranteed access to instruments of labour – that is to say, all those willing and able to work must be afforded the opportunity of gainful employment. Furthermore, everyone must be assured maintenance in times of need. Thus, Hobhouse believed that society must uphold "the 'right to work' and the right to a 'living wage'" as "integral conditions of a good social order."[21] According to Hobhouse the object must be to "restore to society a direct ownership in some things, but an eminent ownership of all things material to the production of wealth, securing 'property for use' to the individual, and retaining 'property for power' for the democratic state."[22]

As for markets, these were to be brought under social control, not abolished. Competition brought benefits to society, not only the ills on which socialist critics insisted. Competition could favor consumer choice; it could encourage improved techniques and products; it could act as a stimulus to individual achievement. However, competition must be confined within socially acceptable channels. Hobhouse did not believe that the entire economic life of the nation could be directed by one central authority. The individual remained the most dynamic element in production.

With respect to the state, Hobhouse favored an activist administration; but this activism was directed towards the empowerment of individuals. He stressed the importance, whenever state action was being considered, of remaining mindful of two basic state characteristics: first, that it acted by means of universal edicts and laws; and second, that it deployed force to compel obedience. Since the state was dependent upon "rules of universal application" and could only "deal with men in masses, and with problems in accordance with what is general and not with what is particular," it was ill-suited to treat "the individuality of life."[23] Furthermore, Hobhouse was insistent that the life of society could not be reduced to the life of the state – there was a vast domain of social interaction with which the state had only marginal

[20] Hobhouse, *Social Evolution*, p. 200.
[21] Hobhouse, *Liberalism*, pp. 83–4.
[22] Hobhouse, "The Historical Evolution of Property," p. 106.
[23] Hobhouse, *Social Evolution*, p. 187.

contact, and this non-state social sphere, the area of voluntary cooperative endeavor, was vital to individual self-realization.

Finally, although Hobhouse did not conceptualize the state's role in
terms of "neutrality," he was resistant to the idea of paternalist administration. Hobhouse envisaged a wider range of state action than that
which earlier liberals had been prepared to consider, but when he came
to justify the deployment of state coercion he did so in terms of
upholding individual rights, and maintaining majoritarian norms.
Except in extreme circumstances, Hobhouse did not countenance the
application of force to promote the good of the coerced individual;
instead, force was always applied to an individual to secure elements of
value for *others*. He discussed regulation of the sale of alcoholic bev-
erages, for example, primarily in terms of "unequal contract" (the liquor
sellers had an unfair advantage over their drink-dependent clients) and
the legitimate coercion of tradesmen through a restriction of opening
hours. It is true that Hobhouse did suggest that in some cases liquor
dependency could impair an individual's capacity for rational judgment,
and to this extent he might justifiably be coerced for his own good. The
danger here, of course, is that by widening the basis on which one
diagnosed individuals as having lost their power of rational self-direction
one could extend the range of paternalist intervention. But this was not
a path Hobhouse was willing to tread. Instead, he emphasized explicitly
his firm belief in the traditional liberal maxim that "a normal human
being is not to be coerced for his own good."[24]

This injunction against coercive state intervention to promote the
good of the coerced individual rested not upon indifference to the
individual good, but upon the analysis of the nature of that good.
According to Hobhouse, "to try to form character by coercion is to
destroy it in the making. Personality is not built up from without, but
grows from within."[25] What state coercion could achieve was the
establishment of optimum conditions under which each individual
could seek his or her own good; it could maintain an external order
under which moral life could flourish. The value of state coercion lay in
the potential that it set free. By restraining the individual for the good of
others, and others for the good of the individual, the state upheld a
common good which allowed each individual to find their own good.

The anti-paternalist thrust of his argument appears clearly in a
passage where Hobhouse compared the ideas of liberty to be found in
the writings of John Stuart Mill and of T. H. Green. Hobhouse wrote:

[24] Ibid., p. 202.   [25] Hobhouse, *Liberalism*, p. 76.

Mill's argument cuts deeper than that of Green (his true successor in the line of political thinkers). Green conceives liberty as the right of a man to make the best of himself – a noble conception, but one that does not meet the vital question, whether a man is to judge for himself what is best for himself. Mill's argument implies that a man has the right to make his own mistakes, or, to put it more fully, that that society is best ordered and contains within it the most seeds of progress which allows men most scope to gain their own education from their own experience.[26]

Self-perception, contemporaneous evaluation, and modern analysis

This second review of issues associated with the descriptions of liberalism with which we started illustrates that Hobhouse did not endorse the anti-liberal positions which rejection of these three doctrines is often held to entail. If Hobhouse repudiated individualism, he did not ignore individuality; if he looked beyond existing property rights, free markets, and a quiescent state, he did not advocate a comprehensive system of state socialism; if he rejected state neutrality, he did not embrace paternalist or *dirigiste* alternatives. As testimony to the liberal character of Hobhouse's approach some readers may find these observations thin. Cannot more convincing evidence of Hobhouse's liberalism be offered than the rather weak affirmation that in a number of important areas his doctrine was not illiberal? One way to approach this issue is to consider matters briefly from the vantage point of three sets of observers: Hobhouse, his contemporaries, and late twentieth-century political analysts.

Hobhouse himself had no doubts about the liberal pedigree of his political theory. He argued that as a movement of ideas liberalism had always emphasized freedom, equality of opportunity, rational debate, representative democracy, and the primacy of right (rather than might) in domestic and international affairs. He saw himself as carrying forward this emancipatory tradition in new circumstances. While Hobhouse acknowledged many of the insights of moderate socialism, and encouraged collaboration between the liberal and the socialist "wings of the humanitarian movement," his primary intellectual attachment remained to liberalism.[27] In a sense, he believed that it was the stronger, more fundamental movement – that it had deeper historical roots and that its accomplishments were more solid. In particular, liberalism stood by "elements of individual right and personal independence of which Socialism at times appears oblivious."[28]

---

[26] Hobhouse, *Democracy and Reaction*, p. 226.
[27] Ibid., p. 239.   [28] Hobhouse, *Liberalism*, p. 108.

To the extent that he thought of himself as a liberal, the most difficult challenge Hobhouse faced was to explain how the vastly extended range of state action which he advocated could be justified according to a doctrine which historically had been so closely associated with the appeal to *freedom from* state interference. This he did by emphasizing both continuity between the underlying preoccupations of the old and the new liberalism, and the altered political and economic conditions which required an innovative response. In particular, Hobhouse pointed to the changed character of the state itself. In the days of Bentham or Cobden, government had resembled a closed corporation with power concentrated in the hands of the aristocracy. But by the outset of the twentieth century British government had been transformed – through the growth of an efficient and relatively impartial professional civil service and progressive extensions of the franchise. Government was "no longer an alien power, intruding itself from without upon the lives of the governed," but had become (though still imperfectly) "the organ of the community as a whole."[29] Thus the success of earlier liberals had cleared the way for the social activism of the modern state.

Hobhouse also emphasized advances in social philosophy which permitted a progressive deepening of liberal self-awareness. He referred to a more profound appreciation of the interdependence of individual and society, and to a more subtle understanding of liberty, and of the social conditions conducive to liberty. He presented the development of liberal theory as a movement which passed from natural rights to utilitarianism, then on through the hey-day of *laissez-faire* to the more balanced views of Gladstone and Mill, ultimately culminating in the new liberal synthesis.

Crucial to Hobhouse's presentation of this synthesis were his views on "personality," "progress," "democracy" and "harmony." Personality was understood as a vital force which required freedom to grow, which could learn though experience, developing moral understanding and self-control. Personality was a universal human attribute, which meant that we both could and should direct "our own lives." Indeed, Hobhouse argued that:

Liberalism is the belief that society can safely be founded on this self-directing power of personality, that it is only on this foundation that a true community can be built, and that so established its foundations are so deep and so wide that there is no limit that we can place to the extent of the building.[30]

While Hobhouse acknowledged that history displayed no even pattern of advance, he argued that over the long-haul there had been forward

[29] Hobhouse, *Democracy and Reaction*, p. 220.
[30] Hobhouse, *Liberalism*, p. 66.

movement – developed social forms in which ethical principles were more soundly established had emerged and proliferated. The modern state was extant proof of the reality of progress for, despite its inadequacies, it constituted the most successful reconciliation of the claims of individuality and community, of personal rights and collective welfare, yet seen. What was distinctive about liberalism was its "understanding that progress is not a matter of mechanical contrivance, but of the liberation of living spiritual energy."[31]

Hobhouse believed democracy to be a core liberal value. It provided the people with a mechanism to control law-makers and administrators, an institutional safeguard against the erosion of other freedoms, and a domain in which organized interests could achieve expression. Democracy was essential to the ethical foundations of the state: the fact that each individual had some say in determining the laws under which all would live cemented the mutuality of the political bond; the fact that each individual could participate in political debate and decision made possible the formation of a genuine popular will, and the collective assumption of responsibility for a shared destiny. In a formal sense democracy meant government dependent upon the ballot-box. In substance it was the orientation of government by the popular will. Majority rule was simply a device to make the substance – popular rule – practicable. Throughout, Hobhouse emphasized that the true foundation of a sound political life was "good will" – that is to say, the shared resolve to promote the common good and to conduct public life according to high moral standards. Democracy could provide no magic solution to social ills; at best it expressed the spirit of a people. And should that spirit be "set on vain things, on amassing wealth which it has not the taste or judgement to spend, on the acquisition of territory which it does not need, or on the unreal show of military glory," the result would not be good.[32] But if the popular spirit was focused on sound things, then it would have "a will worth expressing, and the forms of political democracy" could "give it the means of realization."

Hobhouse invoked "harmony" as his ethical master concept. He spoke of harmony as the "central conception" of "the good or the desirable," and defined "progress" as "the movement by which such harmony may be realized."[33] Hobhouse described the belief that a non-conflictual and mutually reinforcing self-expansion for the personality of each individual was possible as "the fundamental postulate of the organic view of

[31] Ibid., p. 73.
[32] L. T. Hobhouse, "The Prospects for Anglo-Saxon Democracy," *Atlantic Monthly*, 109 (1912), 352.
[33] Hobhouse, *Social Evolution*, pp. 92, 93.

society." But while possible, such ethical harmony could not be a spontaneous product; it would only come about through conscious "effort ... intelligence and will."[34] It was not the case, as an earlier generation of liberals had assumed, that if each man acted according to the principles of enlightened self-interest the outcome would necessarily be the best possible for the community as a whole. In fact, "the line of harmony" was "rather the narrow path," and "every divergence" from it resulted in "collision and more or less of frustration and misery to some one."[35] Constant, conscious, and careful adjustment was therefore required to balance the components of social life. In this process of regulation the state had a central role to play: it was both a mechanism by which the various terms of the social equation could be balanced, and a term which must itself be set in harmony with all other moments.

Furthermore, Hobhouse argued that "harmony" was the "unifying conception" best suited to guide modern liberal movements for social justice.[36] Earlier liberal reformers had upheld "liberty" as the essential dimension of their creed – and their single-minded insistence on the value of freedom had lent power to their efforts. But the earlier understanding of liberty had been "too thin," and modern social problems were too complex to be dissolved by the application of this single remedy. By taking "harmony" as their core value, modern liberal reformers could focus their energies, while reflecting the diversity of the problems to be considered.

Clearly then, Hobhouse thought of himself as a liberal, albeit a liberal of a particular (reform-oriented and socialistic) kind. But was his judgment correct? One way to cross-check such a self-definition is with the perceptions of other thinkers of his day. Did Hobhouse's liberal and non-liberal contemporaries regard the claim of a liberal pedigree for his ideas as outlandish or ridiculous? The straightforward answer is that they did not. Of course, some liberals rebuked thinkers like Hobhouse for abandoning the defence of individual liberty and capitulating to collectivist influences. And some conservatives accused the liberal social reformers of having accepted the subversive program of the socialists. But by the early years of the twentieth century a fairly large body of liberal opinion had become reconciled to the idea of an active social role for the state. In this context Hobhouse's perspective could be appreciated as a legitimate interpretation of liberal principles.[37]

Yet matters cannot be left here. It is possible, after all, that Hob-

---

[34] Ibid., p. 93.   [35] Ibid., p. 86.   [36] Hobhouse, *Liberalism*, p. 126.
[37] Consider Herbert Samuel, *Liberalism* (London: Grant Richards, 1902); J. A. Hobson, *The Crisis of Liberalism* (London: P. S. King, 1909); and W. Lyon Blease, *A Short History of English Liberalism* (London: T. Fisher Unwin, 1913).

house's peers were as mistaken as to the character of his theory as he was himself. We, as observers well removed from the context in which Hobhouse elaborated his views, can bring our own perspective to bear upon this issue. In the first place, we can use our own historical position to consider whether viewing Hobhouse as a liberal was reasonable according to the set of social understandings available to his contemporaries. In other words, were turn-of-the-century British observers correct in their own terms to categorize Hobhouse's perspective as liberal?

This question could be approached from various angles, but let me cite some elements which suggest the contemporaneous evaluation was internally consistent. First, Hobhouse's political vocabulary overlapped substantially with that employed by other liberals. Freedom, the individual, rights, welfare, equality, society, and representative government all played central roles in his theoretical enterprise; and all were deployed in ways that shared a family resemblance with the ways they were integrated into alternative statements of liberalism. Second, the problems which preoccupied him were typically liberal. He was concerned with the reconciliation of individual liberty with social control, personal responsibility with collective responsibility, freedom of conscience with the rights of the majority, government by the people with input by experts, and the destiny of small nations with the fate of existing political entities. Third, the authorities he cited were either liberals, or thinkers who had inspired liberal reflection; among them were Locke, Paine, Rousseau, Hegel, Bentham, James Mill, Comte, John Stuart Mill, Cobden, Bright, Green, and Gladstone. Fourth, Hobhouse was personally attached to long-standing practical liberal causes, notably free trade, anti-imperialism, constitutional reform, Irish Home Rule, and the removal of all privileges for the owners of the land. Fifth, in party political terms, Hobhouse supported the Liberals, and had made a career writing for publications with well-known liberal sympathies.

Thus, we can judge contemporaneous observers to have had good grounds to consider Hobhouse a liberal, within their own understanding of that term. Of course, it could still be argued that these observers were mistaken. Nevertheless, careful consideration must be given to the basis on which such a judgment to "overrule" the evaluation of Hobhouse and his peers might be made. One possibility would be to argue that what we mean by "liberalism" is not what they meant by "liberalism"; and that as we must work with our understanding, their comprehension (which embraced Hobhouse) should be set aside. The problem with insistence upon the primacy of a modern stipulative definition is that it avoids dealing with the reality of a political tradition which has evolved over time, helping to frame the context within which political argument is conducted and serving as a focus for individual allegiance and opposition. Alternatively, it might be claimed that we have now uncovered some inner core of meaning to "liberalism," which allows us to understand the liberal tradition in a deep way inaccessible to Hobhouse and his contemporaries. Armed with such knowledge, we can filter back through time establishing which theories are truly liberal theories. But such a claim requires extraordinary assurance in the coherence of our (new) understanding, and faith in our privileged temporal location.

However, a modern theorist might suggest that turn-of-the-century observers were simply overly generous to Hobhouse: that while in some rather loose sense he might be judged "a liberal," this was not strictly true about his *theory*. In particular, it might be argued that his theory was either so hybridized as to make identification with any specific tradition impossible, or sufficiently confused and incoherent to render classification pointless. In other words, Hobhouse was not a profound liberal; he does not provide a very good example of liberal theorizing. There seems no objection in principle to this type of criticism – certainly it is a judgment that we are entitled to make; it is just that I think it to be mistaken. With respect to "hybridization," I believe that the predominance of liberal over socialist affinities is quite clear, not only with regard to Hobhouse's personal conduct, but also as concerns the structure of his theory. And the "incoherence" argument seems less than convincing in light of the substantial reputation which Hobhouse continues to enjoy as a significant (if perhaps not first-rank) liberal theorist. Of course, on many issues Hobhouse was confused but, with due allowances made for conditions, time, and place, perhaps no more so than many modern theorists of liberalism.

Tracking the liberal political tradition

It is now time to return to the common characterizations of liberalism introduced at the outset: that liberals are individualists, that they are straightforward supporters of free markets, private property, and the minimal state, or that they are advocates of state "neutrality." As we have seen, while none of these descriptions can easily be applied to Hobhouse, there are convincing reasons for considering him a liberal. The inference, then, is that there is something seriously wrong with the casual way in which liberalism is identified with these doctrines. Certainly it is true that a great many liberals have subscribed to one or more of these beliefs. At particular times and places such ideas may well have appeared as near universal attributes of liberalism. But acceptance of even one of these doctrines, as they are normally understood, is not a necessary condition for a thinker to be a liberal.[38]

What of the fact that we found upon reconsideration that with respect to issues which could be approached under these headings Hobhouse's beliefs were not illiberal? Hobhouse did attach significance to the individual; he did believe that private property and markets were useful, and he worried about placing too much reliance upon the state; and he did oppose state paternalism. Does this not suggest that the problem could be resolved by a more flexible formulation of the brief character-izations with which we started? Perhaps they should read something like: "liberals value individuals"; "liberals recognize the importance of private property and markets and resist the complete control of social life by the state"; and "liberals oppose paternalist regulation." The problem, of course, is that as the statements are made sufficiently vague to include all liberals, so they may also become valid descriptions of many non-liberals.

Now it could be argued that despite the fact that descriptions on the first list fail to include all liberals, and those on the second list include many non-liberals, both types of characterization have their place; in fact, they could even be used in tandem. Descriptions of the first type provide a rough-and-ready guide to the typical stance of liberals, while those of the second establish minimum parameters to the range of liberal belief. Thus, for example, we might state that: "liberals are generally individualists," but at the very least "they attach significant value to the individual."

This is an improvement, but the construction of theorems of this type is not a particularly fruitful approach to understanding liberalism. The problem is that the search for such formulas points us in the wrong direction: it suggests that being a liberal is all about accepting a certain set of statements about politics as true, and that the liberal political tradition is simply an assemblage of all those thinkers who share these core liberal beliefs. In fact, being a liberal is about acting towards the world in a certain way: it is about taking part in a particular kind of practice, about engaging in an established pattern of political argument. Being a liberal implies mastering an idiom, it involves accepting a set of inherited concepts, problems, and authorities and applying and ad-justing these elements as one thinks and argues about politics. In short, being a liberal is about inserting oneself in an established tradition of

---

[38] Nor in the case of the first and third of these doctrines is it a sufficient condition. It is possible to be an individualist but not a liberal: consider an anarchist for example; and it is possible to worship private property, markets, and a minimal state, and yet be a conservative.

discourse. Of course, liberals share certain beliefs – but in an important, but paradoxical, sense the central belief they share concerns the special worth of a particular historical form of political behavior and theory, and the significance of belonging to the associated community of practitioners.

On this reading, the liberal tradition is not simply a cross-temporal assemblage of individuals who share one or more premises, but an evolving pattern of interaction: a stream of political actors/thinkers succeeding one another through time, interacting consciously and unconsciously with received concepts, ideas, and authorities. Traditions are loose and open-textured; distinct currents emerge, cross, and recross; central concepts and problems develop and change over time. As each generation adapts its inheritance to changed conditions, dis-agreeing among themselves as they do so, many liberalisms are gener-ated, all sharing a certain resemblance. Liberalism is therefore internally complex and multi-faceted, and there is a dense and to some extent contradictory array of authorities, concepts, and ideas to which any new theorist can turn for inspiration.

What I am suggesting, therefore, is that attempts to sum up liberalism (or any other sophisticated political tradition) in a single phrase, or to capture its "essence" in a belief or small set of beliefs, or to construct a logical model of core liberal understandings, are bound to fail. They fail because they misrepresent what a political tradition actually is; or, putting it more directly, they fail to understand how human beings in modern societies think and behave politically.

Furthermore, unless they are invoked with care, generalizations of the form "liberals believe *x*" are very likely to mislead. Take, for example, the common notion that liberals are opposed to extending popular political participation beyond standard representative-democratic forms. The idea is that antipathy to popular participation is a necessary corollary of liberal principles – particularly liberal individualism.[39] In fact, many liberals have not rested content with the interest-aggregative notion of democracy on which this claim is predicated, and some have come to support the introduction of participatory democratic forms.[40] Even liberals who understood democracy in essentially individualist

---

[39] For various forms of this claim see Carole Pateman, *Participation and Democratic Theory* (Cambridge University Press, 1970); B. Barber, *Strong Democracy: Participatory Politics for a New Age* (Berkeley: University of California Press, 1984); Anthony Arblaster, *The Rise and Decline of Western Liberalism* (Oxford: Blackwell, 1984); and B. Holden, *Understanding Liberal Democracy* (Oxford: Philip Allan, 1988).

[40] J. A. Hobson, the early twentieth-century radical economist, was a prominent liberal advocate of participatory forms. Hobhouse himself supported recourse to national referenda on issues of constitutional import.

and instrumentalist terms have occasionally embraced participatory mechanisms like the referendum – the noted constitutional lawyer A. V. Dicey is a case in point.[41]

Precisely because it is a complex and a historical phenomenon, attempts to capture liberal views in a single phrase, or to construct a simple sketch of "what liberals believe," are bound to be problematic. For example, in a recent study Paul Franco succumbs to the temptation to define liberalism in terms of acceptance of a few key beliefs – essentially acceptance of the idea that the state must pursue no substantive end, but should provide a framework of rights within which individuals and groups are free to pursue their own self-defined goals. He then argues that since Michael Oakeshott accepted these ideas, he was a liberal. Indeed, according to Franco, Oakeshott was not just any liberal, but the most significant liberal theorist of the twentieth century.[42] But surely a contextually sensitive account of post-war British liberalism suggests that Oakeshott is being miscast. Certainly it seems almost perverse to present a thinker, who was himself so sensitive to "tradition," as the epitome of a tradition towards which his attitude was, to say the very least, ambivalent.

As opposed to focusing on a few key beliefs, an adequate understanding of liberalism must (among other considerations) recognize that the tradition can never be understood by logical analysis alone – rather it must be read historically; that attention must be paid to the political and ideational environments within which liberals have been active, particularly to rival approaches in contradistinction to which liberal views have been elaborated; that the tradition has always spoken with multiple voices, and that contention among competing claimants to the "liberal" title has colored the evolution of the theory. We should be concerned with relevant concepts, authorities, and patterns of argument and concern, not just similar beliefs. And we should not overrationalize the tradition; precisely because it has a concrete history, the contingent features shape every specific liberal variant.

As a self-conscious political tradition, liberalism took form during the first half of the nineteenth century. From this point it carried forward, adapted, and ramified. But liberal lineages were also extended backwards in time as liberals (and their critics) sought out resonances with earlier thinkers and movements. By the time Hobhouse wrote, the

---

[41] A. V. Dicey, "Ought the Referendum to be Introduced into England," *Contemporary Review*, April 1890.

[42] According to Paul Franco, Oakeshott has provided "the most sophisticated and satisfying contemporary statement of liberalism" (*The Political Philosophy of Michael Oakeshott* ([New Haven: Yale University Press, 1990], p. 2).

diversity and complexity of existing forms of liberal argument (including national variants) was already apparent; and at the close of the twentieth century this was even more obvious. But what of the unity of the tradition? Clearly liberals share common concerns and patterns of argument, a point to which I alluded when considering whether Hobhouse's contemporaries had good reason to consider him a liberal. Liberals do value liberty and individuality, but, as Michael Freeden has recently argued, concepts such as "progress," "rationality," "the general interest," "sociability," and "limited and responsible power" must also be considered part of the liberal "core." Yet the point which I have tried to make here is that the unity or identity of liberalism is not constituted by an abstract theoretical affinity, but by a historic chain of interaction, involving practical engagement with preexisting ideas and recourse to certain sorts of authority, symbol, and cause. To put this another way, in some respects the fact that Hobhouse turned to Cobden, Mill, and Gladstone as reference points when defining his own views, that he championed free trade and the emancipation of subject nationalities, and that he had faith in a particular kind of reasoned argument are as important in constituting the liberal character of his theory as is the particular conception of "liberty" with which he worked.

Does all this have any particular relevance for contemporary political theory? Some might argue that while such considerations may be pertinent to historians attempting to reconstruct past patterns of doctrinal interaction they can hardly be of great concern to modern thinkers engaged in the first-order theorization of political life. In fact, contemporary theory has much to gain from a more historically grounded appreciation of the complexity and diversity of the liberal political tradition. Such knowledge encourages a certain humility, as one recognizes that the perspectives of past thinkers are invariably more complex than the semi-caricatures with which we are usually presented. It also prompts reflection about causes of change and continuity, as one learns that much of what now passes as "new" and "cutting edge" resonates with debates from a century or more in the past. Above all, by understanding past phases of political debate, the physiognomy of different liberal variants, and the complex historical trajectory of the liberal tradition as a whole, contemporary theorists can better appreciate the focus of current theoretical preoccupations.[43] In other words, knowledge of earlier patterns of political argument can provide a reference

---

[43] For discussion of turn-of-the-century British political thought, consider Freeden, *The New Liberalism*, and Andrew Vincent and Raymond Plant, *Philosophy, Politics and Citizenship* (Oxford: Blackwell, 1984).

point from which to assess the nature and novelty of present political controversies.

Turn-of-the-century British political debate shows how diverse are the currents which can claim a liberal lineage: from Herbert Spencer's "indirectly" utilitarian and liberty-centered political philosophy, through Henry Sidgwick's utilitarian perspective advocating an enhanced "individualist minimum" of state interference and Bernard Bosanquet's Idealist theory of the Real Will and the "removal of obstacles" principle of state action, to Hobhouse's own "new" liberal reconstruction.[44] It shows how political traditions can be re-invigorated by cross-fertilization with other creeds (liberalism with socialism, but also conservatism with liberalism). At a deeper level, the cross-matching of different ontological, epistemological, religious, ethical, and political doctrines suggests that there may be a very loose "fit" between various phases of theoretical endeavour. Similar philosophical "foundations" can lead to widely divergent political views, and similar political programmes can be justified by appeal to widely different "first" principles. The role of intellectual fashion in achieving closure in theoretical debates can be seen with the abandonment of organic imagery – all the rage in the two decades bracketing the turn of the century, but virtually absent thereafter.[45] The relevance of broader political developments for theoretical debate is brought to the fore by the dramatic eclipse of Idealism after 1914 – as much a casualty of the Great War as a philosophical contender beaten by rational debate. Elements such as these, if carefully considered, may alter the way we do theory today. Moreover, arguments such as the contemporary controversy over liberal neutrality can appear in a different light. If it becomes apparent that generations of liberals got on quite well without invoking a category now held to be foundational to the creed, one may be led to consider the sorts of factors which have encouraged late twentieth-century liberals to turn towards neutralist idiom, and to examine the ramifications which neutralist arguments have for the structure of liberal theories and for the potential future development of the tradition. And this can lead on not only to discussion about issues such as the particular place of the Constitution in the US political argument, and the late twentieth-century preoccupation with justifying liberal institutions in plural (or fractured?) societies, but also to the examination of problems such as

---

[44] See Herbert Spencer, *The Principles of Ethics*, 2 vols. (London: Williams & Norgate, 1892, 1893); Henry Sidgwick, *The Elements of Politics* (London: Macmillan, 1891); Bernard Bosanquet, *The Philosophical Theory of the State* (London: Macmillan, 1899).

[45] See James Meadowcroft, *Conceptualising the State* (Oxford University Press, 1995).

the relative de-politicization (or what Rodney Barker has described as the "etherealization") of liberal political theory.[46]

Of course, some theorists might want to draw more direct inspiration from the work of Hobhouse. It could be argued, for example, that Hobhouse's understanding of the relationship between the right and the good – that individual rights must be justified by their contribution to a good in which all may share – is at least as satisfactory (and certainly considerably less tortured) than much modern theory. Hobhouse's version of liberal theory which attempts to balance the claims of individual and society, the provision of social welfare and the assumption of individual responsibility, and the needs for both individual and collective property may also be found appealing. Furthermore, a liberal variant which advocates freedom of conscience but avoids moral relativism, and which explicitly proclaims its confidence in the possibility of progress and its faith in the emancipatory potential of popular democracy, may also attract some modern theorists.

Finally, returning to the characterizations of liberalism with which we started, it is interesting to speculate why the tendency to reduce liberalism to a simple formula is so pronounced. To some extent, the trend may well have been encouraged by liberals themselves. Believing so strongly in rationalism – that the foundations of their own creed are rational, that a rational doctrine can be formulated rationally, and that such a rational statement is the key to political argument – liberals often try to order and simplify their own doctrine, favoring one concept or core belief which will allow the diverse aspects of their ideas to be viewed in their correct interrelation. From Mill we get utilitarianism and then the liberty principle; from Cobden, liberty and *laissez-faire*; from Hobhouse, "harmonious development"; from Dworkin, "equality"; and so on. To some extent it is ironic that a doctrine which emphasizes tolerance and pluralism so often has recourse to mono-theoretic patterns of justification.

Of course, like other ongoing traditions, liberalism also suffers from external pressures. Its opponents are all too happy to suggest pithy characterizations, preferably those that emphasize elements which appear objectionable, suspect, dated, and so on. Thus liberals become "individualists," or defenders of private property. On the other hand, political theorists and analysts must accept a share of the responsibility. Always in search of neat classificatory schemes, and short summaries for our undergraduates, we are only too ready to compress a complex reality into cramped categories.

---

[46] Rodney Barker, "A Future for Liberalism or a Liberal Future?," in J. Meadowcroft (ed.), *The Liberal Political Tradition: Contemporary Reappraisals* (Cheltenham, UK: Edward Elgar, 1996).

6 Bosanquet's communitarian defense of economic individualism: a lesson in the complexities of political theory

Gerald Gaus

The "communitarian critique of liberalism"

"We are witnessing a revival of communitarian criticisms of liberal political theory. Like the critics of the 1960s, those of the 1980s fault liberalism for being mistakenly and irreparably individualistic."[1] In the face of these communitarian challenges, many liberals – like most of the contributors to this volume – seek to show that liberalism is not, after all, "irreparably individualistic." In particular, most of this volume's contributors are inspired by the new liberals of the late nineteenth and early twentieth centuries who, in the face of an earlier wave of "communitarian critiques,"[2] advanced two apparently closely related theses. First, the new liberals insisted that liberalism, understood as a doctrine upholding individual freedom to pursue different ways of living, does not depend on an individualistic or "atomistic" conception of society; indeed, a vibrant liberal theory can (and perhaps must) be built on non-individualistic foundations.[3] Second, it was believed that once we understand the social metaphysics underlying an adequate liberalism, our understanding of the liberal political program will alter – to embrace the welfare state. In Hobhouse's eyes, a "public-spirited liberalism" integrated the core liberal commitment to liberty with a socialistic "solidarity" expressed in state provision for disadvantaged members of

---

[1] Amy Gutmann, "Communitarian Critics of Liberalism," *Philosophy and Public Affairs*, 14 (1985), 308.

[2] Gutmann claims that "the new wave of criticism is not a mere repetition of the old. Whereas the earlier critics were inspired by Marx, the recent critics are inspired by Aristotle and Hegel" (ibid.). Gutmann has a distinctly contemporary conception of "earlier" criticisms – the 1960s. The new liberalism arose directly as a response to Hegelian, but also to Aristotelian, concerns about individualistic analyses of society. As such, it seems very much in the spirit of recent communitarian critiques and liberal responses.

[3] For representative discussions of the new liberals, stressing their anti-individualism, see Stefan Collini, *Liberalism and Sociology: L. T. Hobhouse and Political Argument in England, 1880–1914* (Cambridge University Press, 1979), ch. 2; Alfonso J. Damico, *Individuality and Community: The Social and Political Thought of John Dewey* (Gainesville: University Presses of Florida, 1978), ch. 5.

society.[4] The idea seems straightforward: once we understand the more social or communal foundations of liberalism, we will also see that "freedom is only one side of social life. Mutual aid is not less important than mutual forbearance, the theory of collective action no less funda- mental than the theory of personal freedom."[5]

The political philosophy of Bernard Bosanquet calls into question this seemingly obvious link between a non-individualistic social metaphysic and a non-, or at least less, individualistic economic order.[6] Bosanquet, like Hobhouse, was a student of T. H. Green; indeed, Bosanquet was in many ways the true philosophical disciple of Green, developing Green's Idealist accounts of knowledge, self, and society.[7] Of all the major late nineteenth/early twentieth-century English liberals influenced by Hegelianism, Bosanquet was the most Hegelian, and the least indi- vidualistic in his understanding of society – and on this account was famously attacked by Hobhouse.[8] Yet Bosanquet was an explicit defender of economic individualism and vehement critic not only of socialism, but also of the new liberal welfare state. In this chapter I shall argue that Bosanquet's combination of a thoroughgoingly organic (or communitarian) social metaphysics with a strong defense of economic individualism is not only coherent, but in many ways is a more plausible communitarian program than the new liberals' "semi-Socialism."[9] Bosanquet's political philosophy thus provides a crucial lesson to con- temporary communitarian liberals: in itself, the rejection of "social individualism" has very little in the way of direct implications for liberal political programs or policies – and the "implications" it does have seem surprisingly "capitalistic."

---

[4] L. T Hobhouse, *Democracy and Reaction* (London: T. Fischer Unwin, 1904), pp. 226, 237–43.

[5] L. T. Hobhouse, *Liberalism* (Oxford University Press, 1964), p. 67. See also L. T. Hobhouse, *Development and Purpose: An Essay Toward a Philosophy of Evolution* (London: Macmillan, 1913), p. 9.

[6] For an analysis in the same spirit, questioning whether, in the "liberal–communitarian" debate, "ontological" issues are closely tied to "advocacy issues," see Charles Taylor, "Cross-Purposes: The Liberal–Communitarian Debate," in Nancy L. Rosenblum (ed.), *Liberalism and the Moral Life* (Cambridge, MA: Harvard University Press, 1989), pp. 159–82.

[7] Gerald F. Gaus, "Green, Bosanquet and the Philosophy of Coherence," in S. G. Shanker and G. H. R. Parkinson (general editors), *The Routledge History of Philosophy*, vol. VII: *The Nineteenth Century*, C. L. Ten, ed. (London: Routledge, 1994), pp. 408–36.

[8] Hobhouse blames the "false and wicked" Hegelian theory of the state for the bombing of London. L. T. Hobhouse *The Metaphysical Theory of the State* (London: Allen & Unwin, 1918), p. 6.

[9] See L. T. Hobhouse, *The Elements of Social Justice* (London: Allen & Unwin, 1922), p. 172. Cf. John Dewey's remark that "we are in for some kind of socialism, call it by whatever name you please, and no matter what it will be called when it is realized." *Individualism, Old and New* (London: Allen & Unwin, 1931), pp. 111–12.

Idealism and organicism

Coherence and reality

In the opening paragraph of Bosanquet's greatest work, *The Philosophical Theory of the State*, he explains that a "philosophical treatment is the study of something as a whole and for its own sake."[10] Philosophy, he tells us, endeavors to establish "degrees of value, degrees of reality, degrees of completion and coherence."[11] At the core of Bosanquet's Idealism is the claim that what is most coherent and complete is truest, most valuable, and most real. This is apt to strike contemporary readers as at best odd, perhaps even bizarre. A point of entry that allows us to at least grasp, if not embrace, these core Idealist claims is their theory of knowledge.[12] It is widely accepted today that justified belief is a matter of coherence: the more consistent and comprehensive a system of belief, the better justified are the beliefs that compose it.[13] Contemporary coherence theorists, however, insist that coherence is the criterion of justified belief, but not of truth. A belief, it is typically said today, is true if it *corresponds* to, say, a fact in the world, whereas a belief is justified if it *coheres* with the rest of one's beliefs.[14] Idealists such as Bosanquet did not make this distinction: for them, coherence was the criterion of what beliefs are *justified* as well as what was true. Reality, they supposed, was coherent: it formed what Bosanquet often called a "cosmos" – "a system of members, such that every member, being *ex hypothesi* distinct, nevertheless contributes to the unity of the whole in virtue of the peculiarities which constitute its distinctness."[15] While a coherence theory of *truth* has its difficulties, we should note the Idealist conjunction of coherence theories of knowledge and truth does have at least one advantage over contemporary accounts that combine a coherence theory of knowledge with a correspondence theory of truth. It seems puzzling, at least *prima facie*, why the pursuit of coherent beliefs should lead to knowledge of the world, unless ultimately what is true

---

[10] Bernard Bosanquet, "The Philosophical Theory of the State," in *The Philosophical Theory of the State and Related Essays*, Gerald F. Gaus and William Sweet, eds. (Indianapolis: St. Augustine Press, 2000), p. 47.

[11] Ibid., p. 83.

[12] See Gaus, "Green, Bosanquet and the Philosophy of Coherence."

[13] Lawrence Bonjour, *The Structure of Empirical Knowledge* (Cambridge, MA: Harvard University Press, 1985); David O. Brink, *Moral Realism and the Foundations of Ethics* (Cambridge University Press, 1989).

[14] Bonjour, *The Structure of Empirical Knowledge*, p. 88.

[15] Bernard Bosanquet, *The Principle of Individuality and Value* (London: Macmillan, 1912), p. 37.

is what coheres – what forms a "cosmos" or a "world." If a belief is true if it corresponds to the world, it is not immediately obvious why we should seek coherence: how do we know that coherence in some way maps onto correspondence? Idealists avoided at least this problem by employing coherence as the criterion of both knowledge and truth, ensuring a sort of isomorphism between justified belief and truth.

In any event, once we take coherence as the criterion of truth, we can begin to grasp the Idealist claim that reality is a function of coherence: if what is true is a matter of what coheres this is because reality is ultimately coherent. And so, it is reasoned, what is most real is what is most coherent – coherent being understood here as a comprehensive system of interrelated elements. Thus, ultimately, only the Absolute – the entire cosmos – is real, for only it reaches full unity and comprehensiveness. Bosanquet understands an individual as a self-complete, coherent system: insofar as something is not complete, there is something outside of it, and so it is not fully comprehensive. Thus his claim that "in the ultimate sense there can only be one Individual."[16] As we proceed down from the Absolute, we encounter decreasing degrees of coherence, and so decreasing degrees of reality.

The social organism

It follows on Bosanquet's view that a society is more real than the humans that compose it. To call society an "organism" is to see it as a "whole of parts" – it is a system containing the persons that compose it.[17] It is crucial to keep in mind here Bosanquet's insistence that "it takes all sorts to make a world [or organism]."[18] A "true co-operative structure," he argued, "is never characterised by repetition, but always by identity in difference; it is the relation not of a screw to an exactly similar screw, but of the screw to the nut into which it fastens."[19] Societies are not crowds, the unity of which is explained by similarity of thoughts and motives, but systems of complementary volitions and capacities.[20] For example, if Smith wills to take a train to town, he must will "the existence of the railway, the truth, that is, of thousands of propositions the objects of other wills than his own, which must be true

---

[16] Ibid., p. 72.   [17] Ibid., p. 37.

[18] Ibid., p. 29; Bernard Bosanquet, *Social and International Ideals* (London: Macmillan, 1917), p. 133.

[19] Bosanquet, "The Philosophical Theory of the State," p. 80. See also Bernard Bosanquet, "The Relation of Sociology to Philosophy," in his *Science and Philosophy* (London: Allen & Unwin, 1927), p. 243; Bernard Bosanquet, *The Value and Destiny of the Individual* (London: Macmillan, 1913), pp. 49–50.

[20] See Bosanquet, "The Philosophical Theory of the State," ch. 8.

if it is to be possible for him to go to town by train ..."[21] A social organism, then, is a system of interlocking wills or minds, each implying the others. A social order is a "macrocosm constituted by microcosms ... [a] concrete universal."[22] In comparison to the persons that compose it, the social order is self-complete.[23]

The general will, Bosanquet goes on to argue, "is the whole assemblage of individual minds, considered as part of a working system, with parts corresponding to one another, and producing as a result a certain life for all these parts themselves."[24] Insofar as a person participates in this system of wills, and to the extent the system has achieved coherence, her will is implied by all the others, and she so wills the entire system – the general will.[25] To be sure, Bosanquet often insists that the common life of the members of a society leads them to adopt similar "organising principles," thus providing a common element to the general will.[26] Nevertheless, Bosanquet insists that the general will is constituted by the entire coherent system, and thus no single finite mind in the system can grasp it. Rather than being primarily revealed by reflection, the general will is more apt to be manifested in the workings of the life of the community and in its institutions.[27]

The complex order of the social whole

Unintended consequences, the division of labor, and the general will

This analysis of the general will leads us to the first aspect of Bosanquet's economic individualism. Because the general will is not a common volition, but a system of interconnected volitions, only the entire working of the system truly manifests the general will. And because the general will is primarily a coherent system of volitions, a person expresses the general will not by attempting an overall judgment about what is to be done by society, but by manifesting a will that meshes with others. The division of labor thus expresses the general will:

[21] Bernard Bosanquet, "The Notion of the General Will," in *The Philosophical Theory of the State and Related Essays*, pp. 306–7.
[22] Bosanquet, *The Principle of Individuality and Value*, p. 38.
[23] Bernard Bosanquet, "Hegel's Theory of the Political Organism," *Mind*, 7 (1898), 114.
[24] Bernard Bosanquet, "The Reality of the General Will," in Bernard Bosanquet (ed.), *Aspects of the Social Problem* (London: Macmillan, 1895), p. 325.
[25] Bosanquet, "The Notion of the General Will," pp. 307–8.
[26] Ibid., pp. 306ff.; Bosanquet, "The Reality of the General Will," pp. 323ff.; Bosanquet, *Social and International Ideals*, p. 292.
[27] Bosanquet, "The Reality of the General Will," pp. 325ff.; Bosanquet, "The Philosophical Theory of the State," ch. 11.

Each unit of the social organism has to embody his relations with the whole in his own particular work and will; and in order to do this the individual must have a strength and depth in himself proportional to and consisting of the relations he has to embody. Thus, if the individual in ancient Greece was like a centre to which a thousand threads of relation were attached, the individual in modern Europe might be compared to a centre on which there hang many, many millions. You cannot go back to a simple world, in which the same man can conquer all knowledge, or be versed in all practice. If all are, as we hope, to share in the gains achieved by each, it can only be through the gigantic and ever-increasing labour by which every worker takes account, in his work, of its import for all. There should not be castes of workers, if caste means a social division; there must be classes of workers, because the increasing material of human knowledge and endeavour will more and more consume the entire lives and thoughts of those upon whom its burden falls.[28]

For Bosanquet, then, a person is only on "solid ground" when he considers that part of the general will which reflects the "real necessities of his active life."[29] A person can have reasonably reliable knowledge of that part of the scheme of cooperation that centers on his own life and work. Here his judgments and actions are apt to fit coherently into the overall system, and thus manifest the general will. And this should not really be surprising. The ethic of "my station and its duties" has long been associated with Idealism;[30] and for Bosanquet one's station is focused on one's vocation or occupation.[31]

As one ascends to increasingly abstract perspectives, and so seeks a comprehensive evaluation of social institutions, one exceeds the limits of knowledge. In ways remarkably akin to Austrian economists such as F. A. Hayek – who are as resolutely individualistic as Bosanquet is organicist – Bosanquet insists that, because of the complexity of social life, "no one, not the greatest statesman or historical philosopher, has in his mind, even in theory, much less as a practical object, the real development in which his community is moving."[32] The very complexity and systemic character of the general will thus precludes comprehensive economic planning. Bosanquet explicitly criticizes "Economic Socialism" for failing to grasp that the social whole is composed of the complex interaction of highly differentiated parts rather than essentially identical modules that can be arranged according to a plan. "If you want to treat your social units as bricks in a wall or wheels in a machine, you cannot also and at the same time treat them as elements of an organism

---

[28] Bernard Bosanquet, "The Antithesis Between Individualism and Socialism Philosophically Considered," in *The Philosophical Theory of the State and Related Essays*, pp. 344–5.
[29] Bosanquet, "The Reality of the General Will," pp. 327–8.
[30] F. H. Bradley, *Ethical Studies*, 2nd edn. (Oxford: Clarendon Press, 1927), essay V.
[31] Bosanquet, "The Philosophical Theory of the State," pp. 226, 251n. 277.
[32] Bosanquet, "The Reality of the General Will," p. 328.

... Economic Socialism need not presuppose the social organism. It is, in appearance, a *substitute for* the life of that organism ..."[33] Thus, Bosanquet concludes, socialism arises out of a "blindness to the essential elements of the social organism, which can only exist as a structure of free individual wills, each entertaining the social purpose in an individual form appropriate to its structural position and organic functions."[34]

Two views of human society

F. A. Hayek contrasts two "ways of looking at the pattern of human activities which lead to very different conclusions concerning both its explanation and the possibilities of deliberately altering it."

The first [i.e. constructivist] view holds that human institutions will serve human purposes only if they have been deliberately designed for these purposes, often also that the fact that an institution exists is evidence of its having been created for a purpose, and always that we should so re-design society and its institutions that all our actions will be wholly guided by known purposes ...

The other view, which has slowly and gradually advanced since antiquity but for a time was almost entirely overwhelmed by the more glamorous constructivist view, was that the orderliness of society which greatly increased the effectiveness of individual action was not due solely to institutions and practices which had been invented or designed for that purpose but was largely due to a process described as "growth" and later as "evolution" ...[35]

It would be too simple to depict Bosanquet as a pure anti-constructivist evolutionist: he clearly indicates that institutions arise both by "growth" and by construction. "An institution may have grown up without special ordinance, or may have been called into existence by the public will."[36] Nevertheless, the direction of his thinking is to stress the limits of explicit construction. "[O]n the whole, we are to the structure of legal, political, and economic organisation like coral insects to a coral reef. All these things, and the body of science itself, are on one side natural products – that is to say, that, although conscious purpose works in them, the effect it produces is always part of a system which is more than any particular agent intended."[37] Thus for Bosanquet it is always "*as if*" institutions were established by a public will because they imply a social purpose –

---

[33] Bosanquet, "The Antithesis Between Individualism and Socialism Philosophically Considered," p. 330.

[34] Ibid., p. 334.

[35] F. A. Hayek, *Rules and Order*, vol. I of *Law, Legislation and Liberty: New Statement of the Liberal Principles of Justice and Political Economy* (Chicago: University of Chicago Press, 1973), pp. 8–9.

[36] Bosanquet, "The Philosophical Theory of the State," p. 266.

[37] Bosanquet, "The Reality of the General Will," pp. 328–9.

the organization of many minds implies a social purpose, but it does not follow that institutions are typically created to achieve these complex purposes.[38] The settled institutions of a society are, on this view, the concrete embodiments of that system of correlative ideas and volitions that comprise the general will, a system that is too complex to be fully grasped by any single person. This system of institutions constitutes the foundation of the ethical life of a society.[39] It would certainly seem to follow that, on Bosanquet's conception, we cannot understand all the purposes underlying our society's morality. Bosanquet would certainly concur with Hayek: "If we stopped doing everything for which we do not know the reasons ... we would probably soon be dead."[40] To seek to ignore the institutions of the common life and substitute an imposed conception of the pubic will is to follow Plato in destroying "the social organism by trusting to machinery, instead of morality."[41] "I confess," Bosanquet wrote, "that I believe modern Economic Socialism to rest *in part* on this ineradicable confusion. 'We want a general good life; let us make a law that there shall be a general good life.' "[42]

Another aspect of Bosanquet's anti-constructivism is his anti-rationalism. Michael Oakeshott[43] has, famously, distinguished two types of knowledge: practical knowledge, or the knowledge of an art, and theoretical knowledge.[44] Practical knowledge is a sort of detailed knowing that is gained through exposure to practice and experience; because of its complexity and its role in specific practices, it typically can be only partially articulated. It is, for example, the knowledge of a true cook, who knows what to do but cannot fully describe and codify it. This can be contrasted to theoretical knowledge, which takes the form of abstract principles or theories that can be codified in written form. Such theoretical knowledge is an abstraction from practice: like a cookbook, it captures and codifies some of the cook's knowledge, but at a cost of ignoring the subtlety and detail informing actual practices. Now,

[38] Bosanquet, "The Philosophical Theory of the State," p. 266.
[39] Ibid., ch. 11.
[40] F. A. Hayek, *The Fatal Conceit: The Errors of Socialism*, W. W. Bartley III, ed., (University of Chicago Press, 1988), p. 68.
[41] Bosanquet, "The Antithesis Between Individualism and Socialism Philosophically Considered," p. 332.
[42] Ibid., p. 335.
[43] Michael Oakeshott, "Rationalism in Politics," in his *Rationalism in Politics and Other Essays* (Indianapolis: Liberty Press, [1962] 1991).
[44] For discussions of Oakeshott, with special reference to his place in the liberal tradition, see Kirk Koerner, *Liberalism and its Critics* (London: Croom Helm, 1985); Paul Franco, *The Political Philosophy of Michael Oakeshott* (New Haven, CT: Yale University Press, 1990); John W. Chapman, "Justice, Freedom and Property," in J. Roland Pennock and John W. Chapman (eds.), *NOMOS XXII: Property* (New York University Press, 1980), pp. 289–324.

Oakeshott argues, a rationalist is one who sees theoretical knowledge as the only true knowledge: what cannot be translated into a theory or formula is not real knowledge. Socialism, and many varieties of liberalism, display a distinctly rationalistic frame of mind. The belief that one can "model" the economy and so plan and guide it, or develop a "social theory" that will allow one to organize social life in a conscious and deliberate way, all are manifestations of the rationalist temper. Such an attitude is manifestly related to constructivism: if one can gain theoretical knowledge of society, one can reconstruct it on a rational plan. Bosanquet rejects such rationalism:

> Books cannot contain knowledge in a perfectly vital [and real] form; they are rather instruments or materials of knowledge than knowledge itself. In this science differs from art; poetry, for example, is destroyed if we destroy the particular form it has in a book; but knowledge hardly exists for us till we have destroyed the form which it has in a book. It must be recast in the intelligence, – that is, interpreted and criticised bit by bit till we have made it all of one tissue with our own vital experience – our experience of the matter in question in its most real form, whatever that be, whether given in observation only, or in practice as well. When this is accomplished, and not before, the knowledge is really knowledge – that is, present as intelligence in our view of life and nature, and not as a recollection of something printed in a book. Such intelligence, however wide-reaching, always begins at home, both in social matters and abstract science; there is always some point where we are more especially in contact with reality, and from which our ideas lead by analogy. In all social matters this point is furnished by our own necessarily dominant ideas prescribed by our individual life.[45]

Because true knowledge starts off from one's own life, the dispersed knowledge of individuals operating from their own positions in the social whole is more vital and real than the abstract knowledge of the social planner. This is not to say that there cannot be abstract knowledge of social conditions, but this knowledge is made real and vital when it is applied by individuals in their actual life in the working of the whole.

Bosanquet, then, must be viewed as an anti-constructivist insofar as he insists on the importance of the "unconscious or semi-conscious logic of life in contact with our neighbours,"[46] the vitality and reality of knowledge applied to actual positions in the whole, and his typical complaint that socialism is informed by the conceit that general moral improvement can be arrived at by legislation. Interestingly, he also puts great store in evolutionary competition as the path to social improvement. In social animals, Bosanquet argues, "[t]he struggle for existence has, in short, become a struggle for a place in the community; and these

---

[45] Bosanquet, "The Reality of the General Will," pp. 331–2.
[46] Ibid., p. 330.

places are reserved for the individuals which in the highest degree possess the cooperative qualities demanded by the circumstances."[47] In human society too, he insists, natural selection occurs; more than that, "[n]o social selection ... can be moral except natural selection in the large sense ..."[48] The crux of this particularly human natural selection is a competition for "success in leaving offspring in the widest sense."[49] "[B]roadly speaking, the co-operative individual, as demanded by civilised life, can only be produced in the family"; hence the crux of the competition in modern societies is to "realise the conditions of true family life in its moral and material senses."[50] Thus, it would seem, social progress occurs mainly through this competition between families to produce successful social cooperators.

> If Socialism means the improvement of society by society, we are going on that track more or less to-day, as civilised society has always gone, and the collective organisation of certain branches of production is a matter open to discussion with a view to its consequences. But if Socialism means the total suppression of the personal struggle for existence ... then I think that it really is in hopeless conflict with the universal postulates of the struggle for existence and natural selection, as justly interpreted of human society.[51]

Bosanquet follows the path against which Hayek warns – an evolutionary account that focuses on the selection of individuals (or families) rather than institutions and practices.[52] My concern here is not the adequacy of Bosanquet's evolutionary analysis; rather, I wish to stress that his reliance on natural selection as a prime method for "the improvement of society by society" indicates his general anti-constructivist approach to society and its improvement. And this approach diminishes the scope for the sort of large-scale planned interventions that are usually associated with communitarian and new liberal political programs. Moreover, it seems very plausible indeed for an organic communitarian such as Bosanquet to be a proponent of "an automatic system" of adjustment and a critic of "complete authoritative supervision."[53] Not only is the whole complex, but an Idealist such as Bosanquet has reason to suppose that insofar as individuals are animated by reason and morality, the working of the whole tends towards completion and coherence. Socialism, on this view, manifests not only a conceit – that the purposes of the community can be brought to consciousness and planned – but a lack of confidence in the community

[47] Bernard Bosanquet, "Socialism and Natural Selection," in his *Aspects of the Social Problem*, p. 294.
[48] Ibid., p. 299.   [49] Ibid., p. 298.   [50] Ibid., pp. 299–300.
[51] Ibid., p. 306.
[52] Hayek, *Rules and Order*, p. 23.
[53] Bosanquet, *Social and International Ideals*, p. 220.

to improve itself. Thus Bosanquet's charge that the real root of "Economic Socialism" is a type of individualism: socialism is a substitute for the largely automatic workings of the organic whole, "intended to operate on the egoistic motives of individuals for the good of the whole, which cannot, it is assumed, be attained by the moral power of the social purpose."[54] As Bosanquet saw it, the "Socialistic attitude of mind ... almost amounts to a dread of all processes that chiefly depend on the socialisation of the will."[55]

Private property and social purpose

Private property and the organic whole

This fundamental criticism – that "economic socialism" presupposes "moral individualism" – is nicely brought out in Bosanquet's attack on socialism's rejection of private property. For Bosanquet:

Private property is not simply an arrangement for meeting successive momentary wants as they arise ... It is wholly different in principle, as adult or responsible life differs from child-life, which is irresponsible. It rests on the principle that the inward or moral life cannot be a unity unless the outward life – the dealing with things – is also a unity. In dealing with things this means a causal unity, i.e. that what we do at one time, or in one relation, should affect what we are able to do at another time, or in another relation.[56]

In this essentially Hegelian account,[57] Bosanquet depicts private property as required to express and realize the self – it provides a means for realizing the individual will.[58] In order for property to serve this function, it must, *first*, be "very responsive to the character and capacity of the owner"[59] – it must be up to you to decide what you are going to do with it – and, *second*, it must allow for planning and reflect the unity of a life. This is how a property-owner is distinguished from a child,

who gets what is thought necessary for him quite apart from all his previous action. So too with dress. The dress of a young child does not reflect his own character at all, but that of his mother. If he spoils his things, that makes no difference to him (unless as a punishment): he has what is thought proper to him at every given moment ... What he is enabled to have and to do in no way

[54] Bosanquet, "The Antithesis Between Individualism and Socialism Philosophically Considered," p. 330.
[55] Ibid., p. 342.
[56] Bernard Bosanquet, "The Principle of Private Property," in *The Philosophical Theory of the State and Related Essays*, pp. 349–50.
[57] Jeremy Waldron, *The Right to Private Property* (Oxford: Clarendon Press, 1988).
[58] Bosanquet, "The Principle of Private Property," p. 348.
[59] Ibid., p. 351.

expresses his own previous action or character, except in as far as he is put in training by his parents for grown-up life ... To such an agent the world is miraculous; things are not for him adjusted, organised, contrived; things simply *come* as in a fairy tale.[60]

Given this, the socialist's skepticism about private property translates into a skepticism that individual wills expressed through the use of private property will serve the common good. If, after all, one was convinced that individual wills were informed by the general will, then their outward action in the form of private property would also tend to serve the common good. "Morality consists in the presence of some element of the social purpose as a moving idea before the individual mind; that is, in short, in the social constitution of the individual will."[61] But to doubt that the general will informs the wills of individuals is to doubt the existence of the social organism: to say that a society has an organic character is to say that it "permeates its members."[62] Consequently, on Bosanquet's view, the socialist rejects private property because she rejects the idea that the moral purposes of society are reflected in the realized lives of its members; instead, she supposes an essentially egoistic individual who will only act on the common good if ordered to do so:

Economic Socialism is an arrangement for getting the social purpose carried out just [sic] not by its own force, but by the force of those compulsory motives or sanctions which are at the command of the public power.

... In this point of view at least it naturally rests on Moral Individualism. All compulsion through materialistic necessities of individuals is morally individual-istic.[63]

This is a perfectly coherent – indeed in some ways compelling – communitarian position. If we accept that (i) organic wholes are complex, and cannot be adequately grasped in a single consciousness; (ii) individual human beings are members of the whole in the sense that their lives are informed by the social will – they stand for an aspect of the general will, an aspect informed by their particular location in the complex system, then it seems plausible to conclude (iii) social purposes are best expressed through individual human wills, and (iv) such effective expression requires private property. In this light, "communitarian" or "holist" philosophies that espouse socialism not only manifest an overconfidence that any group – even a "committee of the whole" –

[60] Ibid., p. 349.
[61] Bosanquet, "The Antithesis Between Individualism and Socialism Philosophically Considered," p. 328.
[62] Bosanquet, "Hegel's Theory of the Political Organism," 5.
[63] Bosanquet, "The Antithesis Between Individualism and Socialism Philosophically Considered," pp. 329–330.

can grasp social purposes,[64] but seem also to be based on the supposition that the organic unity of society is deeply flawed: the wills and purposes of property-owning individuals reflect merely their own selfish personal or class interests. But if so, then it is the *lack* of a general will expressed in the lives of individuals that characterizes socialism; socialism seeks to make up for the lack of a social will in individual wills by imposing a social will. Thus Bosanquet advances the interesting thesis that economic socialism is incompatible with "Moral Socialism" – "the view which makes Society the moral essence of the Individual."[65]

Capitalism and the social good

Bosanquet insists that the function of private property – allowing individuals to express their own will, and in so doing an aspect of the social will – cannot be achieved through property rights that greatly hedge the range of decisions open to the owner. "[L]imited ownership is objectionable *per se*."[66] He thus points to reasons against drastically limiting bequest or alienation.[67] More importantly, Bosanquet insists that the benefits of a private property regime are only fully secured when ownership is united with management. "[T]he real utility of systems of ownership is to promote management which is efficient, and efficient in view of all the requirements concerned, which may be summed up in the two extremes, . . . the rights of individuals and the public good."[68] The divorce of ownership and management, Bosanquet argues, endangers this. Our current system, he argues, "has run itself, within a framework of social guidance, by means of the various motives and ideals of individuals, conditioned largely by the need and desire of individuals for profits and earnings . . . [I]t is economic necessity and desire that force the system to work – *i.e.*, force the things that on the whole are wanted to be produced."[69] Under capitalism the "interest of ownership" is to adjust production to "public need":[70] private ownership is a more or less decentralized automatic mechanism for promoting the general will. Bosanquet is especially alive to the creative role of the businessman in this system:

---

[64] See here C. B. Macpherson's notion of participatory economic planning in *The Life and Times of Liberal Democracy* (Oxford University Press, 1977). For a useful discussion, see Chapman, "Justice, Freedom and Property."

[65] Bosanquet, "The Antithesis Between Individualism and Socialism Philosophically Considered," p. 326.

[66] Bosanquet, "The Principle of Private Property," p. 351.

[67] Ibid.

[68] Bosanquet, *Social and International Ideals*, p. 213.

[69] Ibid., p. 219.   [70] Ibid., p. 221.

It must be borne in mind that in industry creative management is everything. One man will make a fortune for himself and his employers, and deal liberally with his workpeople; another will sweat his workpeople, starve himself, and ruin his employers. There is far too much tendency to speak as if business consisted in cheating – the game of grab, we hear. The essence of business is creation.[71]

The upshot of this analysis, Bosanquet argues, is that "the fundamental difficulties which attach in principle to popular Collectivism centre round the question of management without effective ownership":[72]

The want of understanding between ownership and management, which characterises a limited company to-day, is not removed but enormously aggravated under the Collectivist scheme. The ownership, being generalized, is in practice abolished. There is no longer anywhere any special interest of ownership attached to the success or utility of special industrial concerns.[73]

Interestingly, Bosanquet indicates that a planned economy could perhaps only solve the problem of adjusting production and demand by seeking to "imitate or reproduce" the operation of a private property economy.[74]

Socialism and demoralization of property

Emerging from Bosanquet's analysis is not just a communitarian justification of private property, but a distinctively capitalist order in which property rights are held in the means of production. To be sure, even in private property economies the crucial nexus between ownership and management is weakened as private firms become more bureaucratic, but Bosanquet is emphatic that these problems are aggravated, not mitigated, by socialist management. This raises a related objection: by restricting private property to consumption items, socialists undermine the moral purposes of private property.[75] "This is a very serious matter indeed ... In modern Collectivism," he argues, "the accent is laid on free consumption for all. Responsibility for production is not with the producer, but with public authority: there is nowhere any check to the

---

[71] Ibid., p. 222.   [72] Ibid., p. 220.   [73] Ibid., p. 221.   [74] Ibid., p. 219.

[75] The new liberals, for the most part, ranged from indifference to mild hostility to private property in the means of production. Although, for the most part, their goal was to "reform" rather than abolish private property, it is a characteristic of the new liberals that they do not see private property in the means of production as a core liberal commitment. See G. F. Gaus, "Public and Private Interests in Liberal Political Economy, Old and New," in S. I. Benn and G. F. Gaus, (eds.), *Public and Private in Social Life* (New York: St. Martin's Press, 1983), pp. 203–4 and G. F. Gaus, *The Modern Liberal Theory of Man* (London: Groom Helm, 1983), pp. 235–43. See also Michael Freeden, *The New Liberalism: An Ideology of Social Reform* (Oxford: Clarendon Press, 1978), p. 46.

suggestion that all income is for enjoyment alone. Property bears no plain indication of an instrumental function . . ."[76]

"This clean cut between consumption and production endangers the whole character of private life."[77] First, by guaranteeing to each her consumption without tying it to her previous actions (saving, investment), socialism reduces each once again to the status of a child: consumption items miraculously appear, with no clear tie to their causal history. Even if, as with a child, one is coerced to work and then fed, one does not appreciate the link between past action and present consumption, so that one cannot act according to a "plan of life."[78] The function of property in unifying an adult life is thus undermined. Individuals become demoralized; they lose the capacity for a unified life expressing a purpose. Second, by severing the nexus between investment and consumption, a socialist conception of private property – restricted to consumption goods – undermines the understanding that one's holdings are creative and productive, and so serve a social function. This literally de-moralizes one's holdings: instead of understanding them as part of a social purpose aiming at the general will, they become nothing but items for egoistic gratification, again leading to Bosanquet's argument that socialism presupposes (and encourages) not organicism but egoism. "The resources of the state may be more and more directly devoted to the individual's material well-being, while the individual is becoming less and less concerned about any well-being except his own."[79]

Although these arguments are not common, they are cogent, at least in the context of communitarianism. Admittedly to many they will seem naive: if individuals are selfish, they will use their property to pursue individual interests rather than express social purposes. But, again, this really constitutes an acknowledgment of Bosanquet's thesis: the socialist impulse is rooted in a skepticism about the social will or, in contemporary terms, doubts about the deep embeddedness of individuals. If communities are coherent expressions of a way of living (rather than a mere association of individuals) and if individuals are indeed deeply embedded in this way of life, then the wills of citizens will be informed by it, and thus each person's attempt at realizing his purposes will also advance social purposes. As Bosanquet stresses, in such a community a private property market economy allows individuals to express that part of social will intimated to them.

[76] Bosanquet, *Social and International Ideals*, p. 223.
[77] Ibid.
[78] Bosanquet, "The Antithesis Between Individualism and Socialism Philosophically Considered," p. 339.
[79] Bernard Bosanquet, "Some Socialistic Features of Ancient Societies," in his *Essays and Addresses*, 2nd edn. (London: Swan Sonnenschein, 1891), p. 70.

A communitarian critique of the welfare state

The welfare state and dependency

Most of Bosanquet's criticisms were directed at radical forms of social-ism that sought to displace "economic individualism" with central planning or abolish the private ownership of the means of production. As such, one might conclude that, while he was a critic of socialist planning, this criticism does not apply to the new liberal welfare state that (i) retains a basically capitalist economy, but one supervised by the public (i.e., government) for the public good and (ii) does not rely on capitalism to allocate distributive shares, but supplements market dis-tributions with direct state provision of welfare.[80] And this provision, it must be added, is given as a matter of justice to all citizens that qualify.[81] This interpretation of Bosanquet is reinforced by the observation that he was almost as much of a critic of *laissez-faire*[82] or, as he sometimes described it, "administrative nihilism,"[83] as he was of socialism.

Nevertheless, such an interpretation would be quite mistaken: Bosan-quet was an adamant critic of the modern welfare state. As is well known, Helen and Bernard Bosanquet were leading figures in the Charity Organisation Society – a favorite target of the new liberals – which emphasized the importance of non-governmental social work and often opposed uniform government programs for aiding the poor. Bosanquet saw the Poor Law of the nineteenth century as "socialistic" and "lax," producing great evils. "I should say that what is wanted is to lessen the amount of the Poor Law assistance; to make the administra-tion not more lax but more strict; not more lenient, but more harsh"[84] – hardly a new liberal view of the matter.[85] To a large extent this debate between the Bosanquets and the new liberals focuses on the tendency of "charity"-produced dependence. Bosanquet insisted that state provision of "charity" is apt to create dependent characters and ruin lives. "There is moral evil – the confusion of responsibility between the individual and

---

[80] See Gaus, "Public and Private Interests in Liberal Political Economy, Old and New."
[81] Hobhouse, *The Elements of Social Justice.*
[82] Bernard Bosanquet, "Individual and Social Reform," in his *Essays and Addresses*, p. 39; Bernard Bosanquet, "Liberty and Legislation," in his *The Civilization of Christendom* (London: Swan Sonnenschein, 1899), pp. 361, 382.
[83] Bosanquet, "The Philosophical Theory of the State, pp. 25, 92. See also the Editors' Introduction to *The Philosophical Theory of the State and Related Essays*, p. xxix.
[84] Bosanquet, "The Antithesis Between Individualism and Socialism Philosophically Considered," pp. 338–9.
[85] Peter Clarke, *Liberals and Social Democrats* (Cambridge University Press, 1978), pp. 118–27; Peter Weiler, "The New Liberalism of L. T. Hobhouse," *Victorian Studies*, 16 (December 1972), pp. 144–5.

Society as a whole."[86] Bosanquet once again stresses that those who receive their sustenance as gift – dependent on the continuing decisions of others – are demoralized and lose their adult personalities:

the forward look to the unity of life is abandoned, and an adult has accepted the status of a child. So much greater is the need to narrow, instead of widening, the sphere of such slavish dependence. To deny, in principle, the need for a permanent provision for possible work and self-expression is to deny the root-principle of human nature, and the connection of inward and outward morality, or of character and competence. It is also most important to note that the denial of property gives an enormous impulse to animal selfishness. It declares that my share is not for me to work with, to contrive and organise with, to express myself completely with, but simply to meet my wants from day to day. The surplus over the necessary is therefore to be spent on passing enjoyment – a horrible result.[87]

In contrast, although new liberals such as Hobhouse recognized that it was essential for the individual to retain "responsibility for supporting his own household," this was held to be consistent with provision of a uniform "civic minimum."[88] Hobhouse's position, however, is not as far from Bosanquet's as appearances suggest. Hobhouse's civic minimum is an assurance that "every citizen should have the full means of earning by socially useful labour so much material support as experience proves to be the necessary basis of a healthy, civilized, existence."[89] He stresses that the civic minimum paid to a contributing member of the community must be his "true and full property with unlimited right of disposal."[90] Hobhouse explicitly contrasts such contributors to "dependents" – "the helpless, the defective, the idler."[91] Contributors have a claim based on justice for a decent existence whereas dependents "are a charge upon the humanity of the community" and are provided with an allowance "for the specific purpose of meeting their needs."[92]

The "width and depth" of the general will and the limits of government policy

However, Bosanquet's objection to the new liberal welfare state is not simply based on his conviction that government-provided welfare produces dependency;[93] it follows closely from his communitarianism.

---

[86] Bosanquet, "The Antithesis Between Individualism and Socialism Philosophically Considered," p. 340.
[87] Bosanquet, "The Principle of Private Property," pp. 354–5.
[88] Hobhouse, *The Elements of Social Justice*, p. 174; Hobhouse, *Liberalism*, pp. 95–7.
[89] Hobhouse, *Liberalism*, pp. 96–7.
[90] Hobhouse, *The Elements of Social Justice*, p. 138.
[91] Ibid.   [92] Ibid., pp. 138–9.
[93] Bernard Bosanquet, "Character and its Bearing on Social Causation," in *Aspects of the Social Problem*, pp. 103–17.

According to a leading contemporary theorist of the welfare state, "(1) The welfare state intervenes (a) in a market economy (b) to meet certain of people's basic needs (c) through relatively direct means ... (2) The welfare state is a system of compulsory, collective, and largely non-discretionary welfare provision."[94] Understood thus, Bosanquet presents a communitarian critique of the welfare state. A non-discretionary collective mechanism to satisfy needs does not, he maintains, take seriously the complexity and life of the social organism.

We have seen throughout that Bosanquet insists on the complexity of society and the general will, and this leads him to criticize "Economic Socialism" as an impossible scheme to grasp the entire general will and legislate its requirements. Bosanquet advances the same criticism of attempts by government to take over the task of ensuring the social welfare. Current notions of politics – which place the government as the sole effective provider of social welfare – "fail to appreciate the width and depth which belong to the real or general will in a modern nation."[95] The core argument here hangs on Bosanquet's fundamental claim that "[n]o society can be constituted of similars" or "[i]t takes all sorts to make a world."[96] Suppose we adopt a thoroughly communitarian view in which the self is a reflection of part of society: its essence is the specific nexus of social relations in which it is enmeshed. On this view a community is not a collection of essentially similar individuals, but a complex network of persons, each differentiated and incomplete, forming a communal life and a general will. Now because on this complex communitarian view individual persons are highly differentiated, legislation that treats them as essentially similar will typically be inadequate. It will especially be inadequate when it is seeking to help those individuals. That is, when the legislation is treating all as similar to obtain some social goal – say all are accorded an equal right to be unmolested as they walk down the street – it ignores a great deal of the differences between them, but nevertheless helps secure the social goal of safe streets. But if we are trying to assist these individuals, and if because of their various roles in the community they occupy highly differentiated positions and so have very different concerns and problems, legislative attempts to help them are particularly apt to fail. If each has a statutory right to the same treatment but each has very different characteristics and problems, social welfare will not be advanced. "We have found that charity cannot be in 'ironclad' form, as the Americans

---

[94] Robert E. Goodin, *Reasons for Welfare* (Princeton University Press, 1988), pp. 11–12.
[95] Bosanquet, *Social and International Ideals*, p. 127.
[96] Ibid., p. 133.

say; it cannot be purely statutory, though it may co-operate with a statutory committee."[97]

Given this communitarian analysis, Bosanquet quite reasonably upholds the importance of individual casework over statutory guarantees. Bosanquet tells his caseworkers, "Individualise the case; don't classify" – "you must subordinate classification to individualisation."[98] Bosanquet repeatedly stresses just how difficult it is to obtain the specific knowledge of circumstances needed to assist another person effectively. Although it was easy for the new liberals to caricature Bosanquet and the Charity Organisation Society as moralizing middle-class busy-bodies attempting to tell the poor what is good for them, the Idealist and Charity Organisation Society claim that the social welfare cannot usually be advanced by government "machinery"[99] coheres better with the communitarian analysis of society than the new liberal view that government-provided non-discretionary uniform welfare provision manifests the social solidarity of the organic community. As Bosanquet reiterates, plans to obtain social welfare by uniform legislation presuppose that individuals are similar units (and so can be treated as "bricks in a wall") rather than highly differentiated elements, with different needs, in an almost incredibly complex social organism.[100] Consequently, in a complex community an enormous part of the task of securing social welfare falls outside the competency of government. Thus Bosanquet tells us that "[w]e have come to see that the 'general will' ... means the achievement of social welfare in an immense diversity of ways, and with a degree of skill and detailed knowledge which is not only not present in the electors – that is the very point of representative government – but is moreover, as concerns enormous areas of public interests, not in the representatives themselves."[101]

Again, this is not to say that Bosanquet defends "administrative nihilism." Because of his stress on the inadequacy of our knowledge of the social whole, Bosanquet puts great faith in localities as the chief source of conscious government attempts to promote the general welfare:

we look forward to a society organised in convenient districts, in which men and women, pursuing their different callings, will live together and care for one another ... These men and women will work together in councils and on committees; and while fearlessly employing stringent legal powers in the public

[97] Ibid., p. 113.   [98] Ibid., pp. 164–5.
[99] Collini, *Liberalism and Sociology*, p. 142.
[100] Bosanquet, "The Antithesis Between Individualism and Socialism Philosophically Considered," p. 329.
[101] Bosanquet, *Social and International Ideals*, p. 124. See Peter Nicholson, *The Political Philosophy of the British Idealists* (Cambridge University Press, 1990).

interest, yet will be aware, by sympathy and experience, of the extreme flexibility and complication of modern life, which responds so unexpectedly to the most simple interference . . .[102]

Being and becoming fit to contribute to society

In addition to the by-now-familiar problems dealing with the complexity of the general will, we should note another tension between communitarianism and the welfare state. In a communitarian theory such as Bosanquet's, an individual's identity and value is largely a function of his or her role in the community. Thus on this view "[a] right is a power claimed and recognized as contributory to the common good."[103] One can then only have a right to welfare if this promotes the common good. It may seem that given Bosanquet's understanding of an organic community as one in which diverse individuals each play unique roles in articulating social purposes, he would grant that since each person performs a unique function, supporting each person's welfare does indeed contribute to the common good, hence there is arguably a right to welfare provision. But two considerations lead Bosanquet to reject such a right. First, as we saw in the analysis of Bosanquet's views on private property and the market, the market signals to one what functions are required. Because no official or agency has a synoptic view of the general will, central authorities cannot typically direct people to useful functions. As rule, then, market demand is a reasonable – though of course not perfect – indicator of whether one is performing a useful social and economic function. Being responsive to the demands and needs of others is how one becomes fit to serve the common good; hence systems that reward one regardless of one's responsiveness undermine one's incentive to serve social purposes. Second, although a perfect organic whole would be characterized by differentiation rather than repetition, and so each person would have a unique function, Bosanquet clearly does not think that actual societies display perfect

[102] Bosanquet, "Individual and Social Reform," p. 45.
[103] T. H. Green, *Lectures on the Principles of Political Obligation and Other Writings*, Paul Harris and John Morrow, eds. (Cambridge University Press, 1986), p. 79; Bosanquet, "The Philosophical Theory of the State," pp. 193ff. See also William Sweet, *Idealism and Rights: The Social Ontology of Human Rights in the Political Thought of Bernard Bosanquet* (New York: University Press of America, 1997), esp. ch. 2; Nicholson, *The Political Philosophy of the British Idealists*, pp. 83–95; A. J. M. Milne, *The Social Philosophy of English Idealism* (London: Allen & Unwin, 1962), pp. 271–5; Ann Cacoullos, *Thomas Hill Green: Philosopher of Rights* (New York: Twayne, 1974); Gaus, "Green, Bosanquet and the Philosophy of Coherence," p. 429. This is not to deny that the development of one's capacities may itself be a contribution to the common good; see Gaus, *The Modern Liberal Theory of Man*, pp. 55ff.

organic unity. Only the Absolute is perfectly coherent; as we descend from it we encounter increasing degrees of incoherence. Now it seems that one of the ways in which actual societies fall far short of organic unity is that there is genuine repetition: some people, Bosanquet believes, make no special contribution to the world – their contributions are not unique, simply repeating the contributions of others.[104] Given this, we cannot say that, necessarily, everyone is providing a unique contribution to the common good. Some may not be providing a distinctive social service: everything they do may be done better by others. If so, it would not seem that they would have a right to support. It would be an error, I think, to see this conclusion as an idiosyncratic feature of Bosanquet's Idealism. Surely a general characteristic of communitarian justifications of rights – as powers "claimed and recognized as contributory to the common good" – is that they do not provide claims for people who refuse to, or are unable to, fulfill a social function and so are claiming a right independent of their social identity. As one commentator observes (with some uneasiness), it seems that on Bosanquet's view, "if one had no station or function, there would be no obligation for a community to act as if that being had any value whatsoever."[105]

The complexity of political theory

Both liberals and their critics have commonly believed that a "collectivistic," "communitarian," or "organic" social metaphysics is anti-liberal, in the sense that it leads away from traditional liberal political prescriptions.[106] I do not want to suggest that all these thinkers have simply been mistaken, and that liberalism has no relation to an individualistic account of society. But the relations between individualism and liberalism, and between communitarianism and, say, socialism or welfarism, are altogether more complex than most commentators have indicated.

---

[104] See Bosanquet, *Science and Philosophy*, p. 234; Bosanquet, "Philosophical Theory of the State," p. 175.

[105] Sweet, *Idealism and Rights*, pp. 119–20. Sweet seeks to undermine, or at least soften, this interpretation of Bosanquet, for which he admits "there is certainly some evidence" (p. 119).

[106] See G. F. Gaus, "Liberalism at the End of the Century," *Journal of Political Ideologies*, 5 (2000), 179–99. See also Karl Popper, *The Open Society and its Enemies* (London: Routledge, 1945); Hayek, *Rules and Order*, p. 53; Stephen A. Holmes, *The Anatomy of Antiliberalism* (Cambridge, MA: Harvard University Press, 1993); Hobhouse, *Liberalism*; A. F. Mummery and J. A. Hobson, *The Physiology of Industry* (New York: Kelly and Millman, 1956), p. 106; Roberto Mangabeira Unger, *Knowledge and Politics* (New York: Free Press, 1975); Michael J. Sandel, *Democracy's Discontent* (Cambridge, MA: Harvard University Press, 1996); Philip Pettit, *The Common Mind* (Oxford University Press, 1993).

Certainly these relations are not to be understood in terms of inferences or entailments. An appropriate metaphor is perhaps a stream running down a hill; if nothing is done to prevent it, it will follow the easiest course. But it is possible to construct dikes and dig channels, so that the stream may end up on just the opposite side to which it would have "naturally" flowed. So too with social metaphysics and political theories. If one starts out with a collectivist social metaphysics, it seems very easy indeed to end up with deeply illiberal conclusions – such as the claim that we are all part of a common mind, and in some way we should be subservient to it. But, as we see in the case of Bosanquet, if one also adopts an epistemology according to which it is very hard to come to know the general will, and add that the general will so deeply informs individuals that their wills express the social will, then a whole set of arrangements associated with individualism – the market, private property, a limited sphere for politics, and a critique of the welfare state – follow from a deeply communitarian outlook.

Not only does Bosanquet's theory show us the complex ways in which a social metaphysics, an epistemology, a psychology, and economic proposals can be integrated, but he provides a lesson – or perhaps a challenge – to communitarians. For Bosanquet insists that if one really takes seriously a holistic approach, and appreciates the complexity of social systems, the limits of our knowledge, and the deep ways in which individuals are "constituted" by their social relations, then "automatic" adjustments such as the market are more genuinely holistic than conscious adjustments such as state planning. Bosanquet, I think, convincingly demonstrates that whatever the communitarian critics of liberalism hope to achieve, it is not at all clear that they will be freed from that aspect of liberalism they probably most dislike – a private-property based market order. And for much the same reasons, he gives powerful reasons for "non-individualist" liberals to reexamine their supposition that a more communitarian liberalism is inherently a less economically individualistic one.

7 The new liberalism and the rejection of utilitarianism

D. Weinstein

Introduction

The new liberalism and nineteenth-century British utilitarianism were estranged conceptual cousins but they were conceptual cousins nonetheless. Indeed, they were deeply intimate members of an extended conceptual family despite their professed and inflated differences which analytical liberal theorizing in recent decades has only further inflated, as much because of its retrospective amnesia as anything else.

T. H. Green, L. T. Hobhouse, and D. G. Ritchie were pivotal figures in the making of the new liberalism. Yet, as we shall see, their reworking of nineteenth-century liberalism was much less than a thorough reworking. Their debt to British utilitarianism was considerably richer than is now commonly assumed. We should be unsurprised, then, if their respective versions of new liberalism turn out to be fundamentally consequentialist if not fundamentally utilitarian.

This chapter argues that the new liberalism of Green, Hobhouse, and Ritchie was fundamentally consequentialist. For all three, the good was self-realization requiring maximization in the sense of promotion. And for all three, maximizing self-realization fortunately also maximized happiness as well because self-realization and happiness were fused so intractably. Finally, for all three, self-realization was also a common good insofar as each person's self-realization fostered everyone else's, making the new liberalism also part communitarianism. The maximization of self-realization was nevertheless an authentically liberal goal insofar as it was distribution-sensitive by aiming at *everyone's* self-realization. And insofar as the pursuit of this goal was also constrained by respect for stringent moral rights, we have all-the-more reason to honor the authenticity of the new liberalism's liberal credentials.

More is at stake here than the merely historical relationship between nineteenth-century utilitarianism and the new liberalism. Also at stake here is the very meaning of consequentialism. Just as some recent theorists have made a caricature out of liberalism in the name of

communitarianism, others have made a caricature out of consequentialism in the name of liberalism. In truth, consequentialism, as much as
liberalism, is conceptually kaleidoscopic and protean. Thus, some have
tried to defend consequentialism by laboring to accommodate it with
liberalism, much like others have rushed to defend liberalism by infusing
it with communitarianism. And if liberal consequentialism, no less than
communitarian liberalism, is a possible hybrid, then so might a liberalism that is as consequentialist as it is communitarian be one too. The
new liberalism was just such a hybrid.

Self-realization as a moral vocation

For new liberals, moral self-realization was the "unconditional good."[1]
According to Green, realizing our "moral capacity" is "an end desirable
in itself."[2] It is the "fulfilment of man's vocation as a moral being" as the
devoting of ourselves to the "work of developing the perfect character"
in ourselves and others.[3] It is the "attainment of a certain type of
character or some realization of the possibilities of man, not pleasure, as
the end by relation to which goodness or value is to be measured."[4]
Realizing ourselves morally consists in cultivating, exhibiting, and
finding permanent satisfaction in the will to be good.

As our "highest good," moral self-realization is equally a matter of
"free morality."[5] Realizing oneself morally means being fully free by
having more than just the enabling "positive power or capacity of doing
or enjoying something worth doing or enjoying" but actually "doing or
enjoying something worth doing or enjoying."[6] Whereas having the
former is having "outward" freedom, enjoying the latter is enjoying
"inward" freedom. And whereas having the former is a contingent condition of moral self-realization, the latter effectively constitutes moral
self-realization itself. Moral self-realization as "inward" freedom therefore moralizes the meaning of freedom. Being fully free means acting
virtuously.[7]

Furthermore, actually doing "something worth doing" depends on

---

[1] T. H. Green, *Prolegomena to Ethics*, 3rd edn. (Oxford University Press, 1890), sect. 194.
[2] T. H. Green, "Lectures on the Principles of Political Obligation" [1879–80], in T. H.
Green, *Lectures on the Principles of Political Obligation and Other Writings*, Paul Harris and
John Morrow, eds. (Cambridge University Press, 1986), sect. 25.
[3] Ibid., sect. 23.   [4] Green, *Prolegomena*, sect. 164.
[5] Green, "Political Obligation," sect. 221.
[6] T. H. Green, "Lecture on 'Liberal Legislation and Freedom of Contract'" [1881], in
Lectures, p. 199.
[7] For the distinction between "outward" or "juristic" freedom and "inward" freedom in
Green, see especially "On the Different Senses of 'Freedom' as Applied to Will and to
the Moral Progress of Man" [1886], in "Political Obligation," sects. 7–8.

others doing what is worth doing because our identities are so thoroughly interdependent. Developing one's talents, particularly one's moral talents, requires others doing likewise by acting virtuously towards us. And others can only do likewise if we, in turn, act virtuously towards them by exercising self-restraint and by empowering them (both of which are equivalent to granting them "outward" freedom) and by treating them benevolently. As Green says: "In thinking of ultimate good he ['the educated citizen of Christendom'] thinks of it indeed necessarily as perfection for himself; as a life in which he shall be fully satisfied ... But he cannot think of himself as satisfied in any life other than a social life, exhibiting the exercise of self-denying will, and in which ... all men, shall participate."[8]

Moral self-realization was also the axiological hinge of Hobhouse's new liberalism. In *The Rational Good*, Hobhouse says that the "judgement 'This is good'" both expresses an "attitude" and testifies to the existence, as a matter of fact, of "*harmony* between an experience and a feeling."[9] Goodness seems to be a harmonious relationship between types of actions and feelings in the sense in which the feelings generated are pleasurable ones. Pleasure-producing actions are harmonious and therefore exhibit goodness. Pain-producing actions are disharmonious and therefore evince badness. And we naturally approve of the former and disapprove of the latter. Living morally therefore means, in part, living harmoniously by acting in such a way that one's actions give off a steady stream of pleasures. At a minimum, part of what makes the moral life moral is the envelope of pleasure which perpetually shrouds it.

Moreover, living harmoniously also means acting successfully in the sense of accomplishing one's goals.[10] Thus, another part of what makes the moral life moral is the internal coherence or unity of our individual actions. But, of course, the internal coherence of our individual actions depends, in turn, upon their external coherence over time. Unless our ongoing actions are themselves harmoniously coordinated, our individual actions will lack internal harmony. Intention will contend with intention causing action to clash with action and, thus, intention with result. Only harmoniously synchronized lives are self-realizing and display "what we call character."[11] Only such lives are ongoing satisfying wholes whose component actions are typically sheathed in pleasure and constitute the "rational good."

Rational good, then, is a multi-faceted harmony of successful, inte-

[8] Green, *Prolegomena*, sect. 370.
[9] L. T. Hobhouse, *The Rational Good* (New York: Henry Holt, 1921), p. 96; italics added.
[10] Ibid., p. 84.   [11] Ibid., p. 133.

grated actions and their attendant pleasures over a whole life. It is a
certain kind of balanced "personality" that "stands out as a strongly-
marked self-consistent individuality . . ."[12] It is the "actual process of the
full and harmonious life . . . so far as it can be realized in one human
being."[13]

Each personality, Hobhouse also insists, is equally a "meeting point of
a great number of social relations."[14] Thus, because our identities are so
deeply socially constituted, each person's self-realization depends upon
others enjoying guaranteed possibilities of making the most of themselves, of developing their own particular personalities. Each of us must
therefore become, as Green would say, a self-disciplining moral personality. We must accommodate ourselves to one another by negatively
respecting each other's personal integrity and by positively empowering
each other with equal opportunities. In short, our lives must become
externally as well as *internally* harmonious. Indeed, external social
harmony and internal psychological harmony are mutually interdependent. In order to realize oneself as a harmonious coherent personality,
others must likewise flourish which entails that one's relations with
others be harmonious. And the latter, in turn, requires that one realize
oneself morally.

Following Green's distinction between "outward" and "inward"
freedom, Hobhouse also theorizes freedom through the lens of internal
and external harmony. "Moral freedom" is "proportionate to the [self's]
internal harmony," whereas "social freedom" concerns the external
"freedom of man in society."[15] Enjoying the latter is equivalent to
having "outward" or "juristic" freedom, in Green's terminology, while
achieving the former is comparable to what Green calls being inwardly
free or "free to will." For Hobhouse, as much as for Green, being fully
free entails being free in both senses. Being fully free means being not
just negatively free by being left alone and positively free in the sense of
enjoying enabling conditions but being morally free in addition. Being
fully free means living, in the language of harmony, an internally as well
as externally harmonious life.

Ritchie, as much as Green and Hobhouse, made moral self-realization
the conceptual centerpiece of his new liberal normative edifice. In
"Moral Philosophy: On the Methods and Scope of Ethics," Ritchie
reiterates the familiar new liberal claim that self-realization is the

[12] Ibid., p. 142.   [13] Ibid., p. 143.
[14] L. T. Hobhouse, *Social Evolution and Political Theory* [1911] (Port Washington, NY: Kennikat Press, 1968), p. 85.
[15] L. T. Hobhouse, *The Elements of Social Justice* [1922] (London: Allen & Unwin, 1949), pp. 51, 57.

"ultimate end" of "all of mankind."[16] He adds the caveat that happiness may also be considered the ultimate good provided we clearly understand happiness to mean self-realization: "If we use happiness as a term equivalent to self-realization, self-satisfaction, we may say that the end is happiness . . ." However, if "we use happiness in the sense in which it is used in ordinary language, the end is not happiness. Happiness is mainly dependent on the healthy state of the bodily secretions and is a very important means to the attainment of the good life." Moreover, those who achieve self-realization are "happy and pleased in the attainment of it."[17] In sum, happiness in the ordinary sense is both a condition of self-realization and a by-product of it.

In good new liberal fashion, Ritchie further held that self-realization was socially encumbered. "Real civilized" selves flourish "not in distinction and separation from others, but in community with them." Any attempt to understand the "full-grown individual" apart from the "surroundings which make him possible" makes him into an "abstraction." We simply cannot "separate our own interests in an abstract way from the interests of others, nor theirs from ours. The more we learn of nature . . . the more we discover that . . . every atom influences and is influenced by every other."[18]

Moreover, self-realization constituted, for Ritchie, a higher species of freedom, as it did for both Green and Hobhouse. Freedom as self-realization is the "end or aim of morality." It is the freedom "not of lawlessness but of self-government ('autonomy of the will,' in Kant's phrase)." Whereas being free in the "negative sense of freedom" is critical to our well-being, being free in a "higher [self-realizing] sense" dignifies us and separates us from animals. Whereas being negatively free is merely, though importantly, "not being determined by external causes," being positively free means acting in accord with the dictates of reason.[19]

Ritchie's neo-Kantian moralization of freedom as self-realization, coupled with his communitarian theory of personal identity which so closely follows Green's and Hobhouse's, generates much the same mutually reinforcing, perfectionist dialectic between each individual's self-realization that we also saw in Green and Hobhouse. For instance, Ritchie claims that self-realization *qua* self-mastery is the "result of

[16] D. G. Ritchie, "Moral Philosophy: On the Methods and Scope of Ethics," in Robert Latta (ed.), *Philosophical Studies* (London: Macmillan, 1905), p. 299.
[17] Ibid.
[18] D. G. Ritchie, *The Principles of State Interference* (London: Swan Sonnenschein, 1896), pp. 97–8.
[19] D. G. Ritchie, "Free-Will and Responsibility," *International Journal of Ethics*, 5 (1895), 430.

training and discipline which must at first be given us by others, and only afterwards be directed by ourselves."[20] In other words, self-realization is an ongoing process of forbearance towards others that we learn from them. Others train us to forbear because our forbearance makes their self-realization possible. And once we internalize forbearance, their self-realization becomes more secure. Our moral self-realization redounds to their self-realization including, and especially, their moral self-realization. Their self-realization, particularly their moral self-realization, promotes our own in turn as they invest more in training us, as well as subsequent generations, to forbear. To repeat, we flourish "in community" with others. We thrive when they thrive and they thrive when we do. Self-realization and happiness are communal ventures. We achieve them not *apart from* others but *with* others.

So it seems that for Hobhouse and Ritchie as much as for Green, moral self-realization was moral freedom.[21] Acting fully freely meant acting virtuously in the sense of acting in harmony with others by promoting their individuality and flourishing with the hopes of thereby nourishing one's own individuality and flourishing. For all three, in short, moral personality was socially-thick as well as normatively pivotal causing the new liberalism to transcend (by nearly a century) many of the polarizing differences that have afflicted until recently the over-wrought opposition between communitarians and liberals today. What Mulhall and Swift say of Raz's perfectionist liberalism can just as well be said of Green's, Hobhouse's, and Ritchie's:

> By pointing out the extent to which the goals we have as individuals, the attainment of which constitutes our individual well-being, are connected to the services of others and of our community, so that even individual goods are in this sense communal in content, Raz calls into question the whole opposition between individual and community in a way that seems to transcend the terms of debate between liberal and communitarian.[22]

So those who find Raz's communitarian liberalism a bracing palliative to the liberal vs. communitarian debate should find the new liberalism no less analgesic though they may be surprised to learn that this antidote has been available to the philosophically suffering for quite some time now.[23]

---

[20] Ibid., 430–1.
[21] Michael Freeden, by contrast, contends that Green was more of an "ideological halfway house" between Mill and the "communitarian theories" of the new liberals, principally because he shifted carelessly between Millian self-development and new liberal self-realization. See Michael Freeden, *Ideologies and Political Theory: A Conceptual Approach* (Oxford University Press, 1996), pp. 179, 182–3.
[22] Stephen Mulhall and Adam Swift, *Liberals and Communitarians* (Oxford: Blackwell, 1992), p. 286.
[23] Also see Alan Ryan's comparison of Green and Dewey in *John Dewey* (New York: W. W.

Self-realization, in sum, was a core concept around which the communitarian liberalism of the new liberals was constructed but, as we have already begun to see, they each theorized self-realization somewhat differently. These differences should be unsurprising given the hedonic attributes of Hobhouse's and Ritchie's conceptions of self-realization, attributes which appreciably complicate their respective moral theories.

The legacy of Mill

Though Hobhouse's and Ritchie's hedonism separated them from Green, Green's debts to utilitarianism were nonetheless potent. Thus, Michael Freeden correctly claims that nineteenth-century utilitarianism "paved the way" for the new liberalism, including Green's, in crucial respects.[24] Indeed, the way paved by nineteenth-century utilitarianism was remarkably complete and easy to follow.

But what the new liberals appropriated from their utilitarian predecessors was mostly Mill and very little Bentham. Though they disparaged Bentham, they found Mill's improved utilitarianism highly appealing. In Green's view, Mill's theory of good as moral "self-development" resembled his own theory of good, especially when Mill extolled the "higher pleasures" of self-development. By extolling these "higher pleasures," Mill abandoned the "doctrine that pleasure is the ultimate good" and thereby effectively perceived "good in some object, the attainment of which of course is pleasant but which is not itself pleasure."[25] Mill, that is, as much as conceded that good was nothing less than the "attainment of a certain type of character" rather than pleasure.[26] Unfortunately, Mill often retreated into the unimproved utilitarianism of Bentham. He inconsistently persisted in misidentifying good as pleasure because, as is so typical of utilitarians according to Green, he persisted in believing that we overwhelmingly desire maximum pleasure most of all. This mistaken empirical assessment, in

Norton, 1995). Ryan observes that Dewey, like Green, "argued that our true good is the full development of personality and that this development can occur only in a society of like personalities." (p. 94.)

[24] Michael Freeden, *The New Liberalism* (Oxford University Press, 1978), p. 13. Even Green, according to Freeden, "absorbed elements of the utilitarian outlook in his attempt to adumbrate conduct and describe institutions whose end is to supply permanent contributions to the social good." (p. 18.)

[25] T. H. Green, "Lecture E. T. 78," unnumbered MS, T. H. Green Papers, Balliol College, Oxford University. See also *Prolegomena*, sect. 162.

[26] Green, *Prolegomena*, sect. 164. Avital Simhony has suggested to me that Green was much more indebted to Aristotle's notion of self-realization than to Mill's even if the latter's conception resembled Green's in crucial respects.

turn, led him wrongly to conclude that pleasure was good. Had he been a better psychologist, Mill would have seen that we do not desire maximum pleasure over all else and that such desires were, moreover, psychologically unintelligible. Since experiencing aggregate pleasure is impossible insofar as none of us can do any more than experience pleasures sequentially, desiring maximum aggregate pleasure is irrational. And if the desire for maximum aggregate pleasure is irrational, then pleasure is an implausible candidate for good. Green, then, commended Mill for advocating a non-hedonic conception of good though he faulted him whenever he relapsed into Benthamite utilitarianism.[27]

Understanding Green's anti-utilitarianism also requires taking account of his theory of will and good will. According to Green, in willing, we decisively commit ourselves to some of our basic desires. We identify ourselves with them.[28] In effect, we exhibit second-order desires by embracing some of our first-order desires. And when we repeatedly reaffirm our commitment to a subset of first-order desires, we develop character.[29] In good willing, we decisively commit to our basic desire to be moral, to develop a morally good personality. By contrast, willing aggregate pleasure is futile because, as we have seen for Green, aggregate pleasure cannot be experienced. In willing pleasure, we are decisively committing ourselves to an infinite series of fleeting pleasures which is the only kind of pleasurable experience there is. How can one develop durable character and therefore become an identifiable person, let alone a moral person, if one tries to build a stable identity around the pursuit of something so unstable as an infinite series of fleeting pleasures? Willing maximum pleasure is necessarily, for Green, bootless at best and *self*-defeating at worst. But Green's anti-utilitarianism did not make him anti-consequentialist. As we will shortly see, Green was a perfectionist consequentialist for whom maximizing self-realization was the ultimate standard of right.

Hobhouse likewise looked to Mill, as well as to Green, for inspiration.[30] And not surprisingly, given these debts, Hobhouse likewise rejected Benthamism for its illiberalism and for its identity-subverting

---

[27] Undoubtedly with Mill in mind, Green writes that "utilitarianism may be presented in a form in which it would scarcely be distinguishable from the doctrine [Green's] just now stated, the doctrine, viz. that the ground of political obligation ... lies in the fact that these powers [rights] are necessary to the fulfilment of man's vocation as a moral being ..." (Green, "Political Obligation," sect. 23.)

[28] Green, *Prolegomena*, sects. 138, 145, and 146.

[29] Ibid., sect. 101.

[30] "The theory of harmony stands in close relation on the one side to the Utilitarian principle as developed by J. S. Mill, and on the other hand to the form taken by Ethical Idealism in the hands of T. H. Green." (Hobhouse, *Rational Good*, p. 193.)

endeavor to equate good with evanescent pleasures.[31] Like Green before him, Hobhouse held that good had to be more substantial than fleeting pleasures. It had to possess durability so that a life spent pursuing it would not eviscerate selfhood but would, instead, display narrative coherence.[32]

Here, Hobhouse's account of willing is helpful in much the same way that Green's account of willing is helpful. For Hobhouse, in willing we harmonize our impulses, volitions, and desires into a cohesive, ongoing scheme. We forge ourselves into distinct, enduring personalities.[33] And when we will rationally, we forge our personalities around our deepest "root interests" such as our interests in others and in self-respect.[34] We fashion ourselves into thoroughly social personalities by committing ourselves to others' self-realization as well as our own thereby earning the self-respect we also crave. But if we vainly will pleasure, we simply commit ourselves to the vicissitudes of our strongest impulses, volitions, and desires. We foolishly try to unify our lives around transient feelings, insuring that our personalities will never exhibit coherence and depth.

So Hobhouse, like Green, was inspired by Mill's improved utilitarianism. He likewise concurred with Green that Mill implicitly conceded that good was not simply pleasure but was something more enduring insofar as it had to do with the quality of pleasures enjoyed. Mill, in effect, conceded that good was primarily, though not exclusively, what Hobhouse referred to as a "kind of [self-realizing] life."[35]

Mill, then, indeed "paved the way" for a correct theory of good in which, according to Hobhouse, happiness and the "kind of life" in which it was sought were but "two elements of the same whole, as the experience and the feeling-tone which qualifies the experience."[36] Pleasure is "merely another expression" for the ultimate value we find in certain "objects" or "things." Pleasure, therefore, is "in the thing" rather than a "subsequent effect which the thing happens to produce."[37] Though saying that something is one of two elements comprising a whole is

[31] See L. T. Hobhouse, *Liberalism* [1911] (Oxford University Press, 1964), pp. 39–41, and Hobhouse, *Elements of Social Justice*, pp. 17–18.

[32] "To know what objects will permanently satisfy is to possess the secret of happiness . . . and the most serious criticism of Benthamism is that it seems to ignore this necessity . . . We are happy *in* something, and the something must be worth while." (Hobhouse, *Elements of Social Justice*, p. 18.)

[33] Hobhouse, *Rational Good*, pp. v, 46, 49, 52.

[34] L. T. Hobhouse, *Social Development* (London: Allen & Unwin, 1924), pp. 142, 173, 155–7, 169 and 174.

[35] Hobhouse, *Rational Good*, p. 196.

[36] Ibid., pp. 196–7. Also see pp. 156–7 where Hobhouse says: "Viewed as feeling, then, the Rational Good is happiness, viewed as the object of this feeling it is the fulfilment of vital capacity as a consistent whole."

[37] L. T. Hobhouse, *Morals in Evolution* [1906] (New York: Henry Holt, 1919), p. 599.

not quite the same as saying that something is simply an alternative expression for something else, Hobhouse clearly regards happiness as somehow embedded in goodness as a facet of it. And insofar as good is self-realization, for Hobhouse, happiness therefore necessarily accompanies self-realization, for happiness partially constitutes it. Therefore, too, self-realizing lives are equally happy lives, and promoting the latter invariably promotes the former.[38]

Now by claiming that self-realizing lives are always happy ones, Hobhouse is reformulating his claim that in judging an action good, we are testifying to the existence of a certain kind of harmony *qua* feelings of pleasure which certain actions produce. Harmonious lives, recall, are good in the sense that they generate pleasure, making harmony as well part of the meaning of good. So in claiming that self-realization is good, we are equally affirming that self-realization consists, in part, in pleasing activity.

Mill was a catalyst for Ritchie too. Mill, according to Ritchie, often recognized that good was self-realization rather than happiness insofar as he valued self-development and the higher pleasures over the lower ones. Mill, however, inconsistently and wrongly continued confusing pleasure with good. Pursuing pleasure directly is "hopeless" because pleasure is not "something [enduring] that we can hold before us." As a by-product of realizing goodness, it is obtained only by "not being directly pursued."[39]

The futility of pursuing pleasure lies in the fact that we are incapable of holding aggregate pleasure before ourselves as a legitimate object of desire because, as Green and Hobhouse maintained, pleasures were fleeting. By contrast, self-realization is something enduring that we can hold before ourselves and therefore plausibly desire.[40] And whatever we can plausibly desire is a credible possibility for good. Of course, merely establishing something as a credible option does not establish it as the normatively correct option.

The dominion of utility

Ritchie, then, was considerably indebted to Mill, like Green and Hob-

---

[38] Regarding the relationship between self-realization and happiness for Green compared to himself, Hobhouse claims that whereas he treats pleasure as an "integral and essential element" of good, Green treats pleasure merely as a "secondary consequence" of good. (Hobhouse, *Rational Good*, pp. 200–1.)

[39] D. G. Ritchie, "Confessio Fidei," in Latta, *Philosophical Studies*, p. 237.

[40] See especially Ritchie, *Principles of State Interference*, p. 142, where he says, not without ambiguity, and invoking Green, that the "self is . . . something other than a mere series of feelings" as well as "other than a mere subject for pleasurable sensations."

house. And just like them, he nevertheless criticized Mill for never adequately escaping the influence of Bentham's crude psychology of pleasure. But what should we conclude about the new liberalism's relationship to utilitarianism? Could Hobhouse be a utilitarian, especially because happiness was a component of good for him? And if we admit that Hobhouse was a utilitarian, dare we concede the same about Ritchie and even Green?

Like other new liberals, Hobhouse was a perfectionist consequentialist although he was more nearly a utilitarian too. For him, maximizing self-realization consisted in maximizing common good defined as "*each* member of the community" having the opportunity to develop his or her personality.[41] Any truly impartial and therefore rational man must ground the principle of morality "on some good *result* which it serves or embodies" and which takes the "good of *everyone* affected into account."[42]

Nothing said thus far makes Hobhouse a utilitarian consequentialist. But when we recall Hobhouse's view that happiness and unified personality comprised "two elements of the same [self-realizing] whole," then we must conclude that his perfectionist consequentialism was simultaneously a form of utilitarianism. For if maximizing common good *qua* everyone's self-realization also entailed maximizing happiness, because happiness partially constituted self-realization, then Hobhouse was indeed two kinds of consequentialist rolled into one.[43]

We have already established that Ritchie was a perfectionist insofar as he regarded good as self-realization. He was, in addition, a perfectionist consequentialist because, like Hobhouse, he deemed actions as right that promoted everyone's self-realization. However, he did not follow Hobhouse in making happiness a companion element of good and therefore he was not part utilitarian like Hobhouse. Nevertheless, Ritchie unabashedly called himself a utilitarian.

Ritchie, then, was a perfectionist consequentialist who ironically insisted on seeing himself as a utilitarian probably for reasons that were as much historical as theoretical. Utilitarianism shaped the horizon of nineteenth-century British moral philosophizing. Consequently, we should be unsurprised by Ritchie's inability to escape utilitarianism's hegemonic pull. The discourse of utilitarianism was ubiquitous. Those

---

[41] Hobhouse, *Liberalism*, p. 40, emphasis added.
[42] Ibid., p. 68, emphasis added.
[43] See Morris Ginsberg's observation in "The Work of L. T. Hobhouse," in J. A Hobson and Morris Ginsberg (eds.), *L. T. Hobhouse* (London: Allen & Unwin, 1931), p. 184, that Hobhouse, in contrast to Green, retained what he considered to be an "element of value in Utilitarianism, namely, the emphasis on happiness as a feeling attendant upon" successful self-realization.

who we would now call non-hedonist consequentialists had but little choice in calling themselves utilitarians, for *their* conceptual menu was less varied than ours.

Ritchie's self-described utilitarianism was also rooted in his evolutionary account of the development of moral reasoning. According to Ritchie, the theory of natural selection had "vindicated all that has proved most permanently valuable in Utilitarianism," accommodating it with intuitionism though not without rejecting intuitionism's promiscuous subjectivism.[44] For Ritchie, the struggle for survival between societies was equally a contest of differing moral conventions, with those conventions enduring and thriving belonging to societies which endure and thrive. Indeed, societies which succeed do so in part because their moral codes promote comparatively greater social harmony and prosperity. Moral conventions that work are those that last. And because they last, they become moral intuitions that seem to have nothing to do with the promotion of utility. But, of course, they have everything to do with utility. We simply forget their instrumental connection, wrongly taking them as innate, universal, and objective.

Eventually, utilitarian practical reasoning supersedes intuitionism as societies progress and modernize. "Rational selection" replaces natural selection as the engine of social progress and well-being. Instead of moral conventions arising slowly and congealing haphazardly via the mechanism of natural selection, they begin to be systematically reformulated with the deliberate aim of promoting stability and well-being. The utilitarian reformer "anticipates and obviates the cruel process of natural selection."[45] Moral reasoning comes to mean the "conscious and deliberate adoption of those feelings and acts and habits" that advance the "welfare of the community."[46]

Rational selection fully matures as we begin aiming consciously and deliberately, not at maximizing general happiness, but at common good as everyone's self-realization. Because pleasure is a hallmark of self-realization, maximizing the former also promotes the latter. Somehow, by struggling with the assorted difficulties plaguing utilitarianism, like the futility of trying to maximize something so evanescent as pleasure, we eventually begin to attend to self-realization as our aim, for which

[44] D. G. Ritchie, "Darwin and Hegel" [1891], in *Darwin and Hegel* (London: Swan Sonnenschein, 1893), p. 62.
[45] D. G. Ritchie, "Evolution and Democracy," in S. Coit (ed.), *Ethical Democracy: Essays in Social Dynamics* (London: G. Richards, 1900), p. 16.
[46] Ritchie, "Darwin and Hegel," p. 63. See also "Social Evolution," *International Journal of Ethics*, 6 (1896), 170, where Ritchie says: "Natural selection tests the social utility of customs and institutions too late for the benefit of those concerned: utilitarianism ... is the attempt to anticipate and avert, where possible, the cruelty of natural selection."

pleasure is merely emblematic. Our frustration in trying to be utilitarians fuels our discovery that we can succeed as consequentialists nevertheless. All we have to do is stop chasing after maximizing happiness aggregatively and concentrate on promoting everyone's self-realization. In any case, we will fortuitously maximize our happiness while we are at it.

Clearly, Hobhouse and Ritchie were consequentialists whose relationship to utilitarianism was complex and sympathetic. But suggesting as much regarding Green might seem unwarranted, especially given the neo-Kantian motifs in his moral theory. Green's moral theory, however, is knottier than it seems, even to the initiated. For instance, in *Prolegomena to Ethics*, Green says flatly that his moral theory evaluates actions, in part, according to their *effects*. However, they "will be effects, not in the way of producing pleasure, but in the way of contributing to that *perfection* of mankind, of which the essence is a *good will* on part of *all* persons."[47] Green, then, was part perfectionist consequentialist for whom maximizing the moral self-realization of "*all* persons" constituted the criterion of morally right. His consequentialism was, in short, non-hedonic and *distribution*-sensitive.[48] As Michael Freeden says, he decontests liberty as development but not "casual or limited development, but its optimalization" and even "maximization." Furthermore, according to Freeden, "liberty is firmly held in place by what is importantly taken to denote subjective, not objective, optimalization – the *citizens* are those who make the most and best of *themselves*."[49]

Green's consequentialism is equally unmistakable in his differences from Kant. He warns that we are liable to fall into a "false antithesis" if we believe, like Kant, that we must choose between utilitarianism and deontology.[50] We have a middle alternative that combines consequentialist and deontological practical reasoning and therefore resembles what David Cummiskey has recently called "Kantian consequentialism."[51] For Green, there "would be nothing against the spirit of Kant's

---

[47] Green, *Prolegomena*, sect. 294, emphasis added. See also T. H. Green, "Utility as a Principle of Art and Morality," unnumbered MS, T. H. Green Papers, where Green similarly contends that the "rectitude" of actions turns on their "tendency to produce rectitude in others" rather than their "tendency to produce general or individual happiness."

[48] See also D. Weinstein, "Between Kantianism and Consequentialism in T. H. Green's Moral Philosophy," *Political Studies*, 41 (1993), 618–35.

[49] Freeden, *Ideologies*, p. 187.

[50] See especially T. H. Green, "Lectures on the Philosophy of Kant," in R. L. Nettleship (ed.), *Works of Thomas Hill Green*, 3 vols. (London: Longmans, Green and Co., 1885–8), vol. II, p. 140.

[51] See David Cummiskey's stimulating *Kantian Consequentialism* (Oxford University Press, 1996). For a fuller treatment of this idea in Green, see Weinstein, "Between Kantianism and Consequentialism in T. H. Green's Moral Philosophy," pp. 630–4.

doctrine in saying that an act of wise benevolence is good in virtue of its *consequences* so long as these *consequences* are other than the pleasure of the agent and being other than his pleasure, are the *object* for sake of which he does the act."[52]

So Green, as much as Hobhouse and Ritchie, was a consequentialist. However, whereas Hobhouse was both a utilitarian and a perfectionist consequentialist and while Ritchie was a perfectionist consequentialist who nevertheless insisted on calling himself a utilitarian, Green was a perfectionist consequentialist whose consequentialism was camouflaged, being shrouded in the obfuscating mist of neo-Kantian enthusiasms. But he was a consequentialist all the same.

Motives and consequences

Now Green's middle strategy does not abjure the merit of pleasure altogether. In *Prolegomena to Ethics*, Green says that morally good persons do not desire pleasure as an end but "pleasure as an *incident* of a life of which the value or desirability does not consist in its pleasantness."[53] Hence, for Green, pleasure tends to be coextensive with self-realization, making Green what Thomas Hurka calls an "extensional perfectionist." Extensional perfectionists typically claim, according to Hurka, that we tend to desire whatever happens to be coextensive with self-development.[54]

Hobhouse likewise seems to be an extensional perfectionist. But, recall that, for Hobhouse, self-realizing lives are equally happy lives not because happiness is emblematic of self-realization but because happiness is constitutive of self-realization. Whereas for Green, happiness issues from self-realization as an external by-product, it is, as we saw earlier for Hobhouse, "in the thing [self-realization]" instead of being a "subsequent effect which the thing happens to produce." Happiness, that is, is not merely *externally* coextensive with self-realization, as Green claims, but *internally* constitutes it. This internal positioning of happiness is precisely what makes Hobhouse more of a genuine utilitarian.

Ritchie, despite claiming to be a utilitarian, was nonetheless an extensional perfectionist very much like Green insofar as he also regarded happiness as contingently symptomatic of self-realization, particularly moral self-realization. Moreover, he also insisted that feelings of happiness reflected the quality of one's motives inasmuch as having pure motives meant being morally self-realized. In "On the

---

[52] Green, "Lecture E. T. 78," emphasis added.
[53] Green, *Prolegomena*, sect. 238, emphasis added.
[54] Thomas Hurka, *Perfectionism* (Oxford University Press, 1993), pp. 23–30.

Meaning of the Term 'Motive,' and on the Ethical Significance of Motives," he declares moreover:

In the long run ... good motives cannot bring forth bad (i.e. socially mischievous) acts; and when we judge the character and motives, we are inferring the nature of the tree from its fruits. But we may err in very many cases; and it is certainly better to *discuss* the right and wrong acts, where we can directly apply a measure and a standard – viz., their effects on social well-being. The discussion of motives, apart from the acts in which they are apt to issue, is too likely to end in appeals to vague and unanalyzed "intuitive" standards.[55]

In other words, making others happy discloses the purity of one's motives like a tasty fruit reveals the quality of the tree on which it grows. Wherever one finds happiness being generated, one also tends to find pure motives in play. Thus, we can judge the quality of an individual's motives, or the extent to which he or she is morally self-realizing, not only by the happiness or self-satisfaction he or she feels but also by assessing the amount of happiness that he or she elicits in the world. And conversely, promoting general happiness in the world is a surefire strategy for demonstrating one's morally self-realizing worth. If you want to be virtuous, then aim at maximizing everyone's happiness.

Ritchie even confesses that motives may very well be the proper or ideal subject of moral judgment but because they can be "known in their fullness only to an omniscient judge," we are better off just sticking to measuring well-being.[56] Ritchie's reservations about the practicability of neo-Kantianism, all-the-while granting its deeper validity, also suggest a response to those who might insist that Green cannot possibly be a consequentialist, let alone a utilitarian, because, for him, motives, and consequences are the "inner and outer" sides of action. Consequences, so this view protests, express or mirror motives, which are fundamental. Hence, consequences are only important insofar as they provide access to motives which are otherwise inaccessible. Yet, not having God's penetrating omniscience, how else are *we* to evaluate actions than by mirrored consequences? So it seems that in order to make normative judgments, *we* have little choice, as Ritchie would remind us, but to rely on consequences as a second-best strategy. And this sobering predicament may be a reason why Hobhouse was so keen to view happiness more as constitutive of good than as its problematic external marker as with Green.

Having determined that Green and Ritchie were extensional perfectionists while Hobhouse was as much a utilitarian as he was a perfec-

---

[55] D. G. Ritchie, "On the Meaning of the Term 'Motive,' and on the Ethical Significance of Motives," *International Journal of Ethics*, 4 (1893–4), 93–4.
[56] Ibid., 93.

tionist, we are now able to see why all three considered utilitarian practical reasoning so practically serviceable. Obviously, insofar as Hobhouse was part utilitarian because he held that happiness constituted an element of self-realization, strategies promoting the former invariably tended to promote the latter. Because happiness was *internally* interwoven into the very fabric of self-realization, utilitarianism could substitute perfectly for perfectionist consequentialism, especially if maximizing self-realization, happiness notwithstanding, should prove, after all, a harder target to aim for than maximizing happiness.

Even Green concedes that utilitarianism justifies much the same practical strategies as his own moral theory:

> But if the Utilitarian is committed to no more than … the doctrine that the value of actions and institutions is to be measured in the last resort by their effect on the nett sum of pleasures enjoyable by all human, or perhaps all sentient, beings, the difference between him and one who would substitute for this "nett sum, etc." "the fulfilment of human capacities" may be *practically* small. A desire for the enjoyment of pleasure by others … is so entirely different from desire for a pleasure that, if the Utilitarian considers his "Summum Bonum," or any limited form of it, to be a possible object of desire to the individual, he clears himself practically, even though it be at the sacrifice of consistency, from chargeability with any such theory of motives as would exclude the possibility of a "pure heart."[57]

Of course, practical convergence does not entail justificatory convergence. But practical convergence is *practically* significant for Green inasmuch as he allows that utilitarian strategies can profitably substitute for those required by his own moral theory which are harder to specify given the arguably vaguer meaning of self-realization compared to that of happiness.[58] And this replacement efficacy no doubt stems from the way in which happiness mirrors self-realization.

Ritchie likewise, and not surprisingly, held that traditional utilitarianism was practically useful. Utilitarianism overlaps with new liberalism in generating parallel practical strategies because pleasure was extensionally symptomatic of self-realization. Even Green's moral theory, according to Ritchie, resembles Mill's in practice.[59] In Ritchie's view, the "practical tests" that Green applies to the rightness of actions

[57] Green, *Prolegomena*, sect. 356, emphasis added.

[58] See Green, *Prolegomena*, sect. 286 where he admits: "From the difficulty of presenting to ourselves in any positive form what a society, perfected in this sense, would be, we may take *refuge* in describing the object of the devotion, which our consciences demand, as the greatest happiness of the greatest number; and until we puzzle ourselves with analysis, such an account may be sufficient for *practical* purposes" (emphasis added). By contrast, see *Prolegomena*, sect. 361 where Green says that self-realization provides enough practical "definiteness of [normative] direction."

[59] Ritchie, *Principles of State Interference*, p. 145.

"either for the individual or for the State," tend to "coincide" with those recommended by utilitarianism.[60]

Now there is some irony, if not inconsistency, in conceding that utilitarian practical reasoning can, if not should, substitute for new liberal practical reasoning. Recall that for Green, Hobhouse, and Ritchie, desire for greatest pleasure, whether one's own greatest pleasure or everyone's, was futile because pleasures were evanescent. Greatest pleasure was a romance and was therefore not a serviceable criterion of rightness. How, then, could utilitarianism substitute for new liberalism as a more efficacious method for generating strategies of right? If maximizing pleasure is as ambiguous a criterion as maximizing self-realization, then why invoke it in place of the latter?

Clearly, if Green, Hobhouse, and Ritchie held that Benthamism could answer for new liberal practical reasoning, then irony and in-consistency would indeed plague their thinking. But all three have Millian utilitarianism in mind as a substitute strategy. While maximizing pleasure may well be an illusory criterion of rightness, maximizing happiness *qua* self-development in Mill's sense seems a suitably realistic enterprise and therefore a viable proxy for maximizing self-realization. But we still might legitimately wonder what makes Millian self-development any more determinate and accessible than self-realization as a normative goal.[61]

Common good

Common good was a core concept for new liberals as much as self-realization was. Yet, its theoretical importance – an importance that further testifies to Green's, Hobhouse's, and Ritchie's consequentialism as well as their communitarianism – is obfuscated by its interpretative illusiveness.

As we have been arguing, the new liberals were non-aggregating

---

[60] Ibid., pp. 142–3.

[61] Also recall *Prolegomena*, sect. 356 above where Green concedes that universal hedonism can substitute practically in place of his own theory: "A desire for the enjoyment of pleasure by others ... is so entirely different from desire for a pleasure that, if the Utilitarian considers his 'Summum bonum,' or any limited form of it, to be a possible object of desire to the individual, he clears himself practically, even though it be at the sacrifice of consistency, from chargeability with any such theory of motives as would exclude the possibility of a 'pure heart.'" In other words, universal hedonism works for practical purposes because promoting others' pleasures implies some degree of purity of heart. Promoting others' pleasures requires self-restraint and therefore makes one morally self-realizing. It is not so much the content of what one aims to maximize but merely the aim to maximize universally and impartially that exhibits germinal good will. As Green says earlier, in sect. 333, "Impartiality of reference to human well-being has been the great lesson which the Utilitarian has had to teach."

consequentialists who viewed moral self-realization as ultimate good,
insisting that it be maximized by being *equitably* distributed. They
insisted that maximizing good be operationalized in a way that promotes, in effect, an "equal distribution of goods across individuals."[62]
Their consequentialism exemplified what Freeden has called "modified
constrained consequentialism" which incorporates a "communitarian
viewpoint" as opposed to a more traditional "aggregative one."[63]

The "constrained" or "communitarian" maximizing strategy of the
new liberals is palpable as well in their respective theories of common
good. Regarding Green, Avital Simhony correctly observes that
common good "is about securing for all persons the possibilities to make
the best of themselves."[64] As Green says, true freedom is the "liberation
of the powers of all men equally for contributions to a common good."
It "contributes to that equal development of the faculties of all which is
the highest good for all."[65] Hence, inasmuch as common good is our
highest good, it is equally the development of everyone's faculties.

By contrast for Freeden, by common good, Green means an "area of
joint interest" which "secures important aspects of their [individuals']
welfare." It is a "common sphere fashioned consciously by individuals to
their mutual advantage, which is an inescapable by-product of their
rationality, and reacts back on them to ensure their full realization as
individuals."[66] Common good, in short, is a special kind of community
where mutuality thrives insofar as each, in pursuing the best life,
simultaneously helps others to do likewise. Furthermore, according to
Freeden, Green's conception of common good as an arena of mutual

[62] Wayne Sumner, *The Moral Foundations of Rights* (Oxford University Press, 1987),
p. 171. Sumner's second stage in his "three stage" construction of the elements of
consequentialism concerns different strategies for operationalizing the maximization of
good. Though, according to Sumner, aggregation is the most familiar strategy, an
"equal distribution of goods across individuals, or a pattern which attends solely to the
minimum individual share" are legitimate alternatives as well.
[63] Michael Freeden, *Rights* (Minneapolis: University of Minnesota Press, 1991), pp. 89,
98. Also see Rawls' admission that "if the distribution of goods is also counted as a
good ... and the theory [utilitarianism] directs us to produce the most good (including
the good of distribution among others), we no longer have a teleological view in the
classical sense [implying that we have such a view in a more unusual sense never-
theless]." (*A Theory of Justice* [Cambridge, MA: Harvard University Press, 1971],
p. 25.) For Rawls, Hume exemplifies distributive, non-classical utilitarianism: "The
kind of utilitarianism espoused by Hume would not serve my purpose; indeed, it is not
strictly speaking utilitarianism ... For Hume, then, utility seems to be identical with
some form of the *common good*; institutions satisfy its demands when they are to
everyone's interests, at least in the long run." (p. 33, emphasis added.)
[64] Avital Simhony, "T. H. Green: The Common Good Society," *History of Political
Thought*, 16 (1993), 238.
[65] Green, "Lecture on 'Liberal Legislation,'" p. 200.
[66] Freeden, *Ideologies*, p. 252.

flourishing did not just resonate powerfully in the theorizing of later British new liberals but also influenced the American liberal tradition via Dewey. Regrettably, the "trail of influence of British left-liberalism on its American counterpart" seems to have "gone cold in the memory and consciousness of contemporary American liberals."[67] But this trail of influence has hardly "gone cold" in the thinking of other contemporary British liberals besides Freeden who know the liberal tradition better than many of their American counterparts. More than anyone, Alan Ryan has best appreciated Dewey's debts to Green:

> Like the young Dewey, Green wrote as a critic of the empiricist and utilitarian theories of Jeremy Bentham and John Stuart Mill, but in those days Green had rather more sense than Dewey of the real progress that Bentham and Mill represented ... He agreed with the utilitarians that ethics was concerned with the common good, but he denied that individuals were led to promote the common good by getting pleasure in doing so, and he denied that the proper understanding of the common good was that it consisted in the "greatest happiness" of humanity, understood as a maximum of pleasure.[68]

In *Liberalism*, Hobhouse states that common good is a good in which "each man has a share" and that share, in turn, "*consists* in realizing his capacities of feeling, of loving, of mental and physical energy, and in realizing these he plays his part in the social life, or, in Green's phrase, he finds his own good in the common good."[69] Common good "includes *every* individual" and "postulates free scope for the development of personality in *each* member of the community." Moreover, whatever "inequality of actual treatment, of income, rank, office, consideration, there be in a good social system, it would rest, not on the interest of the favoured individual as such, but on the common good." Common good justifies those inequalities that benefit everyone: "If the existence of millionaires on the one hand and of paupers on the other is just, it must be because such contrasts are the result of an economic system which upon the whole works out for the common good, the good of the pauper being included therein as well as the good of the millionaire ..."[70]

So, at a minimum, common good is everyone having the opportunity to flourish. At best, it is everyone actually flourishing. Hence, common good comprises, in part, harmony. The common good is "simply the total of all the lives that are in mutual harmony."[71] The principle of

---

[67] Ibid., p. 255.
[68] Ryan, *Dewey*, p. 90. Ryan is correct in suggesting that Green denied that common good consisted in maximizing happiness but, as we saw earlier, he is wrong in asserting that Green also denied that "getting pleasure" indirectly promoted common good.
[69] Hobhouse, *Liberalism*, pp. 68–9, emphasis added.
[70] Ibid., p. 70, emphasis added. Also see Hobhouse, *Elements of Social Justice*, p. 117.
[71] Hobhouse, *Elements of Social Justice*, p. 108.

harmony disallows any "conflict between the good of one and the good of all" and "holds that acts and institutions are good not because they suit the majority, but because they make the nearest possible approach to a good shared by every single person whom they effect."[72] What is "unambiguously good for a person is good for every person."[73]

Clearly, common good, as the harmonious self-realization of all, precludes people being used. There "is wrong" in the common good insofar as "whatever harmony there be conflicts with an element of good in any member."[74] Its very distribution-sensitive character insures that the pursuit of the common good sacrifices no one's integrity. As Hobhouse says of Green's conception of common good, it is the "well-being actually shared" by each and every member of society.[75]

Common good played much the same important role in Ritchie's new liberalism as in Green's and Hobhouse's. Not unlike Green, Ritchie held that utilitarianism correctly reoriented practical reasoning by making common good (though it understood common good inadequately) its criterion of judgment. Mill in particular, by distinguishing pleasures qualitatively, began correcting utilitarianism's deficient understanding of common good. He was compelled inadvertently to turn to the "standard of 'perfection of character' or of 'the good of the community'" in order to differentiate higher from lower pleasures.[76]

More significantly and not unlike both Green and Hobhouse, Ritchie claimed that good is necessarily "in some sense, a common good" for to be self-realizing is to be, of necessity, "in harmony with other selves."[77] Insofar as each person's pursuit of self-realization harmonizes with that of others, then his or her pursuit facilitates their pursuit negatively by not interfering with theirs and positively by actually contributing to theirs. The very mutuality of self-realization makes it such a dynamic common good. Self-realization, particularly moral self-realization, is *a* shared good that powerfully benefits everyone.

In sum, for new liberals, each person's self-realization is *a* common good, a non-competitive resource for others. It is the "harmony in which *each* individual good is *a* constituent."[78] Hence, common good operationalizes the maximization of good distributively, making common

---

[72] Ibid., p. 107.   [73] Ibid., p. 106.   [74] Ibid., note 1, p. 109.

[75] L. T. Hobhouse, *The Metaphysical Theory of the State* (London: Allen & Unwin, 1918), p. 123. Note as well Green's assessment in *Prolegomena* that the best utilitarianism (presumably Mill's) holds that the *summum bonum* is a state in which all humans "shall live as pleasantly as is possible for them, without one gaining pleasure at the expense of another." (sect. 360.)

[76] Ritchie, "Moral Philosophy," p. 322.

[77] Ibid., p. 296.

[78] Hobhouse, *Elements of Social Justice*, note 1, p. 30, emphasis added. Also see p. 65 where Hobhouse says that the "good of each individual is a part of the common good."

good simply another way of stipulating the maximization of everyone's self-realization as our ultimate criterion of right. Realizing one's non-moral talents means promoting common good by becoming an asset to others. Doing for oneself is simultaneously a matter of doing for others. Realizing oneself *morally* means promoting common good by protecting everyone else's self-realizing opportunities by respecting their rights and by treating them charitably. Doing as one *ought* is never a matter of abusively using others in the name of maximizing some sort of pooled good.

Common good, then, is a distribution-sensitive criterion of moral rightness for the new liberals. Its very distribution-sensitive nature makes their consequentialism authentically liberal insofar as morally right actions foster *everyone's* flourishing. That is why their perfectionist consequentialism is maximizing in the good-promoting, rather than the traditional good-pooling, sense. Good-promoting consequentialism, which maximizes distributively, may be a less familiar variety of consequentialism but it is a legitimate and distinctive variety nonetheless.[79]

Strong rights, of course, reinforce distribution sensitivity by preventing people from egregiously harming each other in the name of speciously trying to maximize self-realization aggregatively. They empower individuals with self-realizing opportunities, enabling them to cultivate their talents as best they can according to their own lights. Hence, they *indirectly* promote everyone's self-realization by giving everyone equal enabling conditions to develop themselves as they see fit.[80] Because self-realization is a "do-it-yourself" concept, securing

---

[79] One might doubt whether good-promoting moral theories are genuinely consequential-ist because, by categorizing them as consequentialist, we risk diluting consequentialism so completely that it ceases being a distinctive moral perspective. But recall Rawls' claim in note 63 that although Humean utilitarianism may not be "strictly speaking utilitarianism" in the "classical" sense because it identifies utility with common good, it may be a form of non-traditional utilitarianism nevertheless.

[80] Hobhouse, in particular, justifies rights in terms of their common good-producing results: "we must regard common good as the foundation of all personal rights. If that is so, the rights of man are those expectations which the common good justify him in entertaining, and we may admit that there are natural rights of man if we conceive the common good as resting upon certain elementary conditions affecting the life of society, which hold good whether people recognize them or not." (*Social Evolution*, p. 198.) For Ritchie too, moral rights are simply "essential conditions" for sustaining common good *qua* everyone's self-realization. Our right to liberty is "not absolute" but is "dependent on some idea of common good or advantage." (D. G. Ritchie, "Law and Liberty: The Question of State Interference" [1892], in *Studies in Political and Social Ethics* [London: Swan Sonnenschein, 1902], p. 60.) For Green, moral rights are likewise necessary conditions for promoting common good. Rights realize our "moral capacity" negatively "in the sense of . . . securing the treatment of one man by another as equally free with himself, but they do not realise it positively, because their possession does not imply that in any active way the individual makes a common good his own." (Green, "Political Obligation," sect. 25.)

everyone equal enabling conditions is the only credible strategy anyway. Strong rights therefore complement common good's distribution sensitivity in sustaining the new liberalism's liberal authenticity.

Remembering the liberal tradition

Will Kymlicka has vigorously argued against Charles Taylor's claim that the "social thesis" favors the communitarian politics of the common good over the liberal politics of neutral concern. For Kymlicka, Taylor mistakenly infers that only a perfectionist communitarian society dedicated to a thick conception of common good follows from our inherent, socially constructed identities. By contrast, Kymlicka holds that accepting the social thesis does not require us to abandon either liberal neutrality or taking rights seriously by making the good prior to the right. On the contrary, "a liberal [neutral] state can be said to promote the common good, since its policies aim at promoting the interests of the members of the community."[81]

Liberalism, in sum, is fully capable of accommodating a robust empirical theory of social identity and a normative theory of thin common good with its traditional commitment to the politics of neutral concern. It can absorb much from communitarianism without ceasing to be an authentic liberalism:

It [liberal justice] expresses an attractive conception of community, recognizing our dependence on a cultural community for our self-development and for our context of choice, yet recognizing the independence we claim, as self-directed beings, from any of the specific roles and relationships that exist in the community. It recognizes the equal standing of the members of the community, through an account of justice, without forcing people to exercise their entitlements at the expense of the people or projects that they care about. The individualism that underlies liberalism isn't valued at the expense of our social nature, or of our shared community.[82]

Now Kymlicka willingly concedes that the politics of neutral concern may need to be considerably egalitarian in advanced capitalist societies.

---

[81] Will Kymlicka, *Liberalism, Community and Culture* (Oxford University Press, 1989), p. 76.
[82] Ibid., p. 127. Also see Kymlicka's "Conclusion" where he resolves that liberalism "is rather an insistence on respect for each individual's capacity to understand and evaluate her own actions, to make judgements about the value of the communal and cultural circumstances she finds herself in." (p. 254.) Moreover, according to Kymlicka, to the extent that communitarians like Sandel and MacIntyre sometimes allow that being constituted by our ends or being embedded in a communal tradition does not preclude us from critically reconstituting ourselves, they fail to say anything distinctively different from liberalism. (pp. 55–7.) Certainly, they fail to say anything distinctively different from the new liberalism.

He invokes Hobhouse's socialist liberalism as a precursor of the kind of communitarian liberalism required by our times.[83] And in his defense of minority rights as not being incompatible with liberal values, he also summons Green and Dewey's commitment to the importance of cultural membership to the flourishing of individuality.[84] He occasionally appeals to these "Hegelian" liberals for inspiration in his efforts to refurbish the theories of "Kantian" liberals like Rawls and Dworkin. But Kymlicka nevertheless fails to say anything beyond these suggestive hints in support of his particular brand of communitarian liberalism. He does not fully exploit the rich historical resources made available by the new liberals and therefore he does not fully appreciate how much he may be renegotiating theoretical terrain they have already negotiated with considerable success. But he is at least aware of these resources, which is unusual enough.[85]

So as modern Kantian liberals go, Kymlicka seems as sensitive as any to liberalism's conceptual flexibility, perhaps because, in part, he is minimally acquainted with its new liberal past. For Kymlicka, there is a "range of possible [liberal as well as communitarian] positions which connect the two issues [the right and the good] in various ways."[86] There are deontological anti-perfectionists, such as Rawls, who prioritize the right over a thin theory of the good as well as teleological anti-perfectionists, such as "liberal utilitarians," who prioritize the good over the right and thereby "deny" that there are any constraints on the "way we maximize social welfare."[87] There are also, for Kymlicka, deontological perfectionists, such as Marx, who "find it unfair to sacrifice one person's pursuit of excellence just because doing so would increase the overall amount of excellence in society." Finally, there are teleological perfectionists though Kymlicka does not specify who they are.[88] Now,

---

[83] Ibid., p. 91. The new liberals denied, however, that political justice could be procedurally sanitized. See especially D. G. Ritchie, *The Moral Function of the State: A Paper Read Before the Oxford Branch of the Guild of St. Matthew* (London: Women's Printing Society, 1887), p. 15. There, Ritchie says, "as I have tried to show, even if the function of the State be limited in the most extreme manner, it is still *indirectly* a moral function, and the moral interests of the community *must* be considered by its legislators."

[84] Kymlicka, *Liberalism*, p. 207.

[85] Even contemporary perfectionist liberals like Raz and Hurka undervalue their new liberal heritage though not as much as neo-Kantians.

[86] Kymlicka, *Liberalism*, p. 36.

[87] Kymlicka misinterprets liberal utilitarianism as advocating the unconstrained maximization of utility. By some accounts, Mill and Spencer were liberal utilitarians who endeavored to accommodate the maximization of utility with potent moral rights. See, for instance, Jonathan Riley, *Liberal Utilitarianism: Social Choice Theory and J. S. Mill's Philosophy* (Cambridge University Press, 1988) and D. Weinstein, *Equal Freedom and Utility: Herbert Spencer's Liberal Utilitarianism* (Cambridge University Press, 1998).

[88] Kymlicka, *Liberalism*, pp. 35–6.

the new liberals certainly exemplify a compelling version of teleological perfectionism. They were what I have called perfectionist consequentialists. Yet, their moral and political theories are also more than modestly deontological as well as perfectionist in the sense that they couple strong, though not indefeasible, rights with a distribution-sensitive conception of common good. In short, the new liberalism is an unconventional blend of Kantianism and consequentialism, as well as perfectionism, that refuses to match the preconceptions that contemporary communitarians and philosophical liberals have hurled at one another (recent efforts at accommodation notwithstanding) in their battle for academic supremacy. There is more conceptual flexibility in liberalism than even Kymlicka concedes, not least because there has been more historical variation to modern liberalism than even he is fully aware of.

Conclusion

Freeden contends that the liberal philosophical tradition consists of a set of core concepts which have been, and continue to be, decontested with considerable variation and innovation. According to Freeden, liberals have always been willing to "entertain multiple rearrangements of their conceptual furniture to a far greater extent" than non-liberals have of their own conceptual furniture because liberals possess an unusual "disposition for conceptual reconfiguration." For Freeden, the new liberalism in particular belies "the mutual exclusiveness or sharp boundaries that ideologies are thought to display" and constitutes "an acknowledgement that their cogent analysis must attend to the multiple forms they adopt."[89] In fine, the new liberalism confirms Stephen Holmes' assessment that a "huge discrepancy" exists between the "legends promulgated by antiliberals and the positions actually defended" by liberals themselves.[90]

But anti-liberals are not the only ones promulgating legends about the liberal tradition. Seminal liberals such as Rawls, Dworkin, and Nozick have promulgated more than enough legends of their own about their own historical identity. Just as communitarians were once prone to

---

[89] Freeden, *Ideologies*, pp. 177, 210.
[90] Stephen Holmes, "The Permanent Structure of Antiliberal Thought," in Nancy L. Rosenblum (ed.), *Liberalism and the Moral Life* (Cambridge, MA: Harvard University Press, 1989), p. 237. Among the "fourteen most common misrepresentations perpetrated and popularized by today's antiliberals," Holmes lists liberalism's purported "hostility toward the common good" second (pp. 239–40). Still, he ignores the new liberals as a fertile resource within the liberal tradition useful in defending liberalism against simplistic distortion.

parody liberalism for ignoring how we are socially constituted and for therefore failing to appreciate how each individual's flourishing requires the flourishing of others, so contemporary philosophical liberals have likewise tended, until very recently anyway, to parody liberalism because, in part, they have neglected much of their very own tradition. Communitarians such as Sandel were thus able to make such apparent short work of philosophical liberalism at the outset, for the latter's theoretical wounds were already in large part self-inflicted. Contemporary liberals have not only impoverished liberalism by ignoring the communitarian legacy of the new liberals. They, along with their communitarian detractors, have also impoverished liberalism by undervaluing the new liberalism's consequentialist and perfectionist heritage.[91] As we have seen, the new liberals not only incorporated communitarian principles into their liberalism but their liberalism was equally consequentialist and perfectionist. Green, Hobhouse, and Ritchie were not only communitarian liberals but perfectionist consequentialist liberals as well. The true story of liberalism has been a rich tapestry of conceptual combinations. Contemporary liberals would have done better by being better intellectual historians. Then, maybe, they could have at least avoided struggling to retrace many of the theoretical moves that earlier communitarian (new) liberals had already made with considerable success. And then, maybe, they could have saved themselves some of the trouble of redundantly refighting battles liberals had previously won.

[91] Both rival groups have likewise impoverished utilitarianism by depicting classical Sidgwickian utilitarianism as the only authentic variety.

8   Staunchly modern, non-bourgeois liberalism

Alan Ryan

Introduction

The title of this chapter is, of course, a gentle tease at the expense of
Richard Rorty's well-known essay on "Post-modernist bourgeois liberalism," an essay that is itself something of a tease at the expense of the
harder left's attack on middle-of-the-road social democrats and their
concern for human rights and non-violent change.[1] I have a non-teasing
purpose, however, and that is to emphasize (as, of course, Rorty himself
does) that Dewey's own conception of his social and political theory was
that it expressed the self-understanding of modern society – "modern"
being no more precise in its denotation than "post-modernist," but
certainly meaning at different times *both* the society that lived off and
built on the scientific revolution of the seventeenth century and the
society that came into existence with the capitalist industrial revolution
of the eighteenth and nineteenth centuries.[2] Dewey's beliefs about the
demands of modernity provide the part of my framework that deals with
modernity.

As to "non-bourgeois," I want to emphasize in a way that many
commentators on Dewey do not that he was a keenly class-conscious

---

This is an abbreviated treatment of issues I tackle at much greater length in *John Dewey
and the High Tide of American Liberalism* (New York: W. W. Norton, 1995); towards the
end, in particular, it gets pretty hasty, therefore.

[1] Richard Rorty, *Philosophical Papers* (Cambridge University Press, 1991), vol. I, pp. 197–
202. I ought to say, what I hope is obvious enough, that Rorty and I are not at odds, but
rather at nuances. I think there is more of a "philosophical metanarrative" in Dewey
than Rorty does, though it surely does not invoke "noumena"; and I demur at the
thought that the institutions that liberalism requires are informatively described as
"bourgeois," especially in the light of Dewey's own attachment to something like Guild
Socialism. But these are complaints from under the same umbrella.

[2] Thus, in *Democracy and Education* (New York: Macmillan, 1916), "modern" means after
the Reformation and the Scientific Revolution of the seventeenth century, while in
Liberalism and Social Action (New York: Putnam, 1935), "modern" means the twentieth
century as opposed to the nineteenth century. There is no particular confusion here:
liberalism of all kinds is a modern phenomenon, but "new liberalism" was a response
within that liberal tradition to new problems as they emerged in the late nineteenth and
early twentieth centuries.

writer. I do not mean that he advocated the politics of class war; quite the contrary. He was, rather, gloomily conscious that the class-divided nature of capitalist societies – sometimes seeing this as a matter of owners versus workers in a more or less Marxist or Weberian style, sometimes seeing it as managers versus the managed in a way more akin to C. Wright Mills – meant that his view of the ways in which modern society opened up novel possibilities of self-expression and social advance was constantly at odds with the immediate facts. One of his many jokes against himself was the observation: "I am very skeptical about things in particular but have an enormous faith in things in general."[3] In social theory, this meant that the organic unity of thought and action, efficiency and free expression, that was latent in modern society was constantly frustrated by conflicts based on misunderstanding and disorganization. What class division pointed to was not the need for a Marxian revolution but for something closer to Guild Socialism and a system of devolved workers' control.[4] His belief in the need for industrial democracy as a complement to political democracy provides at least one "non-bourgeois" element in the framework I use. I should emphasize that this is not entirely at odds with Rorty's essay, though I think Dewey would have thought that "bourgeois" covered too great a multitude of sins to be entirely at home praising bourgeois democracy, and Rorty is far less optimistic about the possibilities of anything resembling workers' control in the context of turn-of-the-century capitalism.

Dewey's views about the peculiar form of freedom available in the modern world make him a liberal. I say this while agreeing, and indeed emphasizing, that until quite late in the day, Dewey's organizing concept is "democracy" rather than "liberalism" – that is, from the very beginning of his discussion of social issues, back in 1888.[5] Dewey thought in terms of the character of a democratic community rather than in terms of the liberal repertoire of individual rights and immunities. When he turns to discussing liberalism in so many words, it is largely in order to argue that American liberalism must be updated, must turn away from *laissez-faire*, and must be redefined as "intelligent social action."[6] None-

---

[3] Letter of April 16, 1915 to Scudder Klyce, quoted in Steven Rockefeller, *John Dewey: Religious Faith and Democratic Humanism* (New York: Columbia University Press, 1991), p. 328.

[4] In this, as much else, he admitted a debt to G. D. H. Cole's work, and espoused a view very like that offered by Russell in *Roads to Freedom* and *Principles of Social Reconstruction*.

[5] "The Ethics of Democracy," in *The Early Works of John Dewey, 1882–1898*, 5 vols., J. A. Boydston *et al.*, eds. (Carbondale: Southern Illinois University Press, 1967–72), vol. I, pp. 227–49.

[6] "Liberalism and Social Action," in *The Later Works of John Dewey, 1925–1953*, 17 vols., J. A. Boydston *et al.*, eds. (Carbondale: Southern Illinois University Press, 1981–7), vol. XI, pp. 46ff.

theless, Dewey's conception of democracy is emphatically a conception of liberal democracy; its origins lie in the ideas of T. H. Green, whose liberal credentials have never been impugned, and its guiding ideal is the strengthening of the organic interconnection of individuals on the basis of freedom and equality. I cheerfully admit that if we define post-modernism in terms of the renunciation of the search for "foundations," and "bourgeois" in terms of the educated middle-class audience for views like Dewey's, we can, stretching a point, talk about post-modernist bourgeois liberalism – but I rather hope we shall not want to.

The mode of analysis I employ is genealogical. I do not mean this in an elaborately Nietzschean or Foucaultian sense, but literally – that is, Dewey is here treated against the intellectual background out of which he emerged because it is easier to understand any writer by seeing where he or she comes from and what assumptions he or she has brought with him or her and has kept or abandoned along the way, and Dewey is discussed to a degree in the political context in which he wrote because some element of contextual understanding is necessary to make sense of what his ideas meant in their own time. It is oddly difficult to do either of these things with any degree of persuasiveness. Assessing just how much baggage he carried with him from his Hegelian youth is difficult because he was obsessed with an issue that hardly bothers us, and yet is one that makes some difference to understanding just what he was up to. That is, his autobiographical sketch "From Absolutism to Experimentalism" gives us Dewey's version of his intellectual progress – an escape from the Absolute. When Russell teased him, none too gently, about the residually Hegelian elements in his thinking, Dewey would angrily insist that he had indeed escaped from Absolutism, and the charge was pre-posterous. But Russell's charge was not that Dewey wished to revive the Hegelian Idea or Notion; it was that Dewey shared Hegel's belief that thought uncovered an organic unity in the world, that the world was a world replete with *meaning* and not just with cause-and-effect connections (which were themselves anyway to be understood as resting on the meaningfulness of the experienced reality as a field of causal forces), and that the empiricist's sharp divisions of fact and value, religion and science, art and utility misrepresented a reality that presented itself to us as a seamless whole. Of course, he was also insistent that he was an "infinite pluralist" as well, and that the world was, so to speak, remaking itself as a differentiated unity. Anti-dualism was quite other than a form of monism. Dewey would also have objected to the suggestion that one is tempted to make: that he was an "experimental Hegelian"[7] – he had

---

[7] Rorty in "Post-Modernist Bourgeois Liberalism" says just what I am tempted to say, that Dewey and others such as Michael Oakeshott "take over Hegel's criticism of Kant's

briefly espoused such a position in the 1880s, arguing that it was empirical evidence in the field of psychology that took us to the understanding that the world was dependent on a Self, and he knew what he had repudiated.[8] What is less easy to decide is how he understood these other "organic" commitments; but it is at least clear that there was more to Dewey's metaphysics than the naturalism of Quine or other successors.[9]

Understanding the connections of his work to matters of the day is not intellectually difficult; the problem is that we have an abundance of Dewey's writings but very little autobiographical evidence with which to illuminate their purpose. That is, a great deal of Dewey's output from the time he moved to New York, and especially after 1914, just is commentary on current politics. This is often politics of a fairly domestic sort. For instance, he wrote against proposals to allow religious instruction in school or to reduce the "progressive" elements in education or to close down art classes and so on, all of which were topics on which Dewey could speak with the authority of the nation's greatest educational theorist, the long-time president of the teachers' union, a founder of the AAUP, sponsor of the ACLU. He also wrote on politics on the grand scale – the American entry into World War I, the Versailles Treaty, and, while he was chairman of the People's Lobby, on the early New Deal policies of Roosevelt – and on much of that one may reasonably have some reservations about his credibility. What is harder to come by is non-public thinking on his political positions. There is an overabundance of prepared material – articles, letters to the editor, and statements of position – but a great shortage of private statements. This makes it hard to see quite how Dewey's political responses tie into his philosophical thinking. As we shall see in conclusion, one thing that happened to Dewey during the 1930s was that he became convinced that he ought to have paid more attention to the importance of the individual; but it is extremely hard to know quite what he meant, and equally hard to know what he wished he had said differently earlier in his career.

conception of moral agency while either naturalising or junking the rest of Hegel." *Philosophical Papers*, vol. I, pp. 197–8. But the interesting issue that this buries is *what* of the rest is "naturalised" and what "junked."

[8] See "The Psychological Standpoint" and "Psychology as Philosophic Method," first published in *Mind*, January and April 1886, in *The Early Works*, vol. I, pp. 122–43, 144–67.

[9] It is true, too, that Dewey could have turned the charge of residual absolutism against Russell if he had thought to; Russell always hankered after what Bernard Williams has called "the absolute conception of the world," and it seems that Dewey really did not. On this, Hilary Putnam, *Renewing Philosophy* (Cambridge, MA: Harvard University Press, 1992), ch. 5, is illuminating.

Although the explanatory tactics here are historical – to show how Dewey employed the intellectual machinery he had constructed by about 1904 to understand the politics of the next forty years – the point of the story is not historical at all. The point I wish to make may surprise some readers, since I claim both that Dewey's work is of great importance and that it is unsatisfactory in crucial respects. Deweyan liberalism is on my analysis very close to the only philosophy of liberal democratic politics that a twenty-first-century reader is likely to find credible. This is not to withdraw any of the skepticism already implied and later spelled out a little about Dewey's contributions to the politics of the day; in particular, it is not to deny that his thoughts on the "outlawry of war" were muddled, incoherent, and laced with wishful thinking, and it is not to deny that his most serious essay on democratic politics, *The Public and its Problems*, is maddeningly evasive, and equally laced with wishful thinking. It is to say that Dewey provides a philosophical basis for twenty-first-century liberalism; or, if you do not like the term "basis," that he provides a uniquely persuasive philosophical gloss on the convictions and commitments of the twenty-first-century liberal. Readers sometimes complain that Dewey's account of twentieth-century politics is shrouded in mist. On the account of the matter offered here, the fog in the photograph sometimes reflects the wobbling hand of the photographer, but is more often a clear representation of a foggy world. Since we all know perfectly well that no philosophical theory can preempt the messy processes of politics and policy-making, and indeed that modern liberalism is committed to taking the messiness seriously, we ought not to ask for a clarity which we cannot have at any price we are ready to pay.

What is Dewey's claim on our attention? Dewey, uniquely, ties the concerns of Jefferson, de Tocqueville, Mill, and writers of a Millian persuasion to a philosophy that escapes the pitfalls of both empiricism and classical Hegelian Idealism. The persuasiveness of contemporary writers such as Charles Taylor and (to a lesser degree) Jürgen Habermas owes a great deal to what they share with Dewey; in particular to the thought that our moral and intellectual horizons are not closed by our social attachments but are, in ways that it is hard to elucidate, nonetheless bounded by communal understandings, and that a modern ethics and politics *must* be individualist at the same time that it must be understood as the product of a particular culture and time, outside which the very idea of the overwhelming importance of individuality would make no sense.[10] It is by now not much disputed

---

[10] The book that makes this case most straightforwardly is Charles Taylor, *The Ethics of Authenticity* (Cambridge, MA: Harvard University Press, 1992), but it is also the burden of Taylor's *Sources of the Self* (Cambridge, MA: Harvard University Press,

that the so-called "liberal–communitarian debate" was nothing of the sort, and that the parodic picture of liberalism offered in Michael Sandel's *Liberalism and the Limits of Justice* served only one valuable purpose, that of forcing liberal political theorists to say more clearly than they had bothered to before just what the sociological and cultural assumptions of their theory were. Once we see that any liberalism must be simultaneously communitarian and individualist, we can work out more delicately in what sense it is true, as Sandel and Taylor have surely persuaded us, that persons would not have selves at all but for the ways they have been shaped by their backgrounds and upbringing, and yet, as Dewey emphasizes, and Taylor's *Sources of the Self* surely persuades us too, that persons fully attuned to the modern world must pursue the project of individual authenticity and social progress that we call liberalism.[11]

Idealism and naturalism 1880–1900

From a purely philosophical perspective, the most interesting years of Dewey's life came between about 1882 and 1899, when he moved gradually through and out of neo-Hegelianism and into the naturalism that was his trademark. Here, there is no room to do more than sketch those parts of this progress that bear on the present topic. But one extraordinary feature of his career is how soon he seized upon the field that became his life's work. It needs to be stressed here not for biographical reasons but as contextual evidence for the claim of this chapter that Dewey was *primarily* a philosopher, not a political commentator propping up his political enthusiasms with philosophy. He graduated from the University of Vermont in 1879 at the age of twenty; he was at something of a loose end until he took up a job teaching high school in a school in Oil City, Pennsylvania run by a cousin. But while he was there, he wrote and sent off to the *Journal of Speculative Philosophy* an essay on "The Metaphysical Assumptions of Materialism" that he hoped would decide whether he should pursue a career in philosophy. The piece – at this distance in time it is almost unreadable – was well

---

1989). Habermas' interest in Dewey goes back to *Toward a Rational Society*, but a perhaps even more interesting link (though not, I think, explored by Habermas) is their common obsession with communication.

[11] This "must" is, of course, mere bullying in the absence of the argument which this remark threatens but does not offer; there is certainly a sense in which Heidegger, say, was *attuned to* the modern world. I am tempted to say that the disastrousness of Heidegger's career is as good an argument as any for that "must," but here at any rate cannot do more than refer the skeptical to Taylor's *Ethics of Authenticity* for the kind of case that we need to make.

received by the editor, W. T. Harris, and Dewey's career was set.[12] Dewey's first philosophical allegiances were to an intuitionism that was commonplace in the late nineteenth-century USA, and was what he had been taught by H. A. P. Torrey at the University of Vermont; it was (oddly, perhaps, but certainly beneficially for Dewey) not shared by W. T. Harris, nor by G. S. Morris who taught him at Johns Hopkins, both of whom were Hegelians rather than followers of President McCosh or Sir William Hamilton. Dewey's attachment to intuitionism dissolved very rapidly. By the time he came to write an article on what he called "Intuitionalism" for an encyclopedia of philosophy during the 1890s he had come to believe that intuitionism was little more than Christian platitudes propped up by wishful thinking. It was not so much philosophy as the assurance that anything we minded about enough had an objective correlate in the real world – a quick way to God, freedom, and immortality. But this was reason conscripted into the service of orthodoxy, unrespectable in motive and argument alike. Dewey's education did him more good than one might have expected it to, however. The piety and conservatism of teachers like Torrey and the university's president, Matthew Buckham, ran off him like water off a duck's back. Indeed, his education had the unintended effect of making him take empiricism and naturalism seriously because it left him a great deal of time to read the British periodical journals to which the University of Vermont subscribed. There he came across Morley, the Stephens, Maine, Henry Fawcett, and Sidgwick and an intellectual life not circumscribed by the conventions of Congregationalist New England.

It seems to have been these writers rather than his philosophy teachers who sparked off an interest in philosophy; it was certainly they who persuaded him that the political options were wider than his teachers supposed. President Buckham was a good citizen but one who believed that all that was needed for social reform was already embodied in the Christian gospels, and that men needed no more than a change of heart to induce them to accept those gospels as a guide. Radicalism seems to have alarmed him and puzzled him in more or less equal measure. Dewey liked Torrey, and continued to study German and German philosophy with him after he graduated; but his verdict on Torrey, too, was that he had hidden his light under a bushel. His constitutional timidity stopped him pressing arguments to their conclusions – and Dewey cited the telling anecdote of Torrey remarking that, philosophi-

---

[12] The story is told in George Dykhuizen, *Life and Mind of John Dewey* (Carbondale: Southern Illinois University Press, 1973), pp. 22–4; the essay is reprinted in *The Early Works*, vol. I, pp. 3–8.

cally speaking, pantheism was the only plausible doctrine, and was only incredible in the light of revelation.

In terms of Dewey's final philosophical stance, it was not a course in philosophy that mattered most at all. Dewey seems to have acquired the belief that naturalism and organicism were consistent with one another in his junior year by reading Huxley's *Physiology*. Fifty years later, in the autobiographical sketch "From Absolutism to Experimentalism" it was Huxley's *Physiology* that he said was the crucial model for successful understanding. He was never tempted by atomistic forms of empiricism; he never subscribed to ethical individualism in the social contractarian sense, nor to the hedonist individualism that underlay Benthamite utilitarianism, but he was always ready to be a naturalist.

The path led through T. H. Green and Hegel. The importance of Green is almost impossible to overstate – even though Dewey himself always had reservations about Green that one imagines he must in part have imbibed from G. S. Morris. Morris' grasp of the history of German philosophy was sufficient for him to teach Dewey that Green was a Fichtian rather than a Hegelian. For all that, Deweyan conceptions of the good of the individual, and Dewey's "democratic" allegiances all his life, had a strongly Greenian flavour. Under the influence of Green, he suggested some remarkable intellectual possibilities. The most astonishing and most dazzling of these was his vision of the eventual transformation of Christianity into democracy:

It is in democracy, the community of ideas and interest through community of action, that the incarnation of God in man (man, that is to say, as an organ of universal truth) becomes a living, present thing, having its ordinary and natural sense. This truth is brought down to life, its segregation removed; it is made a common truth enacted in all departments of action, not in one isolated sphere called religious.[13]

The thought was that the church would eventually cease to exist as a separate institution – a typically Deweyan thought – and would realize itself by dissolving back into the wider community. Eighty years later, a similar fascination with the idea of the *Aufhebung* of state and civil society in the communist utopia was something of a commonplace among readers who had rediscovered the humanist Young Marx, but in Dewey's *oeuvre* the thought stands out because it comes with no account of its pedigree. Its flavour is not unlike that of much else of Dewey's thinking; for instance, in his account of the way the school is to be an aspect of the community's transmission of its own self-understanding rather than a separate institution. But for someone from a Congrega-

---

[13] "Christianity and Democracy," in *The Early Works*, vol. IV, p. 9.

tionalist background it was a bold move to suggest, even in passing, that the church should wither away when the Christian message came to fruition in the lives of a democratic people.

The specific attention to Christianity here, however, points to another important feature of Dewey's work. He always insisted on the religious quality of the democratic faith; however sociological his understanding of philosophy, he never doubted that democracy rested on "faith in the common man," and that that faith was a religious faith. The sense in which it was to be at once religious, philosophical, naturalistic, and scientific is one that takes some elucidation – but unless one accepts that that is what Dewey offered one underestimates his reach. Dewey soon concluded that Green was an inadequate philosophical guide; he suffered from the Kantian tendency to divide the empirical selves that we fully were from the universal self that we aspire to be but can never wholly become. Dewey's anti-dualism repudiated even such a vestigial duality and insisted that we were already one with the universal and that we could rest securely in the sense that the world was not inimical to human aspiration. This was transformed into a reliance on our communal nature by the time he wrote *Human Nature and Conduct*, but the sentiment is much the same:

With responsibility for the intelligent determination of particular acts may go a joyful emancipation from the burden of responsibility for the whole which sustains them, giving them their final outcome and quality. There is a conceit fostered by perversion of religion which assimilates the universe to our personal desires; but there is also a conceit of carrying the load of the universe from which religion liberates us. Within the flickering inconsequential acts of separate selves dwells a sense of the whole which claims and dignifies them. In its presence we put off mortality and live in the universal. The life of the community in which we live and have our being is the fit symbol of this relationship.[14] [Hence his distaste for the "lachrymose" quality of Russell's *Free Man's Worship.*]

Although Dewey's autobiographical essay "From Absolutism to Experimentalism" gives a general sketch of the transformation, it is more difficult to see on the ground. His famous essay "The Reflex Arc Concept in Psychology," however, deserves the place it has in all accounts of Dewey.[15] He wanted to repudiate *both* the idea – very prominent in his earlier *Psychology* – that the study of any empirical phenomena led inexorably to the conclusion that the world was mind,

[14] "Human Nature and Conduct," in *The Middle Works of John Dewey, 1899–1924*, 15 vols., J. A. Boydston *et al.*, eds. (Carbondale: Southern Illinois University Press, 1977–83), vol. XIV, p. 227.
[15] In *The Early Works*, vol. V, pp. 96–107.

and his earlier belief that the only alternative to that metaphysical idealism was atomistic empiricism. But even when Dewey had lost faith in his argument that the world was essentially a Self, the thought that we could understand an organism by building up a system of stimulus–response connections remained incredible. The essay on the reflex arc argued, as Dewey always argued thereafter, that stimulus–response connections made sense because only they were embedded in an organism whose whole constitution was oriented to something like self-maintenance in a problematic environment.

"Experimentalism" was a label Dewey preferred to "instrumentalism" largely because he was less willing than James to scandalize the believers in truth; "instrumentalism" suggests that truth is what it is good to believe, while "experimentalism" suggests only that a major part of all thinking is forming plans or projects for dealing with the world. Dewey's critics were never satisfied that he had given an answer to their questions about the relationship between our thoughts and the world to which those thoughts referred. They were clear that he did not believe in truth as correspondence to fact; but did he think that beliefs were true only to the extent that the world was as we believed it to be? Dewey's refusal to divide "experience" into subjective sensation and belief on the one side and objective fact of the matter on the other thoroughly irritated them. All the same Dewey insisted that all beliefs needed to be tested in experience, and that experience was not in any sense merely subjective. It was, so to speak, the experienced world. One has to be delicate here; although he was less scandalous than James, Dewey was less of an "objectivist" than Peirce. While he was helped to stabilize his own ideas on "warranted assertability" by Peirce's 1878 paper on "The Fixation of Belief," he set no store by the thought that there would be a final convergence on beliefs which in virtue of that "end of the day" convergence one would know to represent "objective" reality. So far as he was concerned, the progress of human understanding would be indefinite and perhaps infinite. Dewey was not hostile to the notion that truths were established, and he certainly was hostile to wishful thinking. Rather, we should take seriously the fact that the search for truth was problem-driven, and (perhaps most crucially) take seriously the injunction to turn from "the problems of philosophy" to "the problems of men," and look for fruitful kinds of cultural criticism rather than hope that a new philosophical wrinkle would resolve the dilemmas that had held up our predecessors.

What this means for Dewey as liberal and democrat is easy to list, but not easy to articulate as the connected philosophical argument he meant it to be. Dewey was best known – after 1899 and the publication of *The*

School and Society[16] – as the great theorist of the school as an institution central to a democratic society. It was a characteristic production, and suggests a good many of the reasons why he was simultaneously regarded with near veneration by the mildly progressive and assailed with some fierceness by the conservative on the one side and the more wildly radical on the other. Much of what he thought about education might appeal to any reader, philosophically inclined or the reverse: for example, the claim that the school must itself be a community in which children learned to respect the rights of others while they learned to claim their own, his fastidiousness about balancing leadership from the instructor and intelligent acceptance of that leadership by the children, and his insistence that education had to become livelier and more interesting, less a matter of rote and more a matter of lived experience. Both friends and enemies, in fact, could seize upon such statements; those who think Dewey conceded too much to vocational education in the sense of job training will read those concessions into his defence of the practical, while those who think he conceded too little will read his impracticality into his insistence that the meaning of the practical must be elicited by reflection – when what the enthusiasts for vocational training usually wished the schools to produce was quick and obedient workmen. According to taste, one could side with those who thought he conceded too much or too little to rote learning, to the authority of the teacher, and to almost any feature of applied pedagogy one cares to name. It is built into the "philosophy of the *via media*" that it should be vulnerable to those who want the brisker and simpler extremes.[17]

The deeper interest of Dewey's educational views, at any rate for us, lies in the philosophical doctrines that all this embodied. In 1894, he sketched in an amazing twenty-page letter a syllabus for the Laboratory School that worked through practical and theoretical tasks, and linked the tasks to the changing seasons, in a sort of Hegelian spiral; this unity of theory and practice, and the ascent to deeper understandings through

---

[16] "The School and Society," in *The Middle Works*, vol. I, pp. 3–109. It was an accidental bestseller; the University of Chicago decided in 1899 to lay on a series of lectures and publications to publicize the University's work, and Dewey's lectures were part of that program. It was also an occasion to reflect on his Laboratory School's work since it had opened in 1896 – the topic of the lectures as delivered, in fact. It very rapidly made its way as a statement of "progressive" views about elementary education, and was a commercial as well as an intellectual hit. There is some unhappy correspondence between Dewey and the publisher at the University of Chicago Press in the Dewey Papers; Dewey was not bashful about money, but the University Press plainly felt that he had been less than open about his plan to have the second printing done by Macmillan. It may also have been a decision provoked by his growing irritation with the University and its administration.

[17] See, for instance, Avital Simhony's discussion of "The Social and Political Ideas of the English Idealists," D.Phil., Oxford University, 1980.

seeing the practical implications of theory and the theoretical questions raised by practice, were supposed to carry the child through the various stages of school and beyond. It embodied one of his many anti-dualisms – in this case the claim that there is no ultimate division between theory and practice – and was an image of his later understanding of science: that science properly was not the piling up of mathematical abstractions but the achievement of an increasingly organic understanding of the *meaning* of events. Whether six-year-olds really understood the full interest of the fact that metal rusting and food cooking are examples of the same oxidization process, one might wonder, but the thought is a fertile one. In practice, in the Laboratory School, Dewey's teachers taught in what a British observer fifty years later might have thought was an enlightened but not an astonishing fashion. Children would spend their first morning at school making boxes for their pens and pencils, and then go on to consider the geometry of what they had created; the sandbox would provide both recreation and an opportunity to think about three-dimensional geometry, the different properties of different materials, and so on. None of this was to be hurried; it is noticeable that Dewey balances his insistence that play must be shaped and directed by an adult understanding of where the child is heading with such statements as this:

The first [stage] extends from the age of four to eight or eight and a half years. In this period the connection with the home and neighbourhood life is, of course, especially intimate. The children are largely occupied with direct social and outgoing modes of action, with doing and telling. There is relatively little attempt made at intellectual formulation, conscious reflection, or command of technical methods ... Hence in the second period (from eight to ten) emphasis is put upon securing ability to read, write, handle number etc., not in themselves, but as necessary helps and adjuncts in relation to the more direct modes of experience.[18]

Or, to put it somewhat uncharitably, a long time was spent on socialization before the three Rs were inflicted on the kids.

In fact, as everyone noticed, Dewey wrote next to nothing thereafter about the details of curriculum issues or pedagogical tactics and strategy. As I have said, pedagogy is subordinate to social theory and social theory is subordinate to what one might call the *Lebensphilosophie* of the modern world. This is not a complaint; Dewey was a philosopher, not a professor of pedagogy – except during the ten years in Chicago when he was indeed Professor of Pedagogy as well as the head of the department of philosophy. The role of the philosopher was not so much to spell out

---

[18] "The University Elementary School: General Outline of Study," in *The Middle Works*, vol. I, p. 337.

ways in which students might be taught more or more enjoyably as to elucidate the place of education in the experience of the community. The opening paragraph of *School and Society* is an obvious illustration; in his first breath, Dewey insists on discussing education as a community concern, not an individual one, that the community must treat *all* its children as devoted parents treat their individual children, and that a society in which their education turns on a competitive struggle between parents seeking the best for their children one by one is a society in disarray. What he then goes on to discuss is not the mysterious quality that makes each child both typical and a unique individual – something to which Russell, for instance, comes closer – but the social background that sets the problems of modern education, such as urbanization, industrialization, the factory, the city, and the slum.[19]

The mature doctrine

Democracy and Education, published in 1916, was the culmination of such thinking. That book, he later said, "was for many years that in which my philosophy, such as it is, was most fully expounded," though he went on to observe that his philosophical critics had taken no notice.[20] It was certainly true that the conception of democracy to which the discussion of education was attached was philosophical rather than political; Dewey made almost no reference to institutions such as the vote, nor to such central liberal institutions as accessible law courts and an uncorrupt police and judiciary. The book makes many references to two basic liberal values – freedom and equality – and Dewey took it for granted, as he always had, that all arrangements in a democratic society should foster freedom and equality, and all its benefits and opportunities should be available to members of the society on a free and equal basis. Nonetheless, what made democracy democracy was, he said, "organic communication." Hilary Putnam has lately written admiringly of Dewey's "epistemological" justification of democracy; but what is striking is not so much that Dewey thinks of democracy as

---

[19] A subject on which I shall not touch is Dewey and the city; critics have been more or less equally divided between complaining that he focused exclusively on the city and thus neglects much else that he ought to attend to and complaining that he hankers after an essentially rural way of life and thus spends his time trying to turn the school into an agency of rural patterns of socialization in spite of its urban setting. See Robert Westbrook, *Dewey and American Democracy* (Ithaca: Cornell University Press, 1991), ch. 5, pp. 150–94, for a great deal on all this. I think it is a non-controversy; Dewey got interested in education in the Chicago of Jane Addams, which was much more like the environment that inspired the British (and of course the American) settlement movement than it was like anything we have encountered in the late twentieth century.

[20] "From Absolutism to Experimentalism," in *The Later Works*, vol. V, p. 156.

"organized intelligence," which he certainly does, as that he *defines* democracy in communicative terms. Democracy is less a political concept in this account than a social one, and its everyday descriptive meaning has been transmuted into something altogether richer; a democratic society is (though this is a thoroughly un-Deweyan thought) one in which the essence of sociability is actualized. A democratic society is one where we can reveal ourselves to one another more deeply and more comprehensively than ever, and therefore come to understand ourselves adequately in the process. There is no such thing as an adequate but solipsistic self-understanding; all self-understanding implies an actual or potential interlocutor, and only a thorough training in explaining oneself to others will provide the basis for any sort of skill in explaining oneself to oneself.[21] For any of this to happen, we had to be educated in such a way that we were self-aware and adept at communicating with our fellows; and for that to happen, we had to share an education with them. Here was the essence of Dewey's emphasis on making the school continuous with the community. The common school was thus, to put it in the simplest way, the basis of a democratic morality; but that slightly pious way of putting it is un-Deweyan, because by this time the usual notion of morality had also suffered a sea-change.

Readers of *Human Nature and Conduct* will remember that an ethics of rules and prohibitions, sanctions and requirements was not what Dewey had in mind at all. Dewey's ethical pragmatism had by the middle of the second decade of the twentieth century become a democratic Aristotelianism, if that is not too sharp a contradiction in terms. Dewey starts from a double departure from what Bernard Williams has abused as "the institution called morality."[22] For him the crucial point was that ethics was not primarily an individual matter; since that is a misleading formulation, one might better say that he thought that beginning with an image of ethical inquiry as a matter of the single individual searching for principles to guide his conduct, or scrutinizing his conscience for its judgments on his behavior, was to start in the wrong place. Ethics begins and largely ends in social practice and socialized habit. In other ways, this was not an anti-individualist argument. It is obvious enough

---

[21] It is not an accident that this kind of claim should sound so much like G. H. Mead; it was Mead and Tufts who got Dewey to come to Chicago, and with the latter Dewey wrote the most successful text in ethics ever to be put before American students, while the former's work on the "I and the Me" so impressed Dewey that he later said he had stopped trying to do any original work in psychology and had simply taken over Mead's results. It is to the Meads, incidentally, that the relatively felicitous prose of "The School and Society" was due; they reconstituted a publishable text from Dewey's lecture notes.

[22] In his *Ethics and the Limits of Philosophy* (London: Fontana Press/Collins, 1985).

that ethical decisions are made by individuals; they draw upon a common stock of solid judgment about what a satisfactory life in a satisfactory community is like, what behavior it requires, which questions are settled, and which open, but it is individuals who draw upon these resources when they engage in decision-making. So the second innovation was to play down the separateness and distinctiveness of *moral* requirements, to remind us that ethics is a form of practical reasoning, and that all forms of practical reasoning have much in common; they are not divided by nature into prudential, ethical, and esthetic forms. (Indeed, though this is by the way, the division of theoretical and practical reason is by no means natural.) They all have a strong means–ends quality, and their goal is always – in formal terms – the satisfactory resolution of a problematic relationship between the organism and the environment. Ethics, like most interesting aspects of experience, is a form of problem-solving. It is a general axiom of Dewey's account of experience and inquiry that without a problem the organism would not think at all, and would on Dewey's analysis scarcely have anything one could call an experience of the outside world. This is not to say that the problem is always what the layman would call a *practical* one; Dewey's analysis of the painting of Cézanne and Matisse is an analysis of problem-solving, but the goal is a form of experience that he calls "consummatory," and the problem thus to enhance that experience rather than attain a further goal.[23]

Dewey's contribution to moral theory is, up to a point, to slide it towards the use of the concept of healthy functioning as its main organizing notion and away from treating either adherence to principle or the pursuit of utilitarian goals as such a notion.[24] Not to belabor the point, a radical and secular re-interpretation of Green might take one a long way towards such a position. A democratic society on this view is a healthy society; surprisingly, in view of their quarrelsome relations, the similarities with the views of Russell's *Principles of Social Reconstruction*

---

[23] "Art as Experience," in *The Later Works*, vol. X, e.g. pp. 143–4.

[24] I say this slightly hesitantly; partly because it leaves out the role of ideals, which certainly mattered a lot to Dewey, and partly because it underplays the role of the individual's *responsibility* and *answerability* to others. If one were to ask what differentiates ethics from other sorts of decision-guiding thinking in Dewey, I think one would have to say that it is the role of "answering to others" for our decisions, and this may sit awkwardly with an emphasis on individual healthy functioning. Of course, in the ideal it does not because in the ideal we find our own satisfaction in seeing our ideals realized in the community's achievements; but even though Dewey was happy to take up the offer of a "moral holiday" that this rather Hegelian thought allows us, he was much too down to earth to ignore the importance of conflicts of interest. The difficulty is that once they are placed in the foreground, the "healthy individual in the healthy community" ideal can easily look like a fudge or wishful thinking.

are striking, though I know of no direct evidence that Dewey read the *Principles*, and I am sure that he would have found too much of the lachrymose tone of *A Free Man's Worship* in the text. But the emphasis on education, the secular religiosity, and the organic account of successful psychological functioning are strikingly alike.

War and depression

If this picture is generally accurate, we can see why Dewey was by 1914 an unusually persuasive philosophical voice. He was optimistic about the potential of society and fiercely critical about the distance between its potential and its actuality. The capacity to be optimistic in general and discontented in particular is one that Americans have always valued very highly. Dewey had it in the most developed possible form. He had a Ruskinian sense of the importance of work in human life that fit into the American self-image readily enough, but with the radical suggestion that work as actually engaged in in the factory or on the stock exchange frustrated the real purpose of work in the moral life, and created ugliness rather than beauty. It was not surprising that he could vote for Eugene Debs in 1912 but for Wilson in 1916: an ideal socialism which closed the gap between utilitarian production and artistic creation was obviously a goal to pursue, but not to the neglect of the here and now. The ideal school was a long way off, but he could easily believe his daughter and Randolph Bourne when they told him "that the 'Gary Plan' put into operation by William A. Wirt in Gary, Indiana, was proof that . . . Dewey's philosophy could be put into practice on a large scale in the public schools."[25] And so it went, more or less across the board. The outbreak of World War I was the beginning of disillusionment.

The Great War severely damaged Dewey's poise. It is easy to overlook this since he published *Democracy and Education* in the middle of the war, but before the entry of the United States, and ended the war writing *Reconstruction in Philosophy* and *Human Nature and Conduct* with apparently undiminished confidence. But he was overtaken by events in the course of the war. He must by war's end have had grave doubts about his own response to Randolph Bourne's attacks on his views; and his reactions to Versailles and the rise of irrationalist politics in the twenties and thirties were inept. His defense of the "outlawry of war" movement was a pure case of willing the end and refusing to will the means, while *The Public and Its Problems* was infinitely less persuasive a defence of democracy than Lippmann's two assaults, *Public Opinion* and *The Phantom Public*, had been criticisms.

[25] See Westbrook, *Dewey and American Democracy*, pp. 179–83.

Dewey's views, it is easy to say in hindsight, were ill adapted to the strains of war, a point that Randolph Bourne made with all the ferocity of disappointed discipleship. The vision of society in its "normal" state as a problem-solving organism did not assert, but nonetheless suggested, an evolutionary process in which ordinary social habit would suffice for everyday activities, until some shock or crisis jolted us into rethinking our habitual behaviors. But this suggested that society was a unity within which the kinds of strain that were revealed by the "Americanization" programmes of the war were invisible; Dewey had always been a "melting pot" theorist, and had assumed that immigration presented the USA with problems of assimilation that might be difficult, but in the long run gave the nation its unique vitality. With the war, it became less easy to believe that American society, jolted out of its everyday existence, would respond imaginatively and productively to new demands. One can see Dewey getting stuck when responding to such militaristic proposals as conscripting all male school students as military cadets; he was, one imagines, simply hostile to it, but in order to oppose it he largely had to stick to the issue of localism versus nationalism and object to its anti-federal aspects. On the other hand, he remained more optimistic than not, and his "What Are We Fighting For?" of 1918 was characteristically upbeat in suggesting that for all the risk of post-war chaos and of a world divided into warring imperialist blocs, the message of the war was the priority of organization over property, the need to employ every able-bodied person when emergency arose, and the ability of nations to cooperate across national divides. If these lessons were incorporated in the peace, there would be a world "made safe for democracy and one in which democracy was firmly anchored." At this stage, early in 1918, he was optimistic about the possibilities of a League of Nations, too; indeed, he was sure that only under a League would the world become safe for democracy.[26]

Nor was the war calculated to show pragmatism at its best, at any rate for anyone as intrinsically pacific as Dewey. For, in a situation where it seemed obvious that American self-interest narrowly construed lay in keeping out of the European conflict, espousing absolute neutrality, and offering good offices as a mediator while the conflict was on and economic aid in reconstruction when it was over, Dewey would swallow neither the idea of an American alliance with the "anti-militarist" powers – Czarist Russia looking particularly implausible as a specimen of that class, and imperialist France and Britain looking hardly more persuasive – nor the sort of realism that would have enjoined giving the

---

[26] "What Are We Fighting For?" in *The Middle Works*, vol. XI, p. 105.

cold shoulder to Britain. Dewey was reduced to arguing that the war demanded *action*, but it appeared to be action in general rather than action to achieve some particular end. Randolph Bourne was later to profess tremendous shock and outrage at Dewey's eventual espousal of the United States' entry into the war on the Allied side, but it was not a surprising result. Once one was committed to the thought that a "cold neutrality" was intolerable, and that the United States must somehow be active but not active militarily, one was a long way down the slippery slope. For as the war went on, it became harder and harder to see what activity was possible that would not eventually drag the country into the war. But it was not an attractive result, even though Dewey said, once it had happened, that he hoped that the result of engagement would be to speed up social development in the United States.

A good deal of Dewey's commentary while the war was on was unpersuasive, though this aspect of it was not, and in fact became commonplace about World War II. But, his reactions to the illiberal, militaristic, chauvinistic, and anti-socialist doings of the government, universities, mobs, and the press were deeply depressing. His first thought was that American illiberalism was "puppyish"; the country was not used to fighting major wars (itself an odd thought from someone whose father had served in the Union army), and so people got boisterously aggressive when pacifists protested.[27] He nearly lost the twenty-year-old friendship of Jane Addams by making silly remarks about the pacifists' lack of moral fibre, and did not much appease her by insisting that *she* did not lack moral fibre but most of her fellow pacifists did.[28] The activities of the president of Columbia, Nicholas Murray Butler, who sacked dissident faculty without the least pretence of going through the procedures established for such purposes, woke him up to a degree, but where Charles Beard resigned from the university, Dewey limited himself to resigning from the disciplinary committee that had been slighted by his president. Late in the day, he saw that the effect of the war on American intellectual life really was disastrous, and said so boldly enough. Still, he seems even then not to have protested against such monstrous actions as the ten-year sentence imposed on Eugene Debs, nor thought that Wilson's refusal to commute it was as vindictive as it obviously was.

Once disillusioned, he swung to extremes. He opposed the Versailles Treaty on entirely decent and rational grounds, but also opposed American membership in the League of Nations and became a propagandist for the "outlawry of war" movement launched by Salmon

[27] "In Explanation of Our Lapse," in *The Middle Works*, vol. X, pp. 292ff.
[28] "The Future of Pacifism," in *The Middle Works*, vol. X, pp. 266–8.

Levinson. This proposed to make war an international crime, but as all
its critics observed, it lacked any means to enforce the world's judgment
of the criminal's misdeeds. Lippmann and others kept urging that only a
system of collective security would be effective in repressing war-
mongering, but Dewey's response was that it was "contradictory" to
employ war to put down war, an argument that, applied to domestic
politics, would suggest that it was contradictory to give police the means
forcibly to restrain muggers and murderers. His isolationism remained
unwavering until Pearl Harbor; as late as 1940, he wrote an essay
entitled "Whatever Happens, This Time Keep Out" that argued, rather
as Russell's *Which Way to Peace?* had done, that the democracies would
only lose their own civil liberties by embroiling themselves in war.
Dewey had more than a touch of the traditional American contempt for
the politics of the European states; the First World War had been an
imperialist squabble that had lured America into what was falsely billed
as a war for democracy, and his was very much a case of once bitten
twice shy. Once the war was on, he wrote nothing on its conduct or on
the post-war settlement; interestingly enough, his most active contribution was to try to disillusion his countrymen about the Soviet Union:
alliance with Russia might be needed to win the war but this was a far
cry from requiring us to think that Stalin was anything other than a
murderous tyrant and the Soviet Union anything other than a slave
society. That, on the whole, seems well judged, but it cannot be said that
international relations were Dewey's strong suit.

Non-Marxian radicalism

Nonetheless, Dewey's ideas about the demands of a modernized liberalism were as rational as anyone's could be. He swallowed too much of a
too simple class analysis and a too simple materialism, and was thus
ready to blame an ill-defined capitalist culture for just about everything
he disliked, but he was steadily anti-Marxist, thinking that neither
revolution nor violence was an effective means for the ends radicals had
in mind. In this, he was much like Russell once more, as he says in his
contribution to "Why I am not a Communist." Unlike Russell, he had
solid philosophical reasons for holding that view; because he refused to
draw a sharp distinction between means and ends it was easier for him
than for Russell to insist that evil means corrupted the ends they were
supposed to serve. The fundamental thought of most of his 1930s
writing was that liberalism needed to be modernized. There were new
threats to liberty and therefore there were needed new forms of organization to overcome these threats. This is the argument of both

Individualism Old and New and *Liberalism and Social Action*. It is often rather thin, but it is never silly nor hysterical. Nor is it vulnerable to charges of wishful thinking. The worst that one might have claimed a quarter-century ago was that Dewey's opponents had all died, and that his work was therefore rather unsurprising. He had spent his energy attacking Marxist revolutionaries to his left and *laissez-faire* conservatives to his right, and in, say, 1975 one might have thought both of them sufficiently discredited by events. After the Reagan counter-revolution, one might reasonably think differently. Even had there not been a Reagan counter-revolution, there was in Dewey an implicit criticism even of the non-*laissez-faire* liberalism of theorists like John Rawls that has some vitality still. Dewey complained that Walter Lippmann, himself a critic of *laissez-faire*, failed to see what new liberalism demanded; that is, Lippmann's conception of freedom was too narrowly political. It did not look for freedom in the workplace as well as the polling booth. This is a charge that one might launch against modern non-*laissez-faire* liberals who are rightly impressed by the difficulties of squaring industrial democracy and civil liberties but who are too quick to renounce the former.

His view of politics was even then frequently inept; defending Dewey against the charge that he underestimated the novelty and effectiveness of the New Deal is a thankless task. It can be done: there is something to be said for the thought that Roosevelt's unprincipled willingess to try anything that would dig the United States out of the slump was not an example of Deweyan experimentalism but simply thrashing about. But, to hold this view, in the way Dewey did, involved much more than pointing to a methodological crux. Dewey, for instance, believed as firmly as anyone that capitalism was simply doomed; nor was this the belief that capitalism defined just in simple nineteenth-century *laissez-faire* terms was doomed; rather it was the belief that the capitalism of large modern government assisted and regulated corporations was also doomed. Whether one ascribes the survival of this economic form to Roosevelt, Keynes, or the military build-up to World War II and the subsequent Cold War, its survival is hard to dispute. Against this sort of disproof by history, philosophical arguments must look thin.

All of this is without regard to his actual political good works. Here we may think the People's Lobby not particularly impressive, Westbrook notwithstanding, and Dewey's persistent hope for a third-party breakaway led by people like the Republican Senator Norris simply misguided. And one might wonder how to evaluate the adventures into which Sidney Hook led him; the Trotsky trial in Mexico City was a heroic adventure, and the Congress for Cultural Freedom a good idea in the late thirties, whatever it turned into after the war. But, Dewey's constant defence of liberalism in education was always admirable, and even if a great deal of what he wrote in the thirties and forties is of more or less antiquarian interest, one never feels embarrassed on his behalf.

Conclusion

In the end the point we must cling to is that Dewey was a philosopher rather than a political activist; Dewey's philosophy is in all sorts of ways practically minded, and it is in some ways anti-philosophical; that is, it largely eschews what Dewey thought of as metaphysical inquiries, and it never allows the traditional formulation of philosophical issues to dictate present analysis. His claim that philosophy was a form of cultural criticism – in fact the criticism of criticisms – conveys a sense of what he was after. Nonetheless, the obvious contemporary figures with whom he is to be compared would be Jürgen Habermas and Charles Taylor.

Dewey's conception of the demands of modernity is strikingly like Taylor's discussion of the ethics of authenticity: there is a form of individualism in ethics that is simply inescapable, but it is inescapable because we learn it in a particular sort of society, not because one could not imagine a different world, nor because it reflects a deep metaphysical loneliness or alienation from our fellow creatures.

Towards the end of his life, Dewey said that he wished he had emphasized the role of individuals in social and political life more than he had done; he felt that he had understated the role of individuals in innovating, and underestimated their role in reforming social and intellectual practices of whatever sort. One can hardly quarrel with his own assessment of his ideas, but it's not clear that he had very much for which to apologize. His argument had never been that reason works behind the backs of individuals, and for that kind of Hegelian teleology he had no taste at all. It had always been that individual projects embody social resources; the individual must either be sheerly unintelligible to himself and to others or must appeal to a stock of concepts and a view of the evidence that he shares with others in his society. The modern project puts upon individuals the burden of making choices about the use of those resources that former societies may not have done, and certainly offers fewer transcendental comforts than the moral projects of earlier ages. But this is not to say that the society supplies the modern project with no resources; the point of an essentially comforting philosophy like Dewey's is to say what those are.

Andrew Vincent

Both the terms "new liberalism" and "citizenship" have intricate relations to late nineteenth- and twentieth-century politics. The term "new liberalism" is still occasionally confused with the term "neo-liberalism" – the latter is usually taken as a synonym for the liberal new right of the 1980s, which stands in overt opposition to the new liberalism. It is important to bear in mind here that liberalism is a complex and intricate body of thought. It is not a uni-dimensional tradition. Classical liberalism has often been singled out by theorists as the most important dimension; however, this seriously neglects other important and distinctive strands of thought within liberalism, not least the powerful and immensely influential tradition of the "new liberalism."[1]

"Citizenship" also embodies an ambiguous conceptual legacy. It is a term which has gone in and out of fashion from the nineteenth century to the present. To raise the issue of the concept of citizenship from the late 1960s, even up to the very early 1980s, was seen as either quaint or archaic. However, times have changed and citizenship is once more fully back in vogue. Unlike "citizenship," however, the term "new liberalism" still has an awkward feel to it in discussions of political theory. Republicanism, classical liberalism and libertarianism, communitarianism, Marxism, feminism, and neo-Aristotelianism flourish in contemporary anglophone political theory, but one hardly ever finds a reference to the new liberalism as a coherent or distinctive view. This might be partly explained by the sheer power, pervasiveness, and hegemonic character of the resurgent classical liberalism of the 1980s, which, for a time, tended to dominate discussion of liberal theory. The new liberalism is also intrinsically a more eclectic doctrine, blending various theoretical elements. We might conceptualize the new liberalism as a form of

---

[1] See Andrew Vincent and Raymond Plant, *Philosophy, Politics and Citizenship: The Life and Thought of the British Idealists* (Oxford: Blackwell, 1984); Andrew Vincent, *Modern Political Ideologies*, 2nd edn. (Oxford: Blackwell, 1995), pp. 30ff. See also Andrew Vincent, "The New Liberalism in Britain 1880–1914," *Australian Journal of Politics and History*, 36 (1990), 388–405 and Michael Freeden, *The New Liberalism: An Ideology of Social Reform* (Oxford: Clarendon Press, 1978).

"liberal communitarianism," although even this does not quite catch the subtle doctrinal nuances.

The focus of this chapter will be on the new liberalism in Britain, although, clearly, variants of new liberal thought appeared elsewhere: in America under the auspices of writers like John Dewey; in Italy in writers like Guido de Ruggiero; and in Germany in the writings of Albert Lange, Karl Vorländer, and Max Weber. The theme of the chapter will be the problematic inheritance of the new liberalism revealed through its deep commitment to citizenship. Part of that problematic inheritance is linked to the very ambivalence over the term "new liberalism" itself and what is expected or implied by it. It is liberal – which, however mistakenly, has individualistic connotations – but it is also more communally or socially orientated. This, in itself, creates a subtle tension in new liberal argument at the most basic foundational level.

The argument of this chapter contends that the idea of citizenship, embedded within late nineteenth-century classical liberalism, was essentially passive in nature. Citizenship implied basic negative rights to, for example, free speech, property, conscience, and worship. It was, therefore, confined to the general obedience to a formal rule of law, preventing coercion or harm between individuals. The correlative duty of such civil rights was forbearance from harming others. In effect, this conception unwittingly devalued any but the most minimal notions of active concern for fellow citizens or positive duties to the wider community. Citizenship, in this civil perspective, was not a self-realizing activity in the service of the community, but rather an assertion of minimal civil entitlements. The new liberal conception of citizenship – which reacted to the classical liberal perspective from the 1880s – was initially theorized in terms of civic duties, as well as a more expansive vision of rights. The civic duty component was crucial to the initial justification of the welfare state in the pre-1914 period. Yet, the stress on rights also maintained a self-conscious continuity with classical liberalism. This continuity had an unexpected cost. The emphasis on rights slowly weakened the idea of public-spirited duties as correlative to such rights. By deploying rights language, new liberals, unintentionally, set the stage for the gradual decline, during the twentieth century, of solidaristic notions of public-spirited duty. From its inception, the new liberalism therefore embodied a complex tension, which has carried through to the present day in Britain. This tension focused on the conflict between civism and civility, between an essentially "rights-orientated" passive recipience vision of welfare and a civic activist vision of duties to the common good.

This tension highlights part of the late twentieth-century sense of crisis within the welfare state – a crisis centered on the conflict between passive entitlements and active duties. Paradoxically, this complex tension was introduced by the new liberalism. In post-1945 thought and practice, new liberal ideas were effectively institutionalized within the burgeoning welfare state. Citizenship, in the 1950s, crystallized around a more administrative, static model of social rights, which side-stepped the issue of civic duties. The internal tension thus became institutionalized. "Duty," for most citizens, mutated into the basic willingness to pay marginally higher levels of progressive taxation, which, over time, became a bureaucratized burden. In consequence, clientalized recipients of welfare claimed passive entitlements without a sense of civic responsibility. In summary, the strong emphasis on the rights of citizenship, the indirect undermining of solidaristic duty, the bureaucratization of social rights, and the gradual decline of communal consensus in the post-1945 world, essentially eviscerated the public-spiritedness which had been implicit in new liberal theory. This opened it up to new right criticism in the 1980s. The assault on the welfare state incorporated an attempt to prise apart the civil and the civic logic. Essentially the new right theories were trying to return citizenship to a more predictable world of passive civil rights. Paradoxically, part of the new right case had already been partly accepted within the logic of new liberal arguments.

This discussion will first examine certain phases of commitment to the concept of citizenship in Britain, placing the new liberal perspective within this framework. The argument will then focus on specific problems encountered in the new liberal standpoint on citizenship, which had repercussions into the late twentieth century.

Phases of citizenship

The term "new liberal" appeared in public discussion in Britain in the 1880s. Other terms, like "radical," "progressive," or "social liberal," also denoted roughly the same conception. Up to 1914, even the term "liberal socialism" often implied, in public discussion, "new liberal." None of these terms was meant to indicate a revolutionary change of view, rather an evolution of policy and ideas. On a formal level, from the 1880s, new liberals can be seen to have reacted critically to certain themes within classical liberalism: notions like atomized individualism, the negative conception of liberty, the *laissez-faire* conception of the economy, and minimal-state theory. They wished to blend or replace these with a more socialized and holistic understanding of the individual, a more positively inclined conception of liberty linked to notions like self-development, a modified conception of a mixed economy, and a more responsive, sensitive, and enabling conception of the state.

The question remains, though, apart from the very formal view of the new liberalism, outlined above, what is the more substantive character of this new liberalism?[2] The picture becomes cloudier at this point. The new liberalism is, in fact, an amalgam of ideas which coalesce around the above formal themes. Whereas there was a greater degree of unanimity in the pre-1914 period, the 1914-18 war experience, the collapse of the parliamentary Liberal Party in the 1920s, and the rise of the Labour Party modified the new liberalism. The new liberalism fragmented during the 1920s – although some of the potential fracture lines were present in the pre-1914 setting. The diversity and fecundity of new liberal thinking from the 1920s onward explains some of the tangled character of later twentieth-century British politics. New liberal thought, in the later twentieth century, involved interpretative shadings across an ideological spectrum.[3] The identity of the new liberalism is thus heterogeneous. Much of the centerist and left of center political debate in Britain has been debate between forms of new liberalism, legatees of the debates of the first few decades of the twentieth century. On the other side of politics, there has been an efflorescence in the 1980s – in the new right – of the very classical liberalism which was attacked by the new liberal theorists from the 1880s onwards.

Citizenship has also gone through complex phases of interest over the last century in British political thought and policy.[4] Three clearer phases can be identified: first, from the 1880s until 1914; second, the immediate post-war period from 1945 to the late 1950s; finally, the mid to late 1980s to the present. There have been explosions of literature corresponding to each period. The new liberalism effectively coincided self-consciously with the first phase, became institutionally embedded in the second, and was challenged and mutated in the third.

T. H. Green's (and Idealism's) intense focus on citizenship provided

[2] There are markedly different perspectives on the coherence of new liberal thought. On the basic incoherence of new liberal thought, see Peter Clarke, *Liberals and Social Democrats* (Cambridge University Press, 1978) and Stefan Collini, *Liberalism and Sociology: L. T. Hobhouse and Political Argument in Britain 1880–1915* (Cambridge University Press, 1979). In defense of its intellectual coherence, Freeden has stressed the role of evolutionary theory, in *The New Liberalism*; John Allett has stressed the role of Hobson's underconsumptionist economic theory, in *New Liberalism: The Political Economy of J. A. Hobson* (Toronto University Press, 1981); and Vincent and Plant have stressed the role of Philosophical Idealism, in *Philosophy, Politics and Citizenship*, chs. 4, 5.
[3] See Andrew Vincent, "New Ideologies for Old?" *Political Quarterly*, 69 (1998), 48–57.
[4] This section draws upon two other articles: Andrew Vincent, "Citizenship," *Contemporary Record* (1990), 15–18; and Andrew Vincent, "Citizenship and Morality," *Bulletin of the Australian Society of Legal Philosophy*, 13 (1989), 90–106.

the theme of the first phase, which then became embodied, with many subtle variants, in the theory and practice of the new liberalism up until 1914. The central category of Green's political philosophy was citizenship. It carried profound theological, epistemological, and ontological implications. The individual citizen assimilates ethical norms by participating in social life. Citizenship denoted a high level of civic awareness, moral character, rationality, and a strong sense of duty. Citizenship was integral to the self-realization of the individual within the wider community. However, Green's legacy on this issue is slightly ambivalent for two reasons. First, Green was essentially trying to adapt active civic citizenship ideas to British liberalism. In so doing, he developed some parallels with civic republican thought. Second, the more antique Greek side of Green's civic legacy is slightly obscured in his writings. The most succinct articulation of the antique vision, which catches the stress on duties strongly implicated with rights, is in the writings of Bernard Bosanquet. Whether Bosanquet should be regarded as a new liberal is open to debate; however, his ideas are certainly *not* classical liberal in their general orientation. In his article "The Duties of Citizenship" (1895), Bosanquet commented ruefully that "[t]he commonest Greek citizen could never altogether forget that his actual existence was bound up with the discharge of civic duty." Bosanquet goes on to complain that even the most educated citizen in Britain, of his time, did not appear to grasp the need for civic duties. Individual acquisitive self-interest was uppermost.[5] Bosanquet's, like Green's, interest in citizenship was deeply duty-orientated. Both lamented the growth of individualist self-interest and stressed the need for strong duties correlative with rights. The citizen was not simply the passive recipient of rights, but rather an active self-realizing being with recognized civic duties to fellow citizens.

Green does discuss the rights of the citizen. Rights, premised upon a moral and legal community, are negative realizations of human powers. Citizenship *per se* implied a consciousness of the ends of human life as embodied within the institutional structures of the state. The state was the organized body within which this consciousness functions. For Green, society and its institutional structures were the means to individual self-realization. Therefore, social institutions or legal practices were justified only to the extent that they furthered the self-realization of individuals. Green viewed all political concepts from this standpoint. Rights, duties, property, or freedom were conditional devices to allow individuals to realize their (ethical) powers and abilities and thus the common good. It is only by willing the common good that citizens

---

[5] Bernard Bosanquet, "The Duties of Citizenship," in Bernard Bosanquet (ed.) *Aspects of the Social Problem* (London: Macmillan, 1895), pp. 5–6.

become truly free. These, and other themes, are explored in his *Lectures on the Principles of Political Obligation*.[6] The nub of Green's vision of politics was therefore that of providing an ethical "enabling state." If there is one important intellectual bequest from Green, it is the ethical theory of citizenship combined with the enabling state. This provided one important undergirding for the early twentieth-century vision of the welfare state.

In the second phase, part of the spirit of the new liberal theory was carried through in the work of William Beveridge, J. M. Keynes, and, especially, T. H. Marshall. For one recent commentator, reformers like Beveridge and Keynes had a "crucial place in defining the terms of the civic bargain that prevailed [in Britain] from 1945 to the 1970s."[7] This bargain entailed guaranteed rights of protection against the effects of illness, old age, and unemployment, as well as opportunities in education. Social rights, financed out of general taxation, provided for social citizenship.[8] Taxation was essentially used to foster civic solidarity, connecting the private to the public realm.[9] The slight ambiguity, at this point, concerns the "duty" which the civic tradition had emphasized. Duty became largely institutionalized into the willingness to pay marginally higher levels of direct taxation. The civic component, in this scenario, began to draw back subtly from its ethical resources.

Marshall, who took over L. T. Hobhouse's professorial chair at the London School of Economics, encapsulated the emphasis on "rights-talk." The rights emphasis was the outcome of a trend in new liberal thinking, through the twentieth century, culminating in the second phase of citizenship in the 1950s. The rights focus was a motif, already strongly present in liberalism *qua* civil rights. Given that new liberal (and Idealist) writers usually wished to stress their continuity with liberalism, it is not surprising that they stressed rights terminology. This tendency became crystallized in the actual legislative work of new

---

[6] These themes are explored in Vincent and Plant, *Philosophy, Politics and Citizenship*. See also Andrew Vincent (ed.), *The Philosophy of T. H. Green* (Aldershot, UK: Gower Press, 1986); and, more recently, David Boucher and Andrew Vincent, *A Radical Hegelian: The Political and Social Philosophy of Henry Jones* (Cardiff: University of Wales Press, 1993).

[7] Michael Ignatieff, "The Myth of Citizenship," in R. Beiner (ed.), *Theorizing Citizenship* (New York: State University of New York Press, 1995), p. 67.

[8] Social citizenship, for Marshall, was the phase which developed after the civil and political citizenship; see T. H. Marshall, *Citizenship and Social Class* (Cambridge University Press, 1950).

[9] It is worth noting in passing that social citizenship arguments *never* really took off in the USA – welfare always has and still does imply a kind of stigma. Thus public hospitals in the USA are usually inferior to private ones; see Nancy Fraser and Linda Gordon, "Civil Citizenship against Social Citizenship? On the Ideology of Contract-Versus-Charity," in Bart van Steenbergen (ed.), *The Condition of Citizenship* (London: Sage Publications, 1994), p. 90.

liberals, in terms of rights to pensions, social insurance, and the like. National *contributory* insurance and pensions, for example, were even justified in the form of a nationalization of "thrift," namely, nationalizing an ontology of individualistic effort and reinforcing the background theme of individual rights or entitlements. Fortuitously, maintaining the continuity with liberalism and stressing the "rights" perspective (particularly rights, *qua* civil rights, which stressed negative or passive duties) brought some unexpected costs later in the century. Primarily, it weakened the idea of public-spirited duties as correlatives to rights. Marshall clearly assumed, in the 1950s, that a moral consensus, community, and public-spiritedness existed in Britain. This assumption, in the immediate post-1945 world, was not far-fetched, although in the world of the 1970s it had less purchase. This moral consensus grounded the notion of social rights in a common good, tempered the ontology of classical liberalism and civil rights, and provided the leitmotif for dutiful civic taxation and redistribution. However, the thinning out of this consensus set the scene for the 1980s.

Many of the major policy initiatives of the British post-1945 Labour government – Keynesian fiscal demand management and Beveridge's social insurance – derived from new liberal thinking. The new liberal Yellow Book of the 1920s formed the prototype of this approach. Beveridge and Keynes remained progressive new liberals into the post-1945 era, although, admittedly, of a different stripe to those of the pre-1914 period. Further, many of the influential personnel of the late-1920s and 1930s Labour grouping, including figures like Haldane, Hobson, Massingham, and Trevelyan, had been new liberals and had moved to Labour after the effective political demise of the Liberal Party in the 1920s. As one scholar has remarked, paradoxically, the disintegration of Liberalism was in part the "triumph of liberalism."[10] From the 1930s, "reformist socialism" became the true home for the new liberalism; the Conservatives, on the other hand, apart from their own partial inheritance of the new liberal theory in the Macmillanite "middle way," also absorbed the sentiments of the older classical liberalism and Whiggery, elements which rose forcefully to the surface again in the 1980s. In many ways, the conflict of the post-1945 era in Britain has been largely one between variants of classical and new liberalism.

In the third phase, it was the resurrection of a messianic classical liberalism, during the 1980s, which again raised to self-consciousness the new liberal perspective on citizenship, at least in its social democratic

---

[10] Robert Eccleshall, *British Liberalism: Liberal Thought from the 1640s to 1980s* (London: Longman, 1986), p. 56; see also Andrew Vincent, "Classical Liberalism and its Crisis of Identity," *History of Political Thought*, 40 (1990), 143–61.

guise. This last phase is, though, more cryptic. Ironically, the importance of citizenship was promoted, initially, by exponents of the new right, during the 1980s, in order to "remoralize" civil society. It entailed an appeal to voluntarism and individual charity, *not* the assertion of rights. The response to this move in social democratic theory was muffled. There were those who self-consciously resurrected and rethought the defense of the social rights of citizenship, *qua* Marshall. However, the impact of this form of argument has been muted by a range of new problems – radical moral pluralism, differential citizenship, and globalism – which were not experienced by earlier theorists and practitioners. These problems relate to the focus on rights and the question concerning what social rights imply.

Rights and citizenship

When we look back to the pre-1914 new liberal perspective on citizenship, what we are observing is, in fact, the embryo of certain problems and issues which were integral to political theory and practice debates in the last three decades of the twentieth century. The debates concerning the new right, communitarianism, republicanism, and liberalism are the latest phase of a debate which resonates with aspects of the new liberal synthesis.

One problematic facet of the new liberalism concerns the issue of rights vocabulary. Citizenship at all levels, in Marshall, is associated with rights. He noted that citizenship had an initial emancipatory role, even in its earliest format, and this was tied to the assertion of individual civil rights. This emancipation is not to be underestimated. Its formal egalitarian implications were clearly destructive of older hierarchical class systems. There is, however, an ambiguity concerning the conceptual tie within civil citizenship between property, emancipation, and rights. Civil rights appeared to bestow equal status on members of the community. At the same time, such rights did not necessarily conflict with the growth of capitalism. Classical liberalism and capitalism have indeed often celebrated civil citizenship as a form of individual emancipation. The egalitarian impulse of capitalism and civil citizenship implicitly challenged hierarchical values. Working ability and equality of contract were preferred to tradition or status. It was thus perfectly reasonable to have equality of civil citizenship, coupled with inequalities of income and even political status. The unequal class structure of early capitalism was thus compatible with civil citizenship. This is something that Marx noted in his writings on rights and law. Property, for capitalism, must be privately owned and tradable. Labor must also be free of feudal hierarchical ties in order to travel where work is needed by capitalists. Law and formal civil rights, in terms of property and contract and tort law, expedited the whole capitalist process. In creating a landless poor ("free labor") and a contractual, formally egalitarian, private-property-based law, the groundwork for capitalism was laid.

The tie between a form of emancipation and civil citizenship did not stop Marx from observing that civil citizenship brought its own enslavement. The rights of civil citizenship were, for Marx, the rights of propertied bourgeois men. They protected individual property-owners and capitalists in their exploitative practices. Rights were associated with individuals who owned them in order to protect private property interests. Civil citizenship thus masked the basic inequalities and exploitative practices of bourgeois commercial society. Marx found this scenario profoundly hypocritical and objectionable.[11] Civil and indeed political citizenship were innocuous categories without some property. (Communism, for Marx, presupposed communal equality of ownership.) Yet, capitalism flourished on unequal property ownership and exploitation.

Property was separated gradually from citizenship by the working-class movements of the nineteenth century. This separation exposed further the partial vacuity of the term in a market society: namely, that civil citizenship was dependent on property and property in capitalism relied on inequality. This view generated, in turn, the move to a more collectivist solution to reduce the contradiction between the *promise* of citizenship and the *reality* in the liberal market economy. From this, interests in social citizenship and the welfare state developed. In effect, to appreciate citizenship, in this reading, is to have some property-based stake in one's society. Marshall (and, in effect, the new liberalism) attempted to undergird the above move with social rights. This was, though, an unwitting coincidence of liberal and civic solidaristic ideals. Protection against illness, old age, and unemployment and guarantees of certain opportunities were both seen as the necessary *rights* of civilized life and part of the *solidaristic* goals of society. Taxation could be used to foster this civic solidarity, connecting the private civil to the public civic interest. This, however, still masked a tension between markets and civic citizenship. This tension was revealed again in the 1980s. The problem, in a nutshell, was that the welfare state *per se* did *not* increase solidarity and markets still generated privileges and inequalities.[12] The public realm in the 1980s was seen largely as an overloaded failure. Citizens tried to opt out of taxation for welfare, or, at least, lower their

[11] See Andrew Vincent, "Marx and Law," *Journal of Law and Society*, 20 (1993), 371–97.
[12] However, this point can be overdone. There are still strong vestiges of solidarism in the health and education services.

commitments to their fellow citizens. The new right were, in effect, trying to prise apart an economic civil logic and a civic logic. They therefore exposed an implicit tension which had lain partially dormant in the new liberal setting. This civil/civic tension is something that recent communitarians, civic republicans, and neo-Aristotelians have been trying to address throughout the last decade.

Rights, even if they were social rights, still embodied the ontology of individualism and classical liberalism. They were reliant on both a flourishing market economy, so that marginal taxation should not necessarily affect the marginal income growth of taxpayers, and a strong underlying communal consensus which legitimated and grounded social rights and redistribution. Once Western economies began to falter in the 1970s, the perception of rights to welfare began to be viewed differently (against the background of the idea that they were still *individual rights*). The communal and moral consensus no longer appeared to underpin and ground such social rights so obviously as in the 1950s. Taxation was viewed increasingly as an imposition on individual freedom and property. Civil citizenship thus began to reassert itself against civic citizenship. Given that the civic perspective utilized a "rights" vocabulary and had virtually lost the language of duties over the century, it was ripe for the picking by classical liberal critics. The new right arguments concerning loss of personal virtue (read "thrift"), individual responsibility, and dependency were premised on the above view. Furthermore, critics of the new liberal perspective argued that the attempt to resurrect full-blown civic-duty language (not just an insubstantial call for more charitable duties from the wealthy) might, in fact, be inconsistent with the spirit of valued civil rights.[13]

Recent defenders of social citizenship ideas still focus on rights as crucial to welfare. The new right view of citizenship, which confined it to civil citizenship and repudiated its extension, is regarded as basically misconceived.[14] The new liberals' most innovative move in argument was always to extend the logic of the classical liberal case. Thus, a basic civil right to, say, freedom, free speech, or free conscience could be modulated. As writers like T. H. Green queried in the 1880s, what does freedom mean? Can one be free and hampered by poverty? He therefore contended that it was justifiable, on the grounds of liberty, to interfere in contractual condition. The Edwardian new liberal Herbert Samuel echoed this directly, remarking that "[t]here could be no true liberty if a man was confined and oppressed by poverty, by excessive hours of

---

[13] See N. P. Barry in Raymond Plant and N. P. Barry, *Citizenship and Rights in Thatcher's Britain* (London: Institute of Economic Affairs, 1990), p. 76.
[14] See Raymond Plant in Plant and Barry, *Citizenship and Rights in Thatcher's Britain*, p. 10.

labour, by insecurity of livelihood ... To be truly free he must be liberated from these things also. In many cases, it was only the power of law that could effect this. More law might often mean more liberty."[15]

The notion of freedom remains, though, profoundly contested. Freedom might still be viewed, in Green's sense, as the positive moral power to do or enjoy something worth doing – in common with others. In this scenario, as Green pointed out, "free" contracts must be shown to contribute to the common good. Furthermore, freedom is inevitably dependent upon resources. Even measured against a more negative freedom argument, "being free" is "being free" *from* coercion, in order to allow the individual to shape their own life. Yet, to shape a life depends upon resources; therefore, real freedom is differentially valuable, depending upon resources. Thus, even the civil right to freedom is conceptually tied to resources. If classical liberals are committed to formal equality, they would also be committed, by the *logic* of their own civil argument, to address the distribution of resources. New liberal argument thus infects the logic of civil citizenship argument.

Rights, duties, and citizenship

Another facet of the new liberal notion of citizenship is the importance attributed to the correlation of rights and duties. The aim was to balance minimal requirements and opportunities with responsible self-development. There was a strong sense, in theorists like Green and later Hobhouse, that the enlargement of rights also entailed the expansion of duties. The new liberal view of citizenship linked the idea of the social minimum and social opportunities with growing civic responsibility. The duty of the state was to provide the minimal conditions, standards, and opportunities necessary for the exercise of civic autonomy. Yet, an important dimension of this autonomy was the correlative performance duties – active and intelligent participation in society. This view of the relation of rights and duties is illustrated in the new liberal attitude to trade unions. If trade unions were conceded rights to their own funds, they ought to demonstrate economic, political, and even moral responsibilities. The attitude of many new liberals to the Taff Vale case and the Trades Disputes Act of 1906 was grounded in this perception. Beveridge, for example, was still arguing this in the 1950s.[16]

[15] Herbert Samuel, *Memoirs* (London: Cresset Press, 1945), p. 25; see also Herbert Samuel's *Liberalism: An Attempt to State the Principles of Contemporary Liberalism* (London: Grant Richards, 1902); J. A. Hobson, *Crisis of Liberalism: New Issues in Democracy* (London: P. S. King, 1909), p. 113; Vincent and Plant, *Philosophy, Politics and Citizenship*, pp. 73–6.

[16] W. H. Beveridge, *Power and Influence* (London: Hodder & Stoughton, 1953), p. 51.

New liberals did not neglect the sphere of duties as the century progressed, but, as social legislation developed, duties increasingly took a back seat. Something changed within the arguments over citizenship, between 1914 and 1945, which switched the onus to more mechanistic arguments for abstract social entitlement rights. The reasons for this development of non-correlative social rights are complex. First, with the early twentieth-century advent of the Fabian and liberal socialist tradition, the emphasis on statism and instrumental rights became fortuitously more entrenched. Socialist writers of both the pre- and post-1914 periods, were at pains to distance themselves, on social questions, from classical liberals and, also, from groups like the Charity Organisation Society (COS). In fact, Fabian critics of the COS often confused it with classical liberal thought. The COS viewed citizenship through the lens of character. This was treated with scorn by most Fabian socialists. Duties, *qua* character arguments, were seen by the Webbs, for example, as antiquated residues of Victoriana. This was particularly the case in the debate between the Majority and Minority Royal Commission reports on the Poor Law in 1909.[17] It also figured in debates on unemployment and old age pensions. Character was, though, a complex term. In T. H. Green's work, it was synonymous with civic *duty*. Repudiating character-based arguments – justifiable as this might be in the context of the cruder renditions of Samuel Smiles – led to a more wholesale repudiation of the thesis of a correlation between rights and duties. In the later Beveridge model of welfare, active duties were also downplayed.[18] The passive recipience model predominated. Rights could, in effect, be administratively embedded in the welfare state. Passive citizens thus took priority over republican or activist citizens. Essentially, the debates on citizenship in the 1950s crystallized around welfare rights and minimized correlative duties.

Second, new liberal writers, in the climate of the post-1918 world, lost much of their ethical evolutionism and perfectibilism. The 1914–18 battlefields largely put pay to the latter urge. Beveridge and Keynes were

The Taff Vale case took place in 1901. It eventually went to the House of Lords and was settled initially in favor of the employers, the Taff Vale Railway Company. It had enormous political ramifications at the time. It focused on the legal liability of trade unions for damages caused by strike action. One central question at issue was whether the legal right to withdraw labor implied any duties, responsibilities, and, ultimately, liabilities. For discussion of the historical context and developments from the case, see Henry Pelling, *The History of British Trade Unionism* (Harmondsworth: Penguin Books, 1969), ch. 7.

[17] See Andrew Vincent, "The Poor Law Reports of 1909 and the Social Theory of the Charity Organisation Society," *Victorian Studies*, 27 (1984), 343–63.

[18] At least, this is the more common view of the Beveridge model. The final upshot of Beveridge's ideas is more contestable.

simply not motivated by morality or communitarian sentiments. In fact, in Keynes, there was a self-conscious ironic distancing from moral argumentation. Their arguments became more technical, economistic, and administrative. The tendency, in Keynes, to blend aspects of an older individualism with administrative statism (within a deftly adminis- tered capitalism) unwittingly coincided with the more instrumental perspective of those advocating the administrative rendition of social rights, although Keynes himself never seemed to be interested in ques- tions of poverty or inequality.

Third, there is a problem in identifying the precise correlative of civic rights. If basic needs are being met, what can be expected correlatively from a recipient? Is it even fair to expect such duties? Whereas civil rights have identifiable correlatives, civic or social rights are far more open-ended. There is a more technical conceptual point here con- cerning the correlatives for different types of right. A right to religious freedom might require that others leave one alone (a correlative dis- ability) and that one has a right to protection and redress from legal authority. A right to franchise implies the state has a duty of forbearance and facilitation. This latter notion has strong echoes of Mill's more educative view of democracy and has not been widely accepted in the twentieth century. A right to receive a minimum wage or social security implies the duty of an employer to provide such a wage and/or the state to guarantee security, but does it correlatively imply anything else? It is easy to focus on rights here and much harder to encourage the notion of civic duty. Entitlements require more straightforward administrative procedural responses; but civic duties imply what?

Fourth, and most problematically, the new liberal argument con- cerning social rights, as it developed in the post-1945 era, implied that a growing market economy would provide the funding for welfare. The new liberalism, in other words, did not abandon the market economy. Rather it relied upon market logic. It tried to combine this with social citizenship. Citizenship, as it was formulated in the pre-1914 period, implied a strong correlative theme of duty (which can be found almost in caricature in the COS and the writings of Bosanquet). In this setting, we have both the rights and duties implicit in the common good. As citizenship became institutionalized in the post-1945 era, it became fixed into social entitlements, with underlying ambiguities still re- maining concerning the correlativities of such entitlements. These ambiguities concerning correlative duties, which still haunt social rights discussion, are the result of an unresolved debate from the late nine- teenth century, and have, in turn, deeper echoes in more antique republican debates.

Fifth, in a peculiar twist of fate, the new right picked up on a criticism of the passivity of rights, expressed in their *social* mode. They premised themselves on the acceptability of passive rights in the civil sphere, with correlative forbearance and disability with regard to rights of property and liberty. However, when it came to the passivity of social rights (or entitlements), the welfare state was seen to *promote* a deplorable passive dependency, which thus perpetuated dependency. Civil rights, however, implied autonomy from others and forbearance in others' behaviour, but they were vigorously asserted and passivity did not imply costs to others' freedom or property. Conversely, the passive right to welfare implied reliance on and costs to others. The response to this in the new right was to promote forms of workfare. Some have also tried to transcribe welfare into market-based or contractual language. This is hardly, though, a free contract on the part of the disadvantaged. Social duress does not usually make for fair contracts or even formal civility.

Sixth, the tendency to stress individual rights has led increasingly to forms of civil privatism. For Jürgen Habermas, for example, citizenship in the late twentieth-century welfare state has been reduced to a client status. The sheer size of the modern public space of the state can be a hindrance to citizens identifying with each other. Administrative state structures have developed their own logic and push citizens to the periphery as supplicant clients. Citizenship today looks more like an aggregation of prepolitical interests (expressed as rights) and directed at bureaucratic agencies with no expectation of duty. There is still an important link between individual autonomy and social security. This link can also be seen as the effective basis for a civilized life and political participation. However, for Habermas, the link is only contingent. He notes that the "rights of individual freedom and social security can just as well facilitate a privatist retreat from citizenship and a particular 'clientelization' of the citizen's role."[19]

Marshall's formulation of social rights encapsulated the mood of the welfare state in 1950. Citizenship focused on social entitlements, which appeared to be indefinitely expandable. But it remained unclear what correlative duties (other than state guarantees) were implied by such rights. From a civic perspective, sharing in a social or civilized heritage implies some form of contribution. Yet, what is the consensual civilization citizens are involved in and contributing to? The shades of civic duties and moral consensus, from the civic citizenship tradition, still haunt the arguments on citizenship. This can be seen in the current civic republican, communitarian, and neo-Aristotelian perspectives which

[19] J. Habermas, "Citizenship and National Identity: Some Reflections on the Future of Europe," *Praxis International*, 12 (1992),11.

also express deep anxiety about the loss of public-spiritedness and communal integrity. However, the individualistic liberal/civil rights tradition has always felt profound unease with the growth of social rights. This latter tradition also believed in duty correlative to rights, but the duty implied, in this civil context, is usually negative forbearance. It also had little sense of community or communal consensus, except in the most minimal sense of a common rule of law. The separation between the private and public realms fixed this sentiment in the liberal ethos. Civil citizenship did not involve positive duties, in the form either of willing contributions to National Insurance and common health care, or of active ethical endeavors for the common good. Citizenship, in the new liberalism, in its compound civic/civil format has thus been caught between the Scylla of classical liberal unease and the Charybdis of administrative social rights, coupled with loss of civic duty.

One way round these arguments would be to question the root distinction which underpins the above discussion. Civil rights are purported to correlate with costless duties of forbearance, whereas the problem with social rights is that they imply that resources must be committed to satisfy the demands for welfare. The duties which do appear in the social rights perspective also appear more open-ended. However, this distinction is only partially accurate. Civil rights to freedom of conscience, speech, property, or association are far from costless. To defend such rights implies complex legal, military, and policing systems which are phenomenally expensive. Further, they might be viewed as paradigm cases of open-endedness. What, after all, is the precise correlative for a right to freedom of speech? The answer might be a general disability which affects everyone who hears! This would be a prime case of open-ended correlativity. If we compare this with a right to a minimum wage, education, or medical assistance in time of ill health, then the latter social rights seem more specific and costed in terms of their correlative state resources. Civil and social rights both involve redistribution of resources. This argument might moderate the strict distinction between types of correlativity, although it does not overcome the "civic duty correlative" argument sketched earlier.

Markets and citizenship

For new liberals, markets were to be encouraged within their place. They were not regarded as appropriate for certain spheres of policy. In terms of employment conditions, health care, education, insurance, and housing, the market was regarded as a crude and unpredictable mechanism. These areas needed sensitive state regulation. This might now be understood as an argument for a more mixed conception of the economy, involving some indicative planning or management. The implication of the latter ideas was that the state had a more active role to play in providing the conditions for the best life of its citizens. It was not merely a ring-holder, but an active agent.

However, the market continued to play an ambiguous role in new liberal thought. The new liberal perspective on social rights reveals the paradoxical need both for the redistribution to satisfy the requirements of social citizenship and consequently for productive markets to fund such rights. There is also an underlying expectation of correlative duties from the citizen, set against the background of, on the one hand, an assumed consensual community and, on the other hand, an individualistic unease with consensual community. New liberal thought thus found itself reliant on the market, not just to finance the requirements of social citizenship, but also because the "rights vocabulary" of liberalism itself contained an insistent ontology which was deeply receptive to and resonant with markets. Further, that ontology, implicit in the rights stance, undermined, implicitly, the community which was the assumed basis for social rights, and thus, unwittingly, acted as an inhibitor of the development of positive ethical duties (correlative on rights).

It is important to realize that the market, *qua* classical liberalism, contains its own insistent ontology. As already pointed out, this latter ontology feels at ease with "civil rights," which are, indeed, part of its *raison d'être*, the correlative duty of such rights being minimalist, namely, paying one's debts, keeping one's contracts, leaving others' property alone, and not interfering with their basic liberties. In the case of political rights, classical liberal ontology feels less at ease (particularly with the loss of a property-holding franchise), partly because democracies can get out of hand and the propertyless, but dutiful, participating citizen conjures up visions of public-spirited Jacobinism and Committees of Public Safety. Liberal democracy needs precautions built into it *against* the people or, more precisely, the mob. Citizen apathy is a sign of civil health. "Social rights," however, are beyond the pale for many classical liberals, and the duties entailed upon such rights, unacceptable.

What the new liberals attempted was to *combine* an "ethically orientated" social rights perspective – implying in its first formulation, *qua* T. H. Green or Hobhouse, ethical duties – with a liberal market ontology. The resulting structure is an amalgam of a more mechanistically administered social rights perspective, a market ontology (whose growth and vigor is the groundwork for financing social rights), and a quasi-individualistic interpretation of social rights as basic entitlements, which imply, in turn, negative correlative duties (although the *expectation* of positive civic duty still haunts the argument). This latter expectation can, in large measure, be seen in the repetitive arguments in Britain and the USA for workfare, or in the comparatively recent Australian discussion of "civil conscription." This, however, is the cruder end of the correlative argument.

Marshall was not unaware of the above scenario. He noted that social citizenship could potentially conflict with the market order. He thus described Britain, in the 1950s, as a "hyphenated society," namely, a "democratic-welfare-capitalism." Britain, on the one hand, was committed to the social element of citizenship. However, on the other hand, social citizenship existed in a permanently tense relationship with capitalism. Despite the crucial need for capitalist enterprise, extreme poverty and deprivation could no longer be tolerated. Social citizenship might provide the important integrating function in modern capitalist society, although Marshall seemed unsure. Essentially, in the post-1945 era, there have been two broad liberal responses to this tension between citizenship and the market, incorporating a number of subtexts.

The first response claims, more optimistically, that we must learn to live with the equilibrated tension, ensuring that neither social welfare nor the market order dominates the other. In addition, we must ensure, if possible, the continued growth of the productivity of the market. These claims, with many subtle variations, largely characterize the new liberal thinking up to the 1950s. In the 1950s one clear and systematic exponent was Anthony Crosland in works like *The Future of Socialism* (1956). For Crosland, Britain was a mixed economy, neither purely capitalist nor command-based. Governments could, via Keynesian and corporatist strategies, regulate, in fiscal terms, economic activity and control levels of unemployment, income distribution, investment, and consumption. Growing abundance would lead to growing expenditure on social welfare. Higher income groups would, he predicted, tolerate a relative decline in income; however, they would not accept, electorally, an absolute decline. Social welfare and the rights of citizenship were thus indissolubly linked to the growth of the market. However, the tension between them remains, but is tolerable as long as markets go on growing.

A second response argues that social citizenship is irreconcilable with a market ontology. There are three possible subinterpretations of this point. The first need not detain us, since it has never functioned in Britain. This maintains that the irreconcilability must lead us to abandon the market in favor of total state regulation. Total economic regulation would ensure equal social rights for all citizens, although it might do so at the cost of certain civil and political rights. This implied a very strong conception of civism. Liberals, from Benjamin Constant to Isaiah Berlin, have been profoundly worried by such arguments as potentially undermining the value of individual liberty and privacy. Ralph Dahrendorf has referred to this communal conception as the "total citizen."[20] The total citizen and the total state would be seen, in this argument, as two sides of the same coin. Such a notion has gone markedly out of favor since the 1980s. The second subinterpretation recognizes the incompatibility of social citizenship with the market ethos, but then argues for the necessity of keeping questions of social citizenship rights distinct from the notion of pure market exchange. Economic exchange does not recognize the moral status of participants, since it works by impersonal criteria. Economic exchange, therefore, of necessity, dehumanizes. Conversely social relations are premised on respect for the moral status of the person. An early exponent of this line of thought was R. M. Titmuss in books like *The Gift Relationship* (1970). Titmuss' basic contention was that blood, as a free social gift, should not be made a commercial entity. Markets should not determine such things. If blood is made subject to commodification, what, Titmuss continues, is to stop its application to "hospitals, nursing homes, clinical laboratories, schools, universities and even, perhaps churches[?]"[21] In the late 1990s, the churches are the last survivor of Titmuss' list. Thus, for Titmuss, social citizenship, and the social relations which characterize it, should be kept distinct from the market. The two should be balanced, but kept separate. The chastened 1980s version of this argument can be found in market socialism. Market socialism has tried to adjust to the anxiety, by accommodating itself more to the market. This chastened anxiety underpins many of the concerns of social democracy and "New Labour" in the 1990s.

The final subinterpretation is premised upon the perceived failure of successive post-1945 governments up to the 1970s, also possibly the purported failure of the Croslandite argument. The contention is that expenditure on social welfare has outpaced market productivity, thus creating an imbalance with the market. The obverse view is taken of the relation of markets and citizenship. Social citizenship, and the social welfare consequent upon it, are seen to be irreconcilable with the market. However, it is social citizenship which is at fault and should

---

[20] R. Dahrendorf, "Citizenship and Beyond: The Social Dynamics of an Idea," *Social Research*, 41 (1974).

[21] R. M. Titmuss, "Who is my Stranger?" in N. Timms and D. Watson (eds.), *Talking about Welfare* (London, Routledge and Kegan Paul 1976), p. 211.

largely be abandoned or curtailed in favor of the market. The welfare state, it is argued, imposes burdens on taxpayers, encroaching on private property rights, undermining negative liberty, and creating dependency. The answer here would be to return citizenship to its civil sense. The civil notion of citizenship, as argued, is not incompatible with markets. In addition, vestiges of any social policy, if retained, would mutate towards civil citizenship and a market ontology. Welfare recipients would become welfare consumers. Welfare providers would be partially deregulated, made to compete as far as possible and also responsible for their budgets like any business. Citizens would be consumers.

Another new liberal solution to the market problem would be to try to invert the civil citizenship argument. First, classical liberals have usually argued that monopolies of market resources are intrinsically harmful and interfere with a civil freedom. Such monopolies (whether public or private) are coercive, by definition, and coercion is contrary to the primary civil right of freedom. Yet, how could a monopoly be coercive and contrary to the civil (negative) right to freedom unless resources were, in some way, tied to liberty? To monopolize is coercive since it prevents freedom, freedom in this case being measured by the inaccessibility or inertia of the monopolized resources. This implies (from the civil citizenship perspective) that there must be some intimate knowledge of key resources required for freedom. Being free is thus tied to having resources to shape one's life, an argument which derives from the civil citizenship perspective. Denial of resources is therefore coercive and an infringement of the civil right to freedom.

Second, arguments on free markets suggest that markets are amoral and impersonal. Some use this as a way of separating out areas, like health, which should not be subject to impersonal exchange; others use this argument for claiming that markets are the best "total" allocator of resources because of their impersonality. Civil citizenship and new right arguments tend to favor the latter. Yet are markets really impersonal, natural, and amoral? Whereas it is difficult to foresee natural events, the effects of many market decisions can be predicted. The decision to deregulate a public hospital in favor of expensive private health care, close a factory, or invest in a low-wage economy, are all intentional acts of which the consequences can be foreseen. If these affect resources and citizens' capacities to act freely, then they are coercive – on the civil citizenship definition. Therefore, it would be incumbent on such classical (civil citizen) liberals to act against such market policies. Such an argument develops points made by the new liberals in the early part of the twentieth-century and yet draws the policy forth from the civil citizenship perspective.

Community and citizenship

The other Achilles' heel of the new liberal view of citizenship is the communal grounding for social rights. Communal individualism implies that the individual citizen could only develop and act responsibly as a citizen when certain basic conditions of life have been guaranteed by the community. Individuality exists within this social framework. Although this implied state action in fostering citizens' lives, new liberals were more immediately concerned with addressing the most basic parameters of civilized life of the socially vulnerable and weak. New liberals were therefore concerned, in the most literal sense, with "social security," that is, security in times of sickness and accident, in caring for and sustaining young children, and in old age. This line of concern was something that Beveridge, although having worked initially on new liberal policies for unemployment insurance and labour exchanges in 1910–11, was eventually to realize in his *Social Insurance and Allied Services* report (1942). The earlier, pre-1914, formulation of this point was concerned with establishing a social minimum or shelf in society to eliminate, as far as possible, the debilitating effects of poverty. Solidaristic goals were deeply embedded in these arguments. Only secure citizens could effectively live, provide for their families, and participate and compete in the market economy. This perspective became institutionalized within Marshall's conception of social citizenship.

Yet, as A. H. Halsey has noted, Marshall saw that "the democratic-welfare-capitalist society had been expected to bring with it consensus over basic issues and values. But even the most cursory glance at the history of Western Europe during the 1960s showed that it did not." Solidarity did not arise with social citizenship. For Halsey, the social dimension of citizenship, developed by Marshall, was an extension of earlier Idealist arguments. He points out that Marshall added a social dimension to the Idealist theory of citizenship, advanced by T. H. Green, whose arguments "had a spectacular . . . impact on liberalism in British theory and practice. Its impact on the twentieth century Labour party was also impressive. But its validity was disputed and undermined by criticism of its metaphysics." Citizenship was still premised, even in the 1950s, on some form of moral consensus. However, as Halsey confesses, such a consensus became more difficult to sustain as the twentieth century proceeded; unfortunately the "bases of social integration in Christian belief, national and imperial success, localised kinship and collective self-help institutions of the urban proletariat were all to decay."[22] This erosion

---

[22] A. H. Halsey, "T. H. Marshall and Ethical Socialism," in M. Bulmer and Anthony M. Rees (eds.), *Citizenship Today* (London: Longman, 1996), pp. 82, 99, 100.

was partially halted in the Second World War siege economy, but the post-1945 welfare state could not recreate this decaying solidarity. The major problem now is that in a situation of increasing pluralism and recognition of difference, it is difficult any longer to get a purchase on metaphysical or moral consensus. Justice and citizenship look increasingly political not metaphysical.

The issue of moral consensus and solidarity is still a major problem for new liberal thought, although it is not alone in this area. The same problem underpins much of contemporary political theory. One way round it is to try to identify certain core foundation concerns or themes. If, as argued earlier, liberty is a crucial human value (which is admittedly contestable – although less contestable in Western liberal democratic societies), and liberty is the space and capacity to shape one's life according to rationally self-formulated ends, uncoerced by others – which, in turn, requires some guaranteed social resources – then, it follows that the capacity to shape one's life is a fundamental human requirement overarching the particular choices that citizens make. Because citizens' substantive "goods" differ so markedly, it needs a form of more rigorous and wide-ranging democracy to represent, while still cementing, such diversity. However, this might still appear as a rather thin and abstracted conception of a communal foundation, although not as thin as classical liberalism. In effect, this argument is a partial reiteration of the liberal "right over the good" claim within a more perfectionist and communitarian setting. The common good in this reading is neither a rich substantive good (as one finds in Green or Hobhouse) nor a minimalist rule of law notion (which might be found in classical liberal thought) but a socialized communitarian liberalism. This might well be the more syncretist path which the new liberalism (and thus social democracy) takes in the early twenty-first century.

Conclusion

The pervasive accounts, over the 1980s, of an overloaded and out of control welfare state reveal or bring to the surface unresolved tensions. The message is not altogether clear, since some would clearly like to return us to a pristine world of civil citizenship, where state budgets are never in deficit and pigs fly. However, the uncertainties over social citizenship rights also reveal a deeper unease. This unease concerns tensions between rights and duties; between civism and civility; between an economic and civic logic; between an essentially passive recipience vision of welfare and a positive civic activist vision. This complex tension was introduced by the new liberalism to twentieth-century politics. This tension also highlights the late twentieth-century loss of solidarity within welfare states – welfare states which, paradoxically, were premised, on the one hand, upon individualistically orientated rights claims and the ontology of individualism, and, on the other, on an ontology of social solidarity, civic service, and active mutualist duty. Two distinct ontologies subsist within the new liberal vision of the welfare state. It is hardly surprising in this context that the welfare state has been subject to vigorous assault by the reinvigorated classical liberal new right – trying to prise apart the economic and civil logic from the civic.

There would appear to be three broad solutions to this tension. First, abandon rights altogether and just speak of duties and public-spiritedness, which implies a return to a pre-liberal civic republican form of culture. This would throw citizens into the warm mutual embrace of undiluted civism. Second, abandon social citizenship (and possibly political citizenship to make the latter abandonment secure – while mass democracy exists there is always the opening for expanding social rights). This would be a return to pristine civil citizenship. Both appear to be non-starters. The Owl of Minerva has flown as regards liberalism, markets, welfare, and rights. The third solution is profoundly tricky (like all third ways). It involves a number of stages, which I have only begun to sketch. First, it implies turning civil rights inside out – showing the logic of civil rights leads to social rights. This, in turn, entails denying the rigid distinctions that Marshall drew between civil, political, and social rights. Second, it implies the harder requirement for encouraging the idea of civic duty as a correlative to the rights of social/civil citizenship. Many might now be prepared to accept the first stage, but not the second (although oddly it is still an insistent voice within social democracy). In the second stage, some form of civic education could be required. We would appear to have outgrown the possibility of a civil religion. However, there are other possible avenues. At the crudest and most worrying end are the workfare or civil conscription policies. Their crudity can be tempered by providing greater and longer-term educational or employment opportunities for citizens, but they still appear as cumbersome and unpredictable devices for generating public awareness or public spirit. The educative side of democracy has been argued for by many theorists, from J. S. Mill onwards. If it is educative then why not make voting compulsory and educate citizens in the arguments involved? "Citizenship studies" could also be made part of a national education curriculum – including within universities. It could be a core curriculum subject for all students throughout their studies. The problem here is that it would either mutate into yet another abstracted social science discipline remote from practice, or, alternatively, would become an underfunded academic sideshow. Mandatory national service of some form has also often been a device favored in the past and could be modified for future use. Good Samaritan laws could be used to ensure or establish the norm of mutual service between citizens, to create a culture of mutuality and solidarity. All the above, however, remain deeply controversial in a society still inflamed by individual freedom and rights. Perhaps the syncretic vision of the new liberals will remain ever more elusive as the public spheres become more global and impersonal, yet more interlocking, and the individual becomes progressively more singular and isolated.

Select bibliography

WRITINGS BY NEW LIBERALS

BERNARD BOSANQUET (1848–1923)

The Civilization of Christendom and Other Studies, London: Swan Sonnenschein, 1889.

Essays and Addresses, 2nd edn., London: Swan Sonnenschein, 1891.

[Editor and contributor] *Aspects of the Social Problem*, London: Macmillan, 1895.

"The Moral Aspects of Socialism," *International Journal of Ethics*, 6 (1895–6), 503–8; continued, 7 (1896-7), 226–9.

"Idealism in Social Work," *Charity Organization Review*, n.s. 3 (1898), 122–33.

"The Meaning of Social Work," *International Journal of Ethics*, 11 (1900–1), 291–306.

The Philosophical Theory of the State and Other Essays, G. Gaus and W. Sweet (eds.), Bristol: Thoemmes Press, 2000.

JOHN DEWEY (1859–1952)

[1889], "The Philosophy of Thomas Hill Green," in J. A. Boydston *et al.* (eds.), *The Early Works of John Dewey, 1882–1898*, 5 vols., Carbondale and Edwardsville: Southern Illinois University Press, 1969–72, vol. III, pp. 14–35.

[1893], "Self-Realization as a Moral Ideal," in J. A. Boydston *et al.* (eds.), *The Early Works of John Dewey, 1882–1898*, 5 vols., Carbondale and Edwards-ville: Southern Illinois University Press, 1969–72, vol. IV, pp. 42–53.

[1908], with James H. Tufts, *Ethics*, New York: H. Holt, 1947.

[1927], *The Public and Its Problems*, Chicago: Swallows Press, 1954.

[1930], *Individualism, Old and New*, Amherst, NY: Prometheus Books, 1999.

Liberalism and Social Action, New York: G. P. Putnam, 1935.

The Early Works of John Dewey, 1882–1898, 5 vols., J. A. Boydston *et al.* (eds.), Carbondale: Southern Illinois University Press, 1967–72.

The Middle Works of John Dewey, 1889–1924, 15 vols., J. A. Boydston *et al.* (eds.), Carbondale: Southern Illinois University Press, 1977–83.

The Later Works of John Dewey, 1925–1953, 17 vols., J. A. Boydston *et al.* (eds.), Carbondale: Southern Illinois University Press, 1981–7.

THOMAS HILL GREEN (1836–1882)

"Popular Philosophy in Its Relation to Life," *North British Review*, 48 (1868), 133–62. Reprinted in R. L. Nettleship (ed.), *Works of Thomas Hill Green*, 3 vols., London: Longmans, Green and Co., 1885, vol. III, pp. 92–125.

[1879], "On the Different Senses of 'Freedom' as Applied to Will and to the Moral Progress of Man," in T. H. Green, *Lectures on the Principles of Political Obligation and Other Writings*, Paul Harris and John Morrow (eds.), Cambridge University Press, 1986, pp. 228–49.

[1879–80], "Lectures on the Principles of Political Obligation," in T. H. Green, *Lectures on the Principles of Political Obligation and Other Writings*, Paul Harris and John Morrow (eds.), Cambridge University Press, 1986, pp. 13–193.

[1881], "Lecture on 'Liberal Legislation and Freedom of Contract,'" in T. H. Green, *Lectures on the Principles of Political Obligation and Other Writings*, Paul Harris and John Morrow (eds.), Cambridge University Press, 1986, pp. 194–212.

Prolegomena to Ethics, A. C. Bradley (ed.), Oxford: Clarendon Press, 1883; 5th edn., 1907.

"Introductions to Hume's *Treatise of Human Nature*" II. Introduction to the Moral Part of Hume's *Treatise*," in R. L. Nettleship (ed.), *Works of Thomas Hill Green*, 3 vols., London: Longmans, Green and Company, 1885, vol. I, pp. 301–73.

"Lectures on the Philosophy of Kant, II. The Metaphysic of Ethics," in R. L. Nettleship (ed.), *Works of Thomas Hill Green*, 3 vols., London: Longmans, Green and Company, 1885, vol. II, pp. 83–155.

The Collected Works of T. H. Green, 5 vols., Peter P. Nicholson (ed.), Bristol: Thoemmes Press, 1997.

LEONARD TRELAWNY HOBHOUSE (1864–1929)

"The Ethical Basis of Collectivism," *International Journal of Ethics*, 8 (1898), 137–56.

"The Prospects of Liberalism," *Contemporary Review*, 93 (1908), 349–58.

[1911], *Liberalism*, James Meadowcroft (ed.), Cambridge University Press, 1994.

Social Evolution and Political Theory, New York: Columbia University Press, 1911.

The Metaphysical Theory of the State, London: Allen & Unwin, 1918.

Morals In Evolution, New York: Henry Holt, 1919.

The Rational Good, New York: Henry Holt, 1921.

The Elements of Social Justice, London: Allen & Unwin, 1922.

Social Development, London: Allen & Unwin, 1924.

Sociology and Philosophy: A Centenary Collection of Essays and Articles, Morris Ginsberg (ed.), Cambridge, MA: Harvard University Press, 1966.

JOHN ATKINSON HOBSON (1858–1940)

[1891], *Problems of Poverty*, New York: A. M. Kelley, 1971.

"Rights of Property," *Free Review* (Nov. 1893), 130–49.

[1893], *The Labour Movement*, London: T. Fisher Unwin, 1912.
The Social Problem, London: J. Nesbit & Co., 1901.
"The Re-Statement of Democracy," *Contemporary Review*, 89 (1902), 262–72.
"John Stuart Mill," *Speaker* (May 26, 1906).
[1909], *The Crisis of Liberalism: New Issues of Democracy*, P. F. Clarke (ed.), London: Allen & Unwin, 1974.
Work and Wealth: A Human Valuation, London and New York: Macmillan, 1914.

DAVID GEORGE RITCHIE (1853–1903)

The Principles of State Interference: Four Essays on the Political Philosophy of Mr. Herbert Spencer, J. S. Mill, and T. H. Green, London: Swan Sonnenschein, 1891.
Darwin and Hegel, London: Swan Sonnenschein, 1893.
"On the Meaning of the Term 'Motive,' and on the Ethical Significance of Motives," *International Journal of Ethics*, 4 (1893–4), 89–94.
"Symposium – Is Human Law the Basis of Morality, or Morality of Human Law?," *Proceedings of the Aristotelian Society*, 2, part II (1894), 124–9.
Natural Rights, London: Swan Sonnenschein, 1895.
"Social Evolution," *International Journal of Ethics*, 6 (1896), 165–81.
"Evolution and Democracy," in S. Coit (ed.), *Ethical Democracy: Essays in Dynamics*, London: G. Richards, 1900, pp. 1–29.
Darwinism and Politics, London: Swan Sonnenschein, 1901.
Studies in Political and Social Ethics, London: Swan Sonnenschein, 1902.
Philosophical Studies, Robert Latta (ed.), London: Macmillan, 1905.
The Collected Works of D. G. Ritchie, 6 vols., Peter P. Nicholson (ed.), Bristol: Thoemmes Press, 1998.

SECONDARY SOURCES

Anderson, O., "The Feminism of T. H. Green: A Late-Victorian Success Story?," *History of Political Thought*, 12 (1991), 671–93.
Arblaster, A., *The Rise and Decline of Western Liberalism*, Oxford: Blackwell, 1984.
Avineri, S. and De-Shalit, A. (eds.), *Communitarianism and Individualism*, Oxford University Press, 1992.
Ball, T., "Political Theory and Conceptual Change," in A. Vincent (ed.), *Political Theory*, Cambridge University Press, 1997, pp. 28–44.
Barker, E., *Political Thought in England, 1848–1914*, Oxford University Press, 1915.
Bell, D., *Communitarianism and its Critics*, Oxford: Clarendon Press, 1993.
Bellamy, R., *Liberalism and Modern Society*, Cambridge: Polity Press, 1992.
  "T. H. Green, J. S. Mill, and Isaiah Berlin on the Nature of Liberty and Liberalism," in H. Gross and R. Harrison (eds.), *Jurisprudence: Cambridge Essays*, Oxford University Press, 1992.
Bellamy, R. (ed.), *Victorian Liberalism: Nineteenth Century Political Thought and Practice*, London: Routledge, 1990.
Benn, S., *A Theory of Freedom*, Cambridge University Press, 1988.

Bentley, M., *The Climax of Liberal Politics: British Liberalism in Theory and Practice, 1868–1918*, London: Edward Arnold, 1987.

Bevir, M., "Welfarism, Socialism and Religion: On T. H. Green and Others," *Review of Politics*, 55 (1993), 639–61.

Bradley, F. H., *Ethical Studies*, 2nd edn., London: Macmillan, 1927.

Brink, D., "Self-Love and Altruism," *Social Philosophy and Policy*, 14 (1997), 122–57.

Brinton, C., *English Political Thought in the 19th Century*, New York: Harper, 1962.

Cacoullos, A., *Thomas Hill Green: Philosopher of Rights*, New York: Twayne, 1974.

Caney, S., "Liberalism and Communitarianism: A Misconceived Debate," *Political Studies*, 40 (1992), 273–90.

Clarke, P., *Liberals and Social Democrats*, Cambridge University Press, 1978.
   "The Progressive Movement in England," *Transactions of the Royal Historical Society*, 5th series, 24 (1974), 159–81.

Collini, S., "The Idea of 'Character' in Victorian Political Thought," *Transactions of the Royal Historical Society*, 5th series, 35 (1985), 29–50.
   Liberalism and Sociology: L. T. Hobhouse and Political Argument in England, 1880–1914, Cambridge University Press, 1979.
   "Hobhouse, Bosanquet and the State: Philosophical Idealism and Political Argument in England, 1880–1918," *Past and Present*, 72 (1976), 86–111.

Condren, C., "Political Theory and the Problem of Anachronism," in Andrew Vincent (ed.), *Political Theory*, Cambridge University Press, 1997, pp. 45–66.

Crittenden, J., *Beyond Individualism: Reconstituting the Liberal Self*, Oxford University Press, 1922

Cummiskey, D., *Kantian Consequentialism*, Oxford University Press, 1996.

Dagger, R. K., *Civic Virtues: Rights, Citizenship and Republican Liberalism*, Oxford University Press, 1997.

Damico, A. J., *Individuality and Community: The Social and Political Thought of John Dewey*, Gainesville: University Press of Florida, 1978.

Damico, A. J. (ed.), *Liberals on Liberalism*, Totowa, NJ: Rowman & Littlefield, 1986.

Den Otter, S., *British Idealism and Social Explanation: A Study in Late Victorian Thought*, Oxford: Clarendon Press, 1996.

Donner, W., *The Liberal Self: John Stuart Mill's Moral and Political Philosophy*, Ithaca, NY: Cornell University Press, 1991.

Essays in Liberalism by Six Oxford Men, London: Cassell, 1897.

Francis, M. and Morrow, J., *A History of English Political Thought in the Nineteenth Century*, London: Duckworth, 1994.

Freeden, M., *Ideologies and Political Theory: A Conceptual Approach*, Oxford: Clarendon Press, 1996.
   "Liberal Communitarianism and Basic Income," in P. Van Parijs (ed.), *Arguing for Basic Income*, London and New York: Verso, 1992, pp. 185–91.
   Rights, Minneapolis: University of Minnesota Press, 1991.
   "Human Rights and Welfare: A Communitarian View," *Ethics*, 100 (1990), 489–502.

"Rights, Needs and Community: The Emergence of British Welfare Thought," in A. Ware and R. E. Goodin (eds.), *Needs and Welfare*, London: Sage Publications, 1990.

The New Liberalism: An Ideology of Social Reform, Oxford University Press, 1978.

Freeden, M. (ed.), *Reappraising J. A. Hobson*, London: Unwin Hyman, 1990.

Gaus, G., "Green, Bernard Bosanquet and the Philosophy of Coherence," in C. L. Ten (ed.), *The Routledge History of Philosophy*, vol. VII: *The Nineteenth Century*, London: Routledge, 1994, pp. 408–36.

The Modern Liberal Theory of Man, London: Croom Helm, 1983.

Gray, J., *Mill on Liberty: A Defence*, London: Routledge & Kegan Paul, 1983.

Greengarten, I. M., *Thomas Hill Green and the Development of Liberal-Democratic Thought*, Toronto University Press, 1981.

Gutmann, A., "Communitarian Critics of Liberalism," *Philosophy and Public Affairs*, 14 (1985), 308–22.

Harris, P., "Moral Progress and Politics: The Theory of T. H. Green," *Polity*, 21 (1989), 538–62.

Harvie, C., *The Lights of Liberalism: University Liberals and the Challenge of Democracy, 1860–86*, London: Allen Lane, 1976.

Holmes, S., *The Anatomy of Antiliberalism*, Cambridge, MA: Harvard University Press, 1993.

"The Permanent Structure of Antiliberal Thought," in N. Rosenblum (ed.), *Liberalism and the Moral Life*, Cambridge, MA: Harvard University Press, 1989, pp. 227–53.

Hoover, K. R., "Liberalism and the Idealist Philosophy of Thomas Hill Green," *Western Political Quarterly*, 26 (1973), 550–65.

Hurka, T., *Perfectionism*, Oxford University Press, 1993.

Irwin, T. H., "Eminent Victorians and Greek Ethics: Sidgwick, Green, and Aristotle," in B. Schultz (ed.), *Essays on Henry Sidgwick*, Cambridge University Press, 1991, pp. 279–310.

Kemp, J., "T. H. Green and the Ethics of Self-Realisation," in G. N. A. Vesey (ed.), *Reason and Reality*, London: Macmillan, 1972, pp. 220–40.

Koerner, K., *Liberalism and Its Critics*, London: Croom Helm, 1985.

Kymlicka, W., *Liberalism, Community and Culture*, Oxford University Press, 1989.

Laski, H. J. [1937], *Liberty in the Modern State*, New York: Viking Press, 1949.

The Rise of European Liberalism, London: Allen & Unwin, 1936.

Lewis, H. D., "Does the Good Will Define its Own Content? A Study of Green's *Prolegomena to Ethics*," in his *Freedom and History*, London: Allen & Unwin, 1962, pp. 15–47.

"Individualism and Collectivism: A Study of T. H. Green," in his *Freedom and History*, London: Allen & Unwin, 1962, pp. 60–89.

"The Individualism of T. H. Green," in his *Freedom and History*, London: Allen & Unwin, 1962, pp. 90–104.

"T. H. Green and Rousseau," in his *Freedom and History*, London: Allen & Unwin, 1962, pp. 105–33.

Macedo, S., *Liberal Virtues: Citizenship, Virtue and Community in Liberal Constitutionalism*, Oxford, Clarendon Press, 1990.

Manent, P., *Intellectual History of Liberalism*, Princeton University Press, 1994.

Martin, R., "Green on Natural Rights in Hobbes, Spinoza and Locke," in A. Vincent (ed.), *The Philosophy of T. H. Green*, Aldershot, UK: Gower, 1986, pp. 104–26.

Meadowcroft, J., *Conceptualizing the State: Innovation and Dispute in British Political Thought, 1880–1914*, Oxford: Clarendon Press, 1995.

Meadowcroft, J. (ed.), *The Liberal Political Tradition: Contemporary Reappraisals*, Cheltenham, UK: Edward Elgar, 1996.

Mill, J. S., *The Collected Works of John Stuart Mill*, 33 vols., J M. Robson *et al.* (eds.), Toronto University Press, 1963–.

Miller, D., "Communitarianism: Left, Right and Centre," in D. Avnon and A. De-Shalit (eds.), *Liberalism and its Practice*, London: Routledge, 1999, pp. 170–83.

Milne, A. J. M., "The Common Good and Rights in T. H. Green's Ethical and Political Thought," in A. Vincent (ed.), *The Philosophy of T. H. Green*, Aldershot, UK: Gower, 1986, pp. 62–75.

The Social Philosophy of English Idealism, London: Allen & Unwin, 1962.

Monro, D. H., "Green, Rousseau and the Culture Pattern," *Philosophy*, 26 (1951), 347–57.

Monson, C. H., "Prichard, Green, and Moral Obligation," *Philosophical Review*, 63 (1954), 74–87.

Moon, J. D., "Communitarianism," in *Encyclopedia of Applied Ethics*, 4 vols., San Diego: Academic Press, 1998, vol. I, pp. 551–61.

Morrow, J., "Liberalism and Idealist Political Philosophy: A Reassessment," *History of Political Thought*, 5 (1984), 91–108.

"Property and Personal Development: An Interpretation of T. H. Green's Political Philosophy," *Politics: Journal of the Australasian Political Science Association* (1981), 84–92.

Muirhead, J. H., *The Service of the State: Four Lectures on the Political Teaching of T. H. Green*, London: John Murray, 1908.

Mulhall, S. and Swift, A., *Liberals and Communitarians*, 2nd edn., Oxford: Blackwell, 1996.

"The Social Self in Political Theory: The Communitarian Critique of the Liberal Subject," in D. Bakhurst and C. Sypnowich (eds.), *The Social Self*, London: Sage, 1995, pp. 103–22.

"Liberalism and Communitarianism: Whose Misconceptions?," *Political Studies*, 41 (1993), 650–6.

Nicholls, D., "Positive Liberty, 1880–1914," *American Political Science Review*, 56 (1962), 114–28.

Nicholson, P. P., *The Political Philosophy of the British Idealists: Selected Studies*, Cambridge University Press, 1990.

"T. H. Green and State Action: Liquor Legislation," in A. Vincent (ed.), *The Philosophy of T. H. Green*, Aldershot, UK: Gower, 1986, pp. 76–103.

Norman, R., *The Moral Philosophers: An Introduction to Ethics*, Oxford: Clarendon Press, 1983.

Pearson, R. and Williams, G., *Political Thought and Public Policy in the Nineteenth Century*, London: Longman, 1984.

Pettit, P., *The Common Mind: An Essay on Psychology, Society, and Politics*, Oxford University Press, 1993.

Pocock, J. G. A., *Politics, Language and Time*, New York: Atheneum, 1971.

Randall, J. H., "T. H. Green: The Development of English Thought from J. S. Mill to F. H. Bradley," *Journal of the History of Ideas*, 27 (1966), 17–44.

Rawls, J., *Political Liberalism*, New York: Columbia University Press, 1993.

"Justice as Fairness: Political not Metaphysical," *Philosophy and Public Affairs*, 14 (1985), 223–51.

A Theory of Justice, Cambridge, MA: Harvard University Press, 1971.

Raz, J., *The Morality of Freedom*, Oxford University Press, 1986.

Richter, M., *The Politics of Conscience: T. H. Green and his Age*, London: Weidenfeld & Nicolson, 1964.

Riley, J., *Liberal Utilitarianism: Social Choice Theory and J. S. Mill's Philosophy*, Cambridge University Press, 1988.

Rorty, R., Schneewind, J. B. and Skinner, Q. (eds.), *Philosophy in History*, Cambridge University Press, 1984.

Rosenblum, N. (ed.), *Liberalism and the Moral Life*, Cambridge, MA: Harvard University Press, 1989.

Ryan, A., *John Dewey and the High Tide of American Liberalism*, New York: W. W. Norton, 1995.

"The Liberal Community," in J.W. Chapman and I. Shapiro (eds.), *Democratic Community, Nomos XXXV*, New York University Press, 1993, pp. 91–114.

J. S. Mill, London: Routledge & Kegan Paul, 1974.

Sandel, M., *Liberalism and the Limits of Justice*, Cambridge University Press, 1982.

Seaman, J. W., "L. T. Hobhouse and the Theory of Social Liberalism," *Canadian Journal of Political Science*, 11 (1978), 777–801.

Sidgwick, H., *Lectures on the Ethics of T. H. Green, Mr. Herbert Spencer, and J. Martineau*, London: Macmillan, 1902.

Simhony, A., "T. H. Green and Henry Sidgwick on the 'Profoundest Problem of Ethics,'" in W. J. Mander (ed.), *Anglo-American Idealism, 1865–1927*, Westport, CT: Greenwood Press, 2000, pp. 33–50.

"Was T. H. Green a Utilitarian?," *Utilitas*, 7 (1995), 121–44.

"T. H. Green: The Common Good Society," *History of Political Thought*, 14 (1993), 225–47.

"Beyond Negative and Positive Freedom: T. H. Green's View of Freedom," *Political Theory*, 21 (1993), 28–54.

"On Forcing Individuals to be Free: T. H. Green's Liberal Theory of Positive Freedom," *Political Studies*, 49 (1991), 303–20.

"Idealist Organicism: Beyond Holism and Individualism," *History of Political Thought*, 12 (1991), 515–35.

"T. H. Green's Theory of the Morally Justified Society," *History of Political Thought*, 10 (1989), 481–98.

Skinner, Q., "Meaning and Understanding in the History of Ideas," *History and Theory*, 8 (1969), 1–53.

Spragens, T. A., "Communitarian Liberalism," in A. Etzioni (ed.), *New Communitarian Thinking: Persons, Virtues, Institutions, and Communities*, Charlottesville: University of Virginia Press, 1995, pp. 35–71.

"Reconstructing Liberal Theory: Reason and Liberal Culture," in A. J. Damico (ed.), *Liberals on Liberalism*, Totowa, NJ: Rowman & Littlefield, 1986.

Sumner, W., *The Moral Foundations of Rights*, Oxford: Clarendon Press, 1987.

Taylor, C., "Cross-Purposes: The Liberal–Communitarian Debate," in N. Rosenblum (ed.), *Liberalism and the Moral Life*, Cambridge, MA: Harvard University Press, 1989.

Thomas, G., *The Moral Philosophy of T. H. Green*, Oxford: Clarendon Press, 1987.

Tyler, C., *Thomas Hill Green (1836–1882) and the Philosophical Foundations of Politics: An Internal Critique*, Lewiston, NY: The Edward Mellen Press, 1997.

Vincent, A., *Modern Political Ideologies*, 2nd edn., Oxford: Blackwell, 1995.

Vincent, A. (ed.), *The Philosophy of T. H. Green*, Aldershot, UK: Gower, 1986.

Vincent, A. and Plant, R., *Philosophy, Politics and Citizenship: The Life and Thought of the British Idealists*, Oxford: Blackwell, 1984.

Walzer, M., "The Communitarian Critique of Liberalism," *Political Theory*, 18 (1990), 6–23.

Weiler, P., *The New Liberalism: Liberal Social Theory in Great Britain, 1889–1914*, New York: Garland, 1982.

"The New Liberalism of L. T. Hobhouse," *Victorian Studies*, 16 (1972), 141–61.

Weinstein, D., "The New Liberalism of L. T. Hobhouse and the Reenvisioning of Nineteenth-Century Utilitarianism," *Journal of the History of Ideas*, 57 (1996), 487–507.

"Between Kantianism and Consequentialism in T. H. Green's Moral Philosophy," *Political Studies*, 41 (1993), 618–35.

"The Discourse of Freedom, Rights and Good in Nineteenth-Century English Liberalism," *Utilitas*, 3 (1991), 245–62.

Weinstein, W. L., "The Concept of Liberty in Nineteenth Century English Political Thought," *Political Studies*, 13 (1965), 145–62.

Welchman, J., *Dewey's Ethical Thought*, Ithaca, NY: Cornell University Press, 1995.

Wempe, B., *Beyond Equality: A Study of T. H. Green's Theory of Positive Freedom*, Delft, The Netherlands: 1986.

Index